THE RELOCATING SPOUSE'S GUIDE TO EMPLOYMENT

THE RELOCATING SPOUSE'S GUIDE TO EMPLOYMENT

OPTIONS AND STRATEGIES IN THE U.S. AND ABROAD

THIRD EDITION

FRANCES BASTRESS

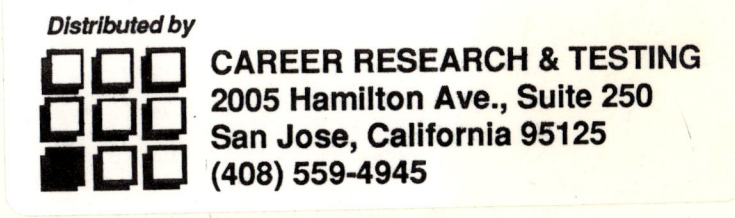

Distributed by
CAREER RESEARCH & TESTING
2005 Hamilton Ave., Suite 250
San Jose, California 95125
(408) 559-4945

Woodley Publications
Chevy Chase, Maryland

Copyright © 1986, 1987, 1989 by Frances Bastress

All rights reserved. No part of this book may be reproduced or transmitted in any form or by any means — except for brief quotations in critical articles or reviews — without written permission from the publisher: WOODLEY PUBLICATIONS, 4620 DeRussey Parkway, Chevy Chase, MD 20815.

Printed in the United States of America.

Library of Congress Cataloging-in-Publication Data

Bastress, Frances.
  The relocating spouse's guide to employment.

  Bibliography: p.
  Includes index.
  1. Job hunting. 2. Job hunting—United States.
3. Married people—Employment. 4. Married people—
Employment—United States. I. Title.
HF5382.7.B375 1989   650.1'4   88-33772
ISBN 0-937623-02-4

For information on distribution or quantity discount rates, call 301-986-9106 or write to Sales Department, WOODLEY PUBLICATIONS, 4620 DeRussey Parkway, Chevy Chase, MD 20815.

To Karl
January 20, 1929 to December 14, 1988

I carry your heart with me
(I carry it in my heart)
I am never without it . . .
e.e. cummings

Contents

Preface xiii
Acknowledgments xvii
Introduction 1

Part I   SELF-ASSESSMENT

Chapter 1
Your Qualifications 7
  The Time Line of Your Life   9
  Training and Education   10
  Work History: A Memory Jogger   12
  Your 'Hidden' Credentials   14
  Building a Work Portfolio   17

Chapter 2
Your Priorities 19
  Evaluating Your Values   19
  The Six Personality Types   20
  What Really Interests You?   22
  Three Types of Skills   23
  Your Dream Job   24
  To Move or Not to Move   25
  Are You a Risk Taker?   26

Part II   EXPLORATION

Chapter 3
Options for a Relocating Spouse 29

You *Can* Take It With You: Six Portable Careers   31
  Counseling • Health Care • Secretarial • Social Work
  • Teaching and Training • Writing and Editing

Careers Compatible With Children   36

Picking Up Portable Skills   37

Selecting a Work Setting   37
  Consulting and Contracting Firms • Corporations
  • Diplomatic Community • Foundations • Government
  • Health-Care Facilities • Home • International
  Nonprofit Organizations • Military Installations
  • Research Organizations • Trade and Professional
  Associations

Alternative Work Arrangements   44
  Contract Work • Part-Time Work • Temporary Work
  • Job Sharing • Flextime • Compressed Workweek
  • Overseas Academics • Volunteering

Chapter 4
Is Self Employment for You? 50

Advantages and Disadvantages   51
How to Decide on a Business   54
Why You Need a Business Plan   57
The Legal and Tax Side   57
Groups That Can Assist You   59
How to Promote Your Business   59
A Word of Caution...and of Confidence   61
Scoring the Entrepreneurial Quiz   61

Chapter 5
Working for the Federal Government 63

The Up Side   63
The Down Side   64
Seeking out the Opportunities   65
How to Get a Federal Job in the United States   66
  The OPM Application Process • The Selection Process
  for a Specific Agency Vacancy • Types of Appointments
  • Reinstatement Eligibility • Direct Appointment
  Eligibility for Spouses of U.S. Government Personnel

Working for the Federal Government Overseas   73
   How to Get a Federal Job Overseas...When Your
   Spouse Already Has One • Types of Overseas
   Appointments • Returning to the United States From
   Overseas

Chapter 6
Exploring Your Options 78
   Read All About It   80
      Sources of Written Information
   Ask Around   83
      Making Contacts • Opening Doors • What to Talk
      About • Make the Most of Your Meeting • How to
      Maintain Your Contacts
   Look Around   93
   Try It on for Size   93
   Career-Related Course Work   94
   Computerized Guidance   94

Part III   CHOOSING

Chapter 7
The Job Market and Employment Trends 97
   Look Before You Leap: Investigating Your New Location   97
   High-Growth Fields in an Era of Change   99
   Is Faster Always Better?   100
   Exotic Jobs of the Future   101

Chapter 8
How to Set and Reach an Employment Goal 102
   Defining Your Goal   103
   Achieving Your Goal   105
      Employment Action Plans • Managing Your Time

Chapter 9
Career Planning Assistance 111
   Workshops and Courses   112
   One-to-One Counseling   113
   Career Resources You Can Use at Home   115

Part IV   TAKING ACTION

Chapter 10
Broadening Your Opportunities With New Skills 119

'Returning to School': Variations on a Theme   120
- Correspondence Courses • External Degree Programs • Special Opportunities for Military and Foreign Service Spouses • How to Pursue Graduate Studies Abroad

Audio and Video Cassettes   125

Learning by Doing   129
- Entry-Level Jobs • Part-Time Work • Temporary Work • Avocations • Volunteering • Internships and Apprenticeships

Self-Development   129

Self-Employment   129

Chapter 11
Tracking Down the Job Openings 131

What Can Your Spouse's Employer Do for You?   131
- Corporations • The Military • The Foreign Service • Other Employers

Long-Distance Strategies   136
- Tips for Seeking Overseas Employment

How to Find Alternative Work Arrangements   142
- Contract Work • Part-Time Work • Temporary Work • Job Sharing • Volunteering

Traditional Job-Hunting Methods (There's Got to Be a Better Way)   144

Self-Directed Job-Hunting Methods (The Better Way)   146

Chapter 12
The Relocation Resume 149

Do You Need a Resume?   149

Why So Many Resumes Fail   150

Categories to Consider   151
- Contact Information • Work Experience • Education • Honors and Awards • Credentials, Licenses, and Special Skills • Publications • Memberships • Languages • Interests • Personal Data • References • Job Objective

The Visual Factor   162

Critique Your Resume   163

Chapter 13
The Customized Cover Letter 170
   Appearance 171
   Address 171
   Opening Paragraph 172
   Body of the Letter 172
   The Clincher Paragraph 173

Chapter 14
The Application Form 178
   Nongovernment Forms 178
      Filling in the Blanks
   SF171: The Application for Federal Employment 180
      Page 1 • Page 2 • Page 3 • Page 4
      After You Complete the SF171

Chapter 15
Interviewing With Confidence 192
   Your Goal in an Interview 192
   Homework That Puts You a Step Ahead 193
   Face-to-Face With the Interviewer 200
   Following Up 203
   Optional Ways to Respond to Interviewers' Questions 208

Epilogue 211

Appendix A
Federal Job Information/Testing Centers 213

Appendix B
Networks and Other Groups 217

Appendix C
**Supplemental Reading Material & Publisher/
Distributor Contact Information** .228

Index 251

Preface

We live in a highly mobile society with workers moving frequently throughout the country and the world. According to the Bureau of the Census, every year for the last 25 years, 20 percent of the U.S. population has changed addresses.

Even though relocation has long been recognized as one of the most stressful events a couple can encounter, until recently it has been accepted as a fact of life. Now, more and more workers are resisting relocation. This phenomenon accompanies the increase in numbers of dual-career couples. The proportion of married couples with both husband and wife in the labor force was 25 percent in 1960, close to 50 percent in 1985, and, according to one projection, may rise to 86 percent by 1990. Since acceptance of a transfer is not as likely when there is an employed partner — either married or unmarried — the relocation factor is having a dramatic impact on many work environments. Rather than face relocation, some employees quit their jobs.

Yet, despite the stress associated with relocation, most couples will continue to move to new locations for a variety of employment reasons. Sometimes individuals have little choice but to follow job opportunities or face career stagnation or even unemployment. For example, many organizations rely on transfers to groom staff for management roles. Similarly, when corporate headquarters or divisions move for more favorable economic or operational conditions, management often assumes that employees will continue their jobs at the new location. In the military and foreign service, frequent relocations are practically a condition of employment. Beyond the control of management, poor economic conditions sometimes create massive layoffs and plant shutdowns, forcing workers to leave their hometowns in search of new jobs.

In other cases, workers voluntarily relocate for jobs higher up the career ladder. For example, scientists, engineers, and university professors frequently follow job opportunities in their specialties. Likewise, clergy in some denominations equate mobility with advancement; many ministers launch their careers with small rural congregations before advancing to larger urban churches.

Whatever the reason for relocation, the experience is likely to be especially trying for the accompanying spouse who also works outside the home. Breaking off a work commitment has an impact professionally as well as personally. Many spouses work simply to add a little extra to the family income without a long-term commitment to their employment; however, more than half of the working spouses in the United States are part of a two-earner marriage whose lifestyle depends on two incomes. Moreover, an increasing number are anxious to reach high levels after having entered professional and executive careers. With specific skills and high expectations, these spouses are especially likely to find that relocation infringes upon their employment plans and hopes.

Career planning and job hunting are difficult tasks for anyone, but spouses accompanying relocating employees face special challenges. They sever valuable networks that could help in locating new employment. Unfamiliar with their new job markets, they may have difficulty identifying people with authority to hire. Employers, wary of work histories of short-term employment periods, may respond negatively to applications from relocating spouses. And if their skills are not in demand where they relocate, these spouses may not be able to find any paid employment in their fields. For reasons such as these, the relocating spouse needs specific and precise information about how to approach the job search under possibly adverse circumstances.

The purpose of *The Relocating Spouse's Guide to Employment* is to enable relocating spouses to overcome the strikes against them in the world of work and to *surpass* the average job seeker in the employment market. Comprehensive and detailed, this resource covers a variety of work options as well as the hows and whys of career planning and the job search, which come alive through 51 firsthand accounts from spouses who have relocated. This guide is intended to help spouses both in remote parts of the world and in large urban areas approach their relocations armed with superior information, techniques, preparation, and work skills. While other employment guides are on the market, there is none of this scope that focuses on the unique requirements and problems encountered by the men and women who choose to accompany relocating employees.

During the past two and a half years, two editions of this guide sold rapidly in the United States and abroad in response to an increasing demand from relocating spouses for meaningful employment assistance. This third edition of *The Relocating Spouse's Guide to Employment* incorporates a number of changes to ease spouses transitions. In particular, it offers valuable new resources and updated contact information on sources of help.

Who can benefit from this guide? It is intended for wives and husbands (or other accompanying partners) and dependent family members of employees in corporations, the military, the foreign service, academia, the ministry, and other work settings, who relocate in the United States and abroad. The material in this resource applies to persons on all levels who move regularly, over and over again, as well as to those who relocate only once or twice. Likewise, this guide is intended both for relocators who plan to pursue full-time, paid employment and for those wanting lesser commitments in the form of part-time, temporary, or even volunteer work.

Finding a new job in a new home is trying, yes; but with solid understanding of one's goals and the strategies for accomplishing them, it can also be a most rewarding adventure.

Frances Bastress
January 1989

Acknowledgments

For starters, I thank all the relocating spouses who provided me with meaningful topics and stories based on their experiences while living *on the move*.

For their ongoing encouragement about my project and their feedback, I thank the staff at Catalyst, the New York-based not-for-profit organization that works with corporations and individuals to develop career and family options.

For generously providing me with material on the progress of spouse employment assistance in the corporate world, I am grateful to the Employee Relocation Council. Located in Washington, DC, this group is the professional membership organization for corporations and relocation service firms concerned with employee transfers.

Through my work with the Military Family Support Center, I first became aware of the acute need for this book. I am obliged to the staff there as well as to my contacts in the family programs offices of the Army, Navy, Air Force, and Marines.

Anne Heard and her assistant Norma Price of the Family Liaison Office (FLO) at the Department of State provided me with excellent material and answered my endless questions. Equally helpful was the staff at the Overseas Briefing Center of the Foreign Service Institute.

Susan McClintock launched me in the spouse employment area in the first place: Soon after her employment with FLO at the Department of State, she invited me to assist with career planning workshops for foreign service spouses. Thank you, Susan!

Unnamed but not unappreciated are my colleagues who let me pick their brains and the authors whose books and articles gave me ideas for this guide. A special thanks to Joyce Picard and Russell Bruch, whose presentations taught me creative approaches for exploring options, some of which are incorporated into Chapter 6.

Finally, for their time and effort in helping to make this book possible, I am especially indebted to Ron Krannich, Laurie Jackson, Dawn M. Eichenlaub, Marlene Hassell, and Becky Eason.

Introduction

While transitions are a normal part of life, you may have been thrust into one not of your own choosing, as the spouse of a relocating employee. You may have feelings of resentment and anger about being uprooted and transplanted to a strange new environment. The relocation experience may be especially wrenching when you have not yet developed new personal or work affiliations in your new location.

With the understanding that relocation may be traumatic, the mission of this book is to help you recognize that even though a door closes behind you when you move, other doors will open. Forced out of your comfort zone, you face new challenges and risks where you can create opportunities out of crisis. By trying yourself out on new tasks in new environments, you will discover facets of yourself you never knew existed. The experience of relocation and reestablishment, while negative to begin with, will be positive and growth-producing in the long run.

Before you read further, it is important to understand the meaning of terms used throughout this guide. As mentioned in the preface, *spouse* here refers to other family members as well as to the married or unmarried partner of a relocating employee. Besides full-time paid work, references to *work* and *employment* will also apply to part-time and temporary work, volunteer work, internships and apprenticeships, and other arrangements between workers and their work environments. Because of this, *career*, in the context of this guide, will not necessarily imply consecutive progressive achievement following a clearly prescribed path to the top. As described in Chapter 3, this term instead may denote an accumulation of knowledge in a field of work. *Dual-career*, for our purposes, designates the employment of both partners, whether or not their jobs provide comparable status and salaries.

The first step to ensuring that your relocation experience develops into something positive is to accept that you are in a state of transition and to express your negative feelings about it to family, friends, and/or outside helpers who can offer the kind of understanding and support you require. After confronting the trauma of relocation, get on with your life by confronting the many decisions that affect all phases of your life — employment being one of them.

As an accompanying spouse or family member, you are faced with more employment decisions than the average career person. While you may hope to continue the same kind of work you have been doing, your new location may not provide employment opportunities in your field. Rather than narrow your options prematurely, keep an open mind and view relocation as a time to reevaluate your career and to explore many previously unconsidered options.

This guide is designed to help you make effective decisions, especially employment-related decisions. Since employment affects many areas of your life, the decision-making process presented here has wide applicability. It will enable you to determine *what* you want to do, *where* you want to do it, and *how* you will do it. As shown here and in the accompanying diagram, this process covers six levels:

I. *Self-assessment:* evaluating what is important to you, including your interests, skills, values, preferred lifestyle, and ideal job specifications.

II. *Exploration:* investigating a wide variety of work and life options after developing good self-awareness.

III. *Choosing:* selecting an employment goal after comparing your options with your priorities and qualifications.

IV. *Taking Action:* applying specific job-search strategies as you pursue your goal.

V. *Adjusting to Transition:* acclimating yourself to your new job or situation and growing in it.

VI. *Reevaluation:* reassessing your position after adjusting to it, and then, perhaps, repeating the decision-making process again beginning with level I. Depending on where and how frequently you move, you may need to be very flexible and to regularly reevaluate your situation.

INTRODUCTION

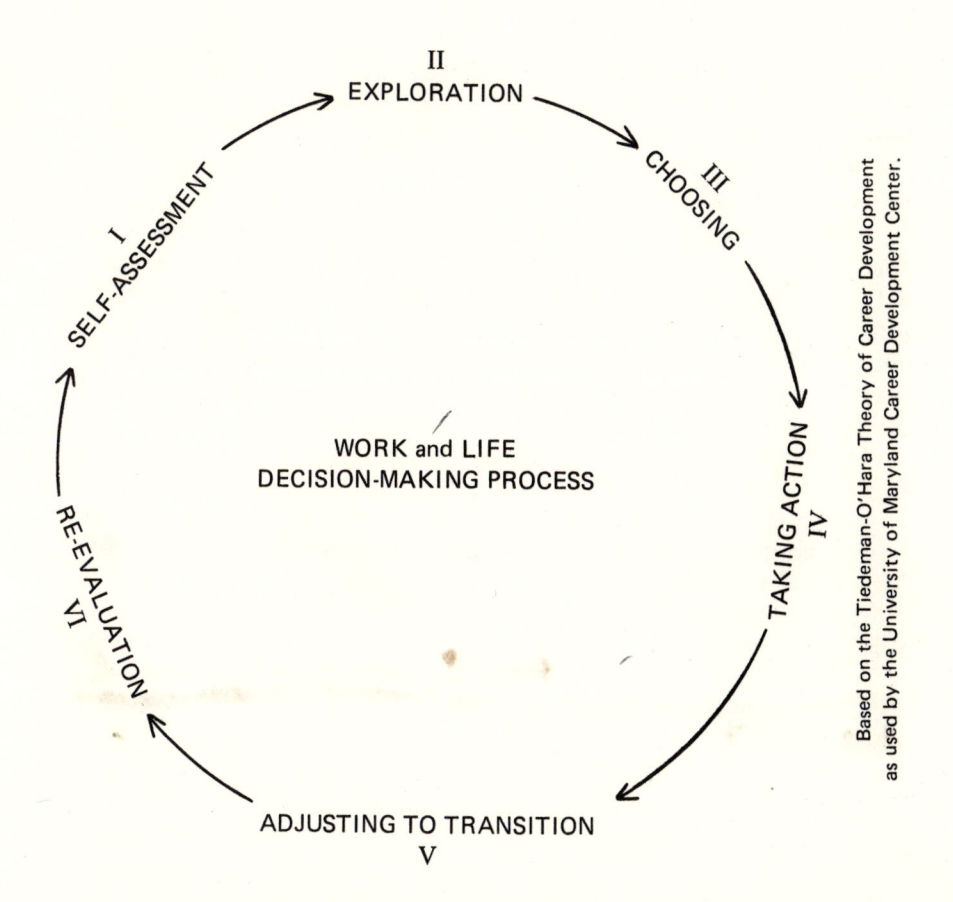

Diagram: WORK and LIFE DECISION-MAKING PROCESS

- I SELF-ASSESSMENT
- II EXPLORATION
- III CHOOSING
- IV TAKING ACTION
- V ADJUSTING TO TRANSITION
- VI RE-EVALUATION

Based on the Tiedeman-O'Hara Theory of Career Development as used by the University of Maryland Career Development Center.

This employment guide is divided into four parts to cover levels I through IV of this work and life decision-making process. Level V is covered in the epilogue. It is advisable to proceed consecutively through Parts I through III, completing one level before moving to the next. Part I is demanding, but if you persevere through the important exercises there, the book becomes more fun.

You can skip chapters that do not apply to you in Parts II, III, and IV, but go to Part IV only when you know *exactly* what work you want to do and can communicate orally and in writing with employers on how your qualifications and priorities meet their needs. While there are many jobs in the marketplace, you will be more likely to identify and locate satisfying employment for the long term if you take time to do the proper planning before entering the job search. Spouses who relocate every few years have found such planning time to be extremely limited; you may find it best to complete Parts I, II, and III *before* relocation in order to hit the ground running *after* relocation. Otherwise, in your impatience to be employed, you might accept the first offer of a job and end up hating it.

The appendices make up a large portion of this book, and should not be overlooked. For the job seeker interested in pursuing work with the Federal Government, Appendix A lists 50 federal job information centers in the United States and its territories. Appendix B lists 131 networks and other groups, many of which provide career information, including training requirements, job duties, salaries, and the employment outlook for specific fields of work. To supplement the information in the guide, Appendix C describes nearly 200 books, pamphlets, directories, and tapes spanning 15 categories — career planning, alternative patterns of work, the two-career family, overseas employment, and more. Especially useful for the spouse in a remote U.S. or overseas location, information is provided on how to contact the publishers and distributors of the career resources listed in Appendix C.

You are about to embark on a career decision-making process that has risks as well as rewards. As you proceed, keep in mind the words of Vauvenargues: "The greatest achievement of the human spirit is to live up to one's opportunities and make the most of one's resources."

I

SELF-ASSESSMENT

Self-trust is the first secret of success.
Ralph Waldo Emerson

1

Your Qualifications

To prepare for making informed decisions about your life and work, you need to periodically reevaluate what is important to you. You can do this best through *self-assessment* — a process that entails recording your work history, education, and other significant experiences, and then identifying your priorities, including your preferred lifestyle, values, work environment, interests, skills, and job specifications.

The self-assessment process is especially important when faced with a major transition like relocation. If you have not been working, moving may provide the impetus to enter paid employment. If you have been steadily working, relocation may prompt you to consider a new career field. Even though you may be very satisfied with what you are doing now — be it a fulfilling career or some other involvement — you may not have the luxury of continuing it after relocation. To avoid setting yourself up for failure, it is important to be open to many possibilities when you move to a new area. By documenting your qualifications and then identifying your priorities, you will be armed with a clear knowledge of what you can do and prepared to consider an array of new options.

Self-assessment is an excellent way to evaluate what you want to do, but, unfortunately, many job-seekers skip this step in favor of entering an active job search. With only a sketchy awareness of their priorities, strengths, and job targets, they are unable to write resumes that attract attention, and are unable to communicate effectively in interviews.

Since this book's approach to self-assessment requires careful documentation of your qualifications, you will be well prepared to communicate with employers orally and in writing once you reach the job search stage. The exercises in both this chapter and the next will enable you to clarify your strengths, what you need for your life and work to be fulfilling, and, perhaps, what you hope to change about yourself. The more you put into the exercises, the more you will get out of them, even though some of the activities will have more meaning for you than others.

CASE IN POINT

Carroll Madison had been teaching world studies in a San Francisco Bay Area high school for nine years when his wife received what she believed to be the job offer of a lifetime. She was invited to join a major New York City investment firm at a salary higher than what she dreamed of making even in 10 years.

A Californian all his life, Carroll had no interest in moving east. He was satisfied teaching motivated teenagers in his affluent community and couldn't imagine doing anything else. "Besides," he fretted, "what else could I do with a history degree?" When thinking about teaching in New York City, he envisioned unruly students and constant disruptions, like a scene out of the movie *Blackboard Jungle*. Nonetheless, Carroll eventually agreed to try East Coast living for a few years so his wife could launch her career.

Unsure about wanting to teach or being able to teach in New York City, Carroll sought the assistance of a career development authority and took steps to determine what to do next. Describing the process, he says, "I forced myself to go away for a weekend to a friend's vacant house to evaluate my past by writing a work autobiography. I wrote 20 to 30 pages about everything I'd done work-wise from the very first thing I'd ever considered work. I also described my interests and hobbies and other things that were important to me. Reviewing those pages, I looked for the common elements — what I liked and disliked, what was fun for me, and what components I needed to have in my future work and in the rest of my life."

That exercise clarified for Carroll that, if he must relocate to New York City, he wanted to live in Manhattan with only a short commute to work, he wanted to stay in education but not in the public school system, and he wanted to try working with adults. Furthermore, the self-assessment process was the catalyst he needed to become aware of the many skills he had acquired from teaching, from his community work, and from the other experiences in his life.

THE TIME LINE OF YOUR LIFE

As the starting point for clarifying many important things about yourself, create a time line of your life:

1. Draw a vertical line down the length of a piece of paper that measures at least two by three feet.
2. Start with the current year, and mark off the line in two-year time periods, allowing two or more inches for each segment. Continue in this reverse chronological order until you reach a time when you began doing some form of paid or unpaid work, perhaps your mid-teens. If necessary, use the back of your paper or a second page.
3. *Significant Life Events:* Close to the left of the line, next to the appropriate years, list significant events from all periods of your lifetime; for example, high school and college graduations, marriages, births of children, deaths of loved ones, relocations, and awards.

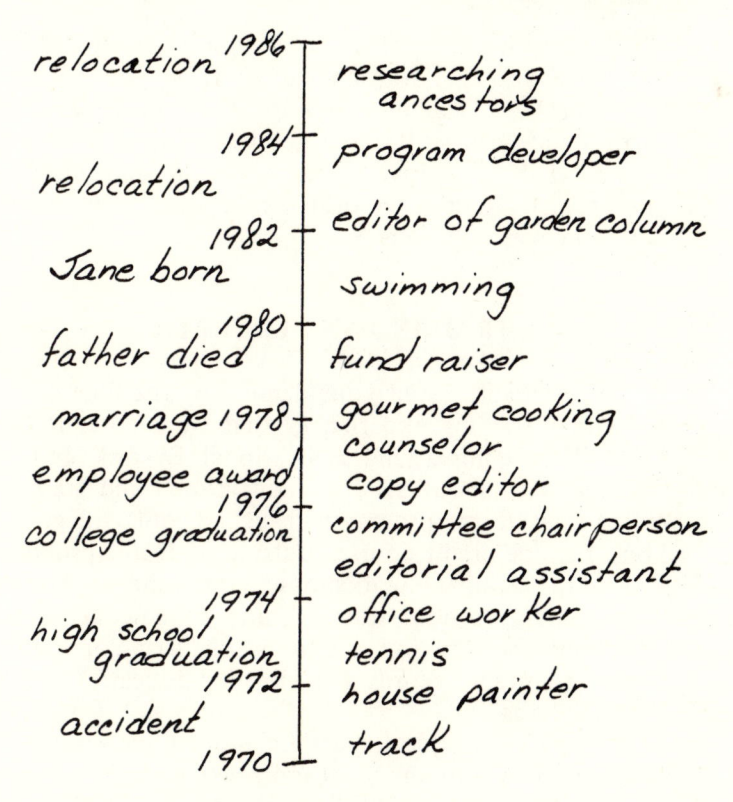

```
relocation      1986 ─┬─ researching
                      │   ancestors
                 1984 ─┼─ program developer
relocation            │
                 1982 ─┼─ editor of garden column
Jane born             │
                      │   swimming
                 1980 ─┼─
father died           │   fund raiser
                      │
marriage         1978 ─┼─ gourmet cooking
                      │   counselor
employee award        │   copy editor
                 1976 ─┼─
college graduation    │   committee chairperson
                      │   editorial assistant
                 1974 ─┼─ office worker
high school           │
  graduation          │   tennis
                 1972 ─┼─ house painter
accident              │
                 1970 ─┴─ track
```

Sample Time Line

4. *Roles:* Also to the left of the line, you may want to list roles you have had during your lifetime; for example, spouse, parent, or helpmate.

5. *Hobbies and Major Activities:* Next, close to the right of the line and close to the appropriate years, enter hobbies and major activities from all periods of your life, including participation in social, community, or work-related groups and events.

6. *Work (Paid and Unpaid):* Again to the right of the line and next to the appropriate years, write in job titles for all the work you have performed during your lifetime. Besides full-time, paid work, include internships and apprenticeships as well as part-time, temporary, and volunteer work from all aspects of your life — professional or civic organizations, the community, school, and church or synagogue. If your work had no job title, create one; for example, aide, assistant, expediter, analyst, program developer, negotiator, thrift shop salesperson, fund raiser, counselor, and chairperson.

7. Examine your time line. Does it adequately represent who you are? Have you left out anything? Have you covered all the periods of your life? Take a few minutes to fill in any gaps.

8. Now stand back and take a good look at your time line. Concentrate on what is positive about your life and what *you* value from it — forget about what others may value. Our needs, hopes, and goals make us who we are.

TRAINING AND EDUCATION

While you probably listed your degrees on the time line, you may have had other training experiences that were not entered. Create forms like the accompanying Educational Record, and record on them the specifics about all your educational and training experiences other than degree programs in high school, college, and graduate school. Include credit courses outside of degree programs, career and leadership training, workshops, conferences, Armed Forces training, vocational school training, and other educational experiences from membership organizations, civic or community work, and school. Maintain records for all your educational experiences on an ongoing basis.

In case employers request specifics about your educational background or you decide to apply for more schooling, it's a good idea to keep transcripts of your credit work on hand as well as certificates of participation for your other training endeavors.

YOUR QUALIFICATIONS 11

EDUCATIONAL RECORDS

Course Title _____ Dates Attended _____

Sponsoring Organization _____

Name of Instructor _____ Telephone _____
    (if known)   (if known)

Location _____

Description of Course (give details):

Skills or Knowledge Acquired:

Method of Recognition, i.e., certificate, continuing education units (specify number), college credits (specify number of semester or quarter hours), or other forms of recognition:

WORK HISTORY: A MEMORY JOGGER

To increase your awareness of your qualifications, write out the details of your past employment, whether paid or unpaid. Besides clarifying your skills, this method is excellent preparation for writing resumes and employment applications and for interviewing with employers. Since this documentation approach appears tedious to many job-seekers, few bother with it. If you take time to follow a few easy steps, you will substantially improve your chances for employment.

To get yourself going, pick a job you especially liked. On your time line, to the right of that job, list 10 to 15 of your responsibilities. At a minimum, list a verb with an object; for example, "trained patients," "counseled youth," "gave presentations," "wrote proposals."

To give more details about your important work responsibilities, consider this approach: First, list a *verb* and a *subject* to describe a job from your time line; for example, "typed documents." Then insert another element — perhaps the *kind* of document you typed — and the phrase may become "typed statistical documents." Next, add *for whom* you typed the documents, and your finished description may read "typed statistical documents for mental health practitioners."

For guidance as you work to enhance the quality of your descriptions, refer to the accompanying model and examples. Select one of the 10 to 15 job responsibilities you listed on your time line, and fill in as many of the elements on the model as appropriate.

MODEL FOR DOCUMENTING YOUR EXPERIENCE

Action
   verb:

Object
   what:
   quantity or size:
   subject, type, or kind:

Outcome
   for whom:
   purpose:
   final results:

Examples of Sentences Combining Elements from the Model

1. Filed medical records for large hospital surgical department to
   (verb) (type) (what)   (for whom)

   simplify billing procedures.
   (purpose)

2. Wrote 16-page systems booklet, "How to Conduct Leadership
   (verb) (size) (type) (what)   (subject)

   Training Programs," for coordinators of volunteers to promote
                         (for whom)   (purpose)

   staff development in the agency. Received an award for superior writing quality from headquarters personnel. (final results)

3. Organized 20-member youth group to canvass suburban
   (verb)   (size)   (kind) (what) (purpose)

   community to increase support and collect funds for political candi-
                                                     (for whom)

   dates. Efforts resulted in campaign pledges of $5,000 after only three days of canvassing. (final results)

4. Planned and presented a seminar for the professional develop-
   (verb)   (verb)   (what)   (purpose)

   ment of 200 people in an organization.
        (for whom)

When you feel comfortable with the method described here, document the details of all your work experiences, both paid and unpaid, on forms you create like the Job Description Record, shown later in this chapter. If you have trouble getting more than a few sentences, it may be that you need to think in smaller terms; for example, "supervised three employees" may have entailed recruiting, interviewing, delegating, evaluating, assisting, and training. The accompanying list of action words will help you in remembering your responsibilities.

ACTION WORDS

communicated	performed	prioritized	determined
managed	counseled	scheduled	reorganized
reported	encouraged	supervised	disciplined
wrote	achieved	reviewed	adjusted
interpreted	instructed	composed	corrected
researched	persuaded	explained	solved
planned	motivated	illustrated	identified
designed	trained	advised	contracted
conceived	stimulated	enabled	established
analyzed	attained	listed	reduced costs
defined	summarized	facilitated	sold
evaluated	inspected	clarified	prepared
perceived	compared	modified	invented
forecast	reviewed	typed	presented
estimated	maintained	structured	served
programmed	negotiated	referred	was promoted
organized	renegotiated	anticipated	oversaw
selected	adjusted	collaborated	taught
brought	reconciled	simplified	handled
enlisted	recommended	observed	expanded
developed	updated	screened	operated
administered	improved	generated	edited
applied	reevaluated	created	exhibited
coordinated	assigned	experimented	contacted
directed	enforced	demonstrated	cut
dealt	completed	integrated	diagnosed
implemented	improvised	visualized	chaired
responded	identified	guided	appraised
assessed	led	prepared	surveyed
delegated	mediated	recognized	molded
initiated	collected	produced	decided
expedited	inspired	tested	promoted

YOUR 'HIDDEN' CREDENTIALS

Besides education and work, you may have other experiences in your background that will be relevant to future employers' requirements and, therefore, enhance your qualifications. One relocating spouse says, "What I most disliked about being a foreign service spouse — organizing diplomatic events, supervising household staff — gave me management skills. Soon after I returned to the United States, I got several job offers. In these employers' eyes I had been a manager."

YOUR QUALIFICATIONS 15

Examine your activities, interests, and hobbies to see how they may contribute to your credentials.

CASE IN POINT

The daughter of missionaries, Gita Larson spent much of her youth in Nigeria. She says, "I was a prime organizer of boarding school activities while in Nigeria. Back in the States, I did a lot of speaking in churches with my parents, and I traveled alone as a teenager to summer camps and churches where I was paid to give speeches about my life in Nigeria. Through these experiences, I learned a great deal about giving presentations and organizing materials."

Years later, while raising twins in Lynchburg, VA, Gita worked as a member of five community and regional boards. She managed projects, organized people, planned and presented programs, worked with groups, sold ideas, and developed a childbirth education curriculum. Through the League of Women Voters, she met two women who, like herself, were ready to translate their volunteer skills into paid jobs. Gita says, "Using a career development book, we worked together to assess our interests and skills. I realized I loved training and had picked up many valuable skills through my volunteer activities. Although I had been teaching here and there since I was a teenager, I decided after my self-assessment to work with adults rather than youth."

Now in Rockville, MD, where she relocated as the spouse of a corporate employee, Gita is employed full-time with Montgomery College as program director for business and industry training. Enthusiastic about her work, Gita says, "I do needs assessment, market programs, select instructors, evaluate programs, and, whenever I can, I do stand-up training on the side."

Review all periods of your life and consider your experiences in church or synagogue, camp, membership groups, school, community, personal activities and hobbies, politics, and recreation. On your time line document things you could use, by any stretch of the imagination, in your future career. Some examples: coordinated social event for 75 foreign dignitaries, solicited contributions from members of community nonprofit organization, created floral arrangements for display windows. If your responsibilities in any one area are substantial enough to be equivalent to an unpaid job, describe your work on one of your job description records.

JOB DESCRIPTION RECORD

Job Title _____ Dates of Work _____

Organization Name _____ No. of Hours per week _____

Address _____ Telephone _____
         (if known)   (if known)

Supervisor _____ Title _____

Description of work (Using the action/object/outcome format, give specifics):

Special Accomplishments:

Skills Developed on the Job:

Awards, Commendations, Nominations, etc.:

Additional Comments:

BUILDING A WORK PORTFOLIO

After you have documented your qualifications, keep these papers and your other credentials together in a *work portfolio*, which could be a folder or large envelope. Serving as an *autobiography* of your career, your portfolio will allow you to produce on-the-spot information for employment and academic purposes. The following documents and materials are appropriate additions to a work portfolio for a relocating spouse:

- educational records and job description records
- your time line and other self-assessment information
- academic transcripts
- workshop certificates
- copies of submitted employment application forms
- recent resumes
- copies of cover letters
- work samples, such as brochures, handbooks, writing samples, and art work
- news clippings and program notes indicating your participation
- personnel actions, such as letters offering you employment, promotions, and salary increases
- certificates of awards

Also include letters of recommendation from individuals who can attest to your work-related abilities rather than your character. It is important to get these letters before relocating. Save the originals, and offer copies to future employers. If for some reason you cannot obtain a reference letter from a supervisor, you may have to take the initiative to write your own and get it signed by the supervisor.

CASE IN POINT

Adele Watkins, a 36-year-old public health worker now in Atlanta, GA, composes her own recommendations and then submits them to her supervisors for approval and signatures. Besides describing her work and skills, she includes honest comments about her personal qualities. The following are sample sentences from her letters:

- "Adele has an analytic mind, attacks assignments in innovative ways, and is a lucid writer."
- "She is competent at coordinating project work and is very partic-

> ular about deadlines."
> - "She is skillful in bringing people together and acting as a catalyst to organize and coordinate their interaction."

Set aside time to develop your portfolio for past years, and then keep it up to date. After compiling a comprehensive and organized work portfolio, your job search will be more efficient and your employment communications — applications, resumes, and others — will be easier to compose.

For safekeeping, make copies of all documents in your portfolio and store them in a separate location. During your moves, hand-carry your portfolio containing the original documents rather than pack it with your household belongings. This prevents possible loss or a delay in securing employment.

After documenting your credentials and creating your work portfolio, you will be prepared to determine your priorities.

2

Your Priorities

It is not unusual for a wife or husband who accompanies a relocating employee to feel like a victim of the spouse's mobile career. Instead of taking the reins of their own lives, relocating spouses often respond with a passive, fragmented approach to work.

To succeed at this business of relocating, you need to take an active approach. This requires, first of all, that you determine your priorities. Maybe that means working, or volunteering, or child rearing, or any combination of these. You need to decide whether you want consistent employment and income, or would prefer to work only now and then to supplement your spouse's salary. Is your career a major force in your life, or do you work primarily for the fringe benefits offered by employment? Are you motivated by career advancement, or by making a useful contribution to your community? Focus on the realities of *your* existence, and let your choices be reasoned ones.

As an aid in determining your priorities, complete the exercises in this chapter and then examine the results to find the common elements.

EVALUATING YOUR VALUES

Values are things that hold great meaning and importance for you. You will be more likely to locate satisfying employment if you identify your personal values and your work values and remember them as you make career decisions.

Personal Values: What do you need in your life for it to be satisfying for you? Affection? Popularity? Approval? Plenty of discretionary income? Plenty of discretionary time? Time spent with your children? A minimum of stress? Personal values affect your way of life, including your career. Refer to your time line and documentation in Chapter 1, and list your personal values. Keeping in mind you may not be able to have them all, star the values you couldn't do without.

Work Values: What is it you need in a job for it to be satisfying for you? Excitement? Creativity? Public contact? Recognition from others? Opportunities for advancement? Security? Competition? Good fringe benefits? A fast pace? A high salary? Refer to your documentation in Chapter 1, and make a list of the things that are important to you in your employment. Star those values that are essential to your work satisfaction.

What working conditions have annoyed you during your past work experiences? Too many rules? Lack of challenges? No variety? No chance for advancement? Lack of appreciation? Inflexible hours? Lack of feedback? Not enough vacation? Too long a commute? Since deciding what you don't want in a job is a step toward locating satisfying employment, list 10 to 15 working conditions that would bother you.

THE SIX PERSONALITY TYPES

According to John Holland, author of *Making Vocational Choices: A Theory of Careers,* most people in our culture can be characterized by their resemblance to one of six personality types. He goes on to say there are six kinds of work environments, each of which is dominated by a given type of personality, and people seek out environments that allow them to exercise their skills and abilities, express their attitudes and values, and take on agreeable problems and roles.

To assess your personality type and preferred work environment according to Holland's theory, read each of the following categories, and choose three that best describe you.

Realistic: Prefer to work with objects, machines, tools, plants, or animals, or to be outdoors. Have mechanical or athletic ability. Tend to have a practical outlook, and prefer to work on activities that have a specific outcome.

Investigative: Enjoy observing, investigating, and analyzing situations and solving abstract problems. Tend to have a need to understand how things work and why they are the way they are. Tend to be task-oriented and prefer to work independently of others.

Artistic: Have creative abilities in art, music, drama, language, or writing. Tend to be imaginative and have a need for individualistic expression. Prefer to work alone in unstructured environments, using creativity.

Social: Like to inform, help, train, develop, or cure people. Feel responsible for helping others who need assistance. Tend to be sociable and skilled with words.

Enterprising: Enjoy leadership roles, including management of others. Tend to be good with words and enjoy influencing and persuading others. Tend to be goal-oriented and prefer organizational environments — either their own or others. Tend to value political or economic achievement, including power, status, and material wealth.

Conventional: Prefer clearly defined activities using clerical, computational, and/or business system skills. Fit well into organizations and enjoy office work. Tend to follow the instructions of others rather than lead others.

Write the first letters of your first, second, and third choices; i.e., R, I, A, S, E, C.

_____	_____	_____
my first choice	my second choice	my third choice

Note that the realistic personality types prefer to use skills with *things*. The investigative and artistic types prefer to use skills with *ideas*. The social and enterprising personality types prefer to use skills with *people*. The conventional personality type prefers to use skills with *data*. From most preferred to least preferred, indicate how you prefer to use your skills; for example, (1) data, (2) people, (3) ideas, and (4) things.

Career centers often organize career information according to Holland's six categories, and several popular interest inventories are based on his theory. When you explore your options, keep the results of these exercises in mind.

A different approach to personality type assessment was developed by Isabel Briggs Myers. By taking the *Myers-Briggs Type Indicator* from a qualified counselor, you may learn about your temperament, including how you like to look at things and how you like to go about deciding things. The Indicator can help you understand where your strengths are and what kinds of work you might enjoy and succeed in.

WHAT REALLY INTERESTS YOU?

Interests are things you like doing, and they profoundly affect career choice. According to Tom Jackson in *The Hidden Job Market*, "An interest without a skill is happier and even more profitable than a skill without an interest . . . A high interest can be the motivation for developing skills and a full landscape of pleasures."

Rick Maurer, a human resource development consultant and former musician, believes that you can improve your chances for career satisfaction by looking toward things that excite you rather than looking at a category of skills and saying, "I can do that." He says, "I could probably make a living playing trumpet if I wanted to get back in shape. Unfortunately, I'd be playing for dances, and it would not offer the kind of challenge I want. If we only concentrate on our skills, we may make that kind of mix-up."

You may be able to learn more about your interests by taking the *Strong Campbell Interest Inventory*, the *Career Assessment Inventory*, the *Self-Directed Search*, or other interest inventories. On the other hand, since many of these instruments do little more than *inventory* your interests, your own knowledge of your interests may be quite sufficient.

CASE IN POINT

Married soon after high school, Lorraine Rudowski lived abroad for 15 years in six different countries as the spouse of a U.S. Government employee. When she returned to the United States in 1976, Lorraine was ready to prepare for a career. She says, "To determine what to train for, I considered my past experiences and what interested me: I had chaired the American Red Cross volunteers in Turkey and found that experience gratifying. I had taught many swimming classes overseas and liked working with teens and young adolescents. Finally, I really enjoyed raising five children — I had wanted to have six. These experiences helped me realize

YOUR PRIORITIES

> I'm a very service-oriented person."
>
> With this in mind, Lorraine investigated correctional work, education, and nursing. She wanted a profession that didn't set an age limit, and was attracted to nursing for this reason. She says, "I was 44 when I started my undergraduate nursing program in 1976 at George Mason University in Fairfax, VA. After finishing my bachelor's, I worked as a nurse and then returned for my master's. Now I do part-time nursing and am teaching nursing fundamentals to junior-level students at George Mason as well as working in their international nursing program. Soon, I will enter a Ph.D. program. I have always been able to work around my family, and they have been very supportive — they just don't want to go to any more graduations!"

Determine the degree of your interests in various activities by thinking about your work, your play, and your learning. What is it that gives you the most pleasure? What is it that you do first when you have a choice? What gives you energy and enthusiasm? Refer to your time line and documentation in Chapter 1, and then list 5 to 15 of your interests. Star those you might want to have as a part of your employment.

THREE TYPES OF SKILLS

While job search skills are important for locating employment, concrete, work-specific skills are essential for getting hired and advancing in your career. After carefully documenting your work history, education, and other significant experiences, you will be more confident about your skills and prepared to identify those you prefer. According to Richard Bolles, each of us has three different kinds of skills: (1) *transferable* or *functional skills*, (2) *work-content skills*, and (3) *self-management skills*.

The skills you pick up as you go through life and carry from one career field to another are *transferable* or *functional* skills, sometimes called *soft* skills; for example, writing news articles, counseling teenagers, maintaining accurate records, and nurturing young children. Your transferable skills will be prominent and obvious in the sentences you created for your job description records in Chapter 1. Select 5 to 15 of the transferable skills you have enjoyed using and hope to use in your future employment. Record them by listing, at a minimum, an action verb and an object.

Work-content skills, sometimes called *hard* skills, generally require you to remember something in particular in order to do a job; for example, operating a calculator, speaking Spanish, using word processing software, administering and scoring aptitude tests, and having a knowledge of adult development theory. Although you can acquire work-content skills on your own through independent study, people typically learn them in school or on the job. Whereas transferable skills help you advance once you are established in a career field, relevant work-content skills are necessary, more often than not, to get hired. After reviewing your educational records and your job description records, list 5 to 15 of the work-content skills you have enjoyed using and hope to use in your future employment.

Self-management skills, better known as personal traits, are related to temperament. We acquire many of our self-management skills early in life as a result of relationships with our family, peers, and environment, but we can acquire new traits later in life with determination or intensive education. The following are examples of self-management skills: adaptability, altruism, assertiveness, charm, creativity, perseverence, empathy, optimism, precision, and self-confidence.

A common misconception is that self-management skills are not relevant to the world of work. To the contrary, many fields of work require specific personalities.

Record your self-management skills that may be useful, even remotely, in future employment. If you get stuck, call upon your friends, family, and colleagues to help you identify your personal traits.

For additional help in identifying your skills, refer to the resources in Appendix C.

YOUR DREAM JOB

Make a list of the things you hope to get in a job. Among other things, include values you want fulfilled, working conditions you hope to avoid, interests and skills you hope to use, and anything else that is important to you in your employment, such as location, hours of work, and vacations. You might also include work settings that appeal to you; for example, corporations, the diplomatic community, financial institutions, government, schools, and health-care organizations. While you may change some of your specifications after reading the remaining chapters, this exercise will help you narrow your options.

TO MOVE OR NOT TO MOVE

For spouses of transferred employees, an intrinsic part of the self-assessment process is assessing the impact such a relocation would have on their lives. When relocation, childbirth, or other factors cause you to leave a job, your career is unavoidably affected. The severity of any negative effects depends on the number of interruptions, your particular field of work, and, if relocating, where you will be living. For example, one or two relocations within the United States for a nurse or teacher will not create as severe a disruption as four or five worldwide relocations for a corporate lawyer. If your relocation is likely to have major detrimental career repercussions, you and your spouse may want to examine other options.

The conventional expectations for marriage have been for couples to live together regardless of the circumstances. Today, however, it is not always assumed that the spouse automatically will follow the transferred employee. Now that huge numbers of women are in the workplace with serious investments in their careers, many challenges face the concept, "whither thou goest, I will go."

An alternative, when distances are manageable, is for a dual-career couple to move halfway between their employers. Consider the case of John and Mary who lived and worked in Washington, DC, until John's employer transferred him to New York City. To enable Mary to continue her employment in Washington and to distribute the hardship of commuting between them, the couple relocated to Philadelphia, which is approximately halfway between their former home and John's new work site.

Another option is a so-called "commuter marriage," in which husband and wife maintain separate residences at the sites of their respective employment, and rendezvous whenever possible. A commuter marriage is unlikely to survive indefinitely if long distances and financial burdens prevent regular meetings. Foreign service spouses may be interested to know that the Foreign Service allows an employee to request, for personal reasons, a separate maintenance allowance for dependents. With this benefit, interested spouses are able to continue employment without interruption, but, because of the distance factor, must endure long separations from their partners.

Unconventional choices, of course, should be carefully weighed with consideration for your career commitment, your family relationships, and the other circumstances in your life and your family's life.

ARE YOU A RISK TAKER?

How strong is your willingness to risk, compared with your desire for security? Risking usually involves giving up something in order to get something. By moving, you demonstrate at least some willingness to risk. If, at the same time, you plan to make a transition to a new career, the risks become much greater.

The willingness to risk varies from person to person. While you may be willing to risk in one area of your life, you may not be willing in other areas. Spend some time reflecting on your willingness to risk in the personal, professional, and financial areas of your life. Consider the positive and negative effects risking may have for you in the long run.

A relocating spouse and successful career changer once said, "Being a risk taker is critical for making it in any environment. Even though they may fall hard, too, it's the risk takers who are the big winners."

II
EXPLORATION

*Life is either a daring adventure or nothing.
To keep your face toward change and behave
like free spirits in the presence of fate
is strength undefeatable.*

Helen Keller

3

Options for a Relocating Spouse

The exploration phase of the decision-making process is a time to let yourself go and fantasize about how it would feel to be employed in a number of fields, work settings, and work arrangements.

As a relocating spouse, you need to be more flexible than the average career person because, depending on where and how frequently you move and what you want to pursue, you may not be able to find your ideal job. Rather than narrow your options prematurely, view relocation as a time to explore many previously unconsidered options.

Career can be defined in several ways. *Webster's Third New International Dictionary* defines it as "pursuit of consecutive progressive achievement especially in public, professional, or business life." But *career* can also be an individual's accumulation of knowledge in one or several fields of work. If you foresee relocations to places with a high demand in your field, you may have no trouble maintaining a career as *Webster's* defines it. However, if you foresee relocations to job markets where there is a low demand (or no demand) for your line of work, your career may be more like the second definition.

In a particularly difficult environment where there are many limitations, look for and investigate the positives. You could maintain your career through course work, volunteering, writing, or by taking a lower-level job in your field.

CASE IN POINT

Linda Calvin had been secretary to the president of a Seattle-based manufacturing firm for five years when its headquarters closed down. Her husband Lucas, employed with the same firm, was told to either transfer to the plant's new headquarters in rural Washington State or look for another job. Linda could not transfer to the new plant at her present level because of an internal reorganization, nor could she find a comparable job with another company in such a remote location.

While Linda's first thought was to remain in Seattle in the same kind of work and commute to Lucas on weekends, she eventually decided to follow him. "I was frustrated and angry at first," Linda says, "but my semidepressed state prompted me to examine my options in new ways. When I stopped assuming I must continue doing what I had always done, I reconsidered one of my old dreams — to run a bed-and-breakfast operation. The idea seemed outlandish at first, but I began to realize it was a very practical business idea. While the new plant was to be a focus for considerable business activity, few lodging accommodations were accessible."

In brief, Linda and Lucas bought and renovated a large Victorian home. Besides five well-appointed guestrooms, they set up a conference room for guests wanting to conduct business away from the plant. Linda reports, "What began as a jolt to my career has resulted in an exhilarating experience for me."

Here is a sampling of fields to start you thinking about the diversity of career options available.

EXAMPLES OF FIELDS OF WORK

Administration
Banking
Beauty Services
Biological Sciences
Bookkeeping
Child Care
Clerical
Community Affairs
Construction
Counseling
Culinary

Health Care
Hospitality and Leisure Services
Human Services
Journalism
Law
Lobbying
Meeting Planning
Personnel
Program Development
Promotion
Public Relations

Data Processing
Engineering
Entertainment
Financial Analysis
Food Service
Fund Raising
Graphic Design

Real Estate
Retailing
Sales
Social Work
Teaching and Training
Volunteer Management
Writing and Editing

If you foresee frequent relocations in your future, you may want to consider employment options where your progress is based on your knowledge as demonstrated by the results of your work rather than time in a job following an inflexible path to the top.

CASE IN POINT

Barbara Yoder speaks three languages and has lived in four countries in nine years — most recently, she lived in East Berlin. With her formal training in music and dance, and her experience in gymnastics, she has this to say: "The jobs followed me around. In many cases, people came to me and asked me to work, and in other cases I saw a need and devised a program. Among other things, I have designed physical education curricula and gymnastics programs for children, I have taught aerobics to youth, and I have done translating." By adapting to her environment and asking herself, "What are the restrictions and what are the possibilities?" Barbara has been able to work everywhere she's wanted to work.

YOU CAN TAKE IT WITH YOU: SIX PORTABLE CAREERS

A research report by the Employee Relocation Council suggests that spouses of employees with *highly* mobile careers select complementary careers with the following four characteristics:

1. a predicted labor shortage
2. openings not limited by geographic area
3. income not dependent on developing a clientele
4. advancement or benefits not dependent on tenure.

The report concluded that "couples with complementary careers seem less likely to have problems than couples with noncomplementary careers."

As you explore career options, you may wish to give special consideration to portable careers that are compatible with a highly mobile lifestyle. These include counseling, health care, social work, secretarial work, teaching and training, writing and editing, and more.

Counseling

In addition to well-known counseling positions such as school counselor and career counselor, a growing number of variations are cropping up in this profession. These include foreign student counselor, relocation counselor, leisure counselor, learning disabilities counselor, and rehabilitation counselor. With the threat of terrorism abroad, there may be an increase in opportunities for mental health practitioners to work either in agencies or in private practice overseas. To learn about the variety of special interest groups in the counseling field, contact the American Association of Counseling and Development (Appendix B).

As the counseling field gains in popularity, professional standards and monitoring are becoming tougher. For information about credentialing and licensure, contact the National Board for Certified Counselors through the American Association of Counseling and Development.

Health Care

The Department of Commerce reports that health care is the largest industry in the U.S. economy. The increased attention toward improving the health of the population worldwide and use of technology in health-care facilities has resulted in increased opportunities and new occupations spanning a variety of specialty areas and skill levels. Among others, there is an increased demand for occupational, physical, and inhalation therapists; medical, bloodbank, and cyto technologists; medical secretaries; physicians and surgical assistants; and opthalmic dispensers. The list of new occupations includes diagnostic medical sonographers; radiation therapy and nuclear medicine technologists; and cardiology, dialysis, and biomedical equipment technicians. While formal programs provide the most comprehensive training, on-the-job training is offered for many of these new occupations. *Career World* (March 1986) suggests a new concept — become a *multicompetent allied health professional* by acquiring training in more than one health field and thereby improve your chances of employment. This is a good suggestion for the spouse who foresees relocations to places with limited opportunities.

Even in traditional health-care occupations, such as nursing, many changes are apparent. For example, a number of nurses are channeling their skills into two new growth areas — home care and administration. In addition, there is a growing need for registered nurses with advanced degrees and specialities in geriatrics, primary care, and intensive care. Depending on their work settings, nurses are becoming involved in programs for stress counseling, sex education, alcoholism, nutrition, work safety, drug control, and smoking.

If you are relocating to a developing country, you will never want for challenging health-care opportunities, because according to a spokesperson for the National Council for International Health, programs there operate at a very fundamental level and are perpetually understaffed. Desperate for hands-on clinical staff, these programs often elevate competent personnel to higher levels than they could get in the United States. Even without a prior health-care background, your efforts are likely to be welcomed. Whether for pay or no pay, you can make an enormous difference by contributing, and will come away with new skills and unforgettable experiences.

Be aware that in some foreign economies you may have licensing problems if you are a doctor, dental technician, or are in another occupation requiring credentials that may be country-specific.

To become better informed about opportunities in health care, send for a free copy of "200 Ways to Put Your Talent to Work in the Health Field." Besides describing more than 100 health-related occupations, this booklet lists 110 associations that can provide you with additional information. Send $.45 in postage or a stamped, self-addressed, business-sized envelope to the National Health Council (see Appendix B).

Secretarial

With secretarial skills, you can almost always find a job anywhere in the world on a full-time, part-time, or temporary basis. If you want to take a year or two off, you will have no trouble reentering the secretarial field after your absence. According to the U.S. Department of Labor, salaries for secretaries have been rising, with executive secretaries in the United States now averaging more than $26,000 a year.

With the advances in technology, the stereotyped image of a secretary tied to a typewriter is rapidly disappearing. New electronic office systems have revolutionized the secretary's job and have opened up new career paths with more time spent on decision making. The predictions are that tomorrow's secretary will be an *office information manager* using electronic spreadsheets and computer graphics software.

Social Work

Like counseling, social work takes many forms: psychiatric social work, geriatric social work, family therapy, clinical social work, and social work associated with the courts, to name but a few. Stress caused by a mobile lifestyle has created a need for marriage therapists, especially in the diplomatic, military, and corporate communities abroad. Social work involves many skills that can be transferred to different fields as well as to new places. For example, social workers often rely on the management skills they have developed in their field to move into careers in administration.

Licensing and registration laws regarding social work practice and the use of professional titles have gained in importance, and the master's in social work is now the recognized degree in this field. For additional information, contact the National Association of Social Workers (Appendix B).

Teaching and Training

While advancement in the teaching field depends on length of service, teachers are almost always in demand worldwide and the profession has many nuances besides preschool, elementary, secondary, and postsecondary education. Learning disabilities specialists are increasingly sought out, and ESOL teachers (English to Speakers of Other Languages) have multiple opportunities both in the United States and abroad. By tutoring, you can easily work part-time. Moreover, if you plan to operate as both an employee and a parent, what work schedule could be more compatible than teaching? Since credentials are important in this field, keep them current as you relocate and move in and out of the profession.

While some overseas schools recruit teachers in the United States, others recruit them abroad, but whenever possible, contact the hiring institution before going abroad. A master's degree is often sufficient for teaching at the university level abroad. The University of Maryland is an example of a U.S. university with overseas branches. As

OPTIONS FOR A RELOCATING SPOUSE

described later in this chapter, overseas teaching opportunities are often provided by contract work arrangements. For books about teaching overseas, refer to Appendix C.

Training, a related field, involves the development of adults rather than the development of children and youth. Training is a growing, $40 billion to $60 billion industry in the United States that lures many teachers away from traditional classrooms. Besides effective presentation and interpersonal skills, the teaching-based skills most transferable and marketable to the consulting and training field are the following, according to Maggie Bedrosian, international speaker and former teacher:

- preparation of proposals
- design, delivery, and evaluation of education/training
- development of program materials
- coordination and management of programs
- evaluation and assessment of participants' skills
- review of literature and application
- facilitation of group interaction
- selection of appropriate audiovisual materials
- recognition and resolution of conflicts

Trainers in industry often need knowledge of adult development and some technical background relevant to the industry to which they are applying. Since many trainers serve as independent consultants, a career in training can be portable. To learn more about the training field, read the author's book, *Teachers in New Careers: Stories of Successful Transitions*, and contact the American Society for Training Development (Appendix B) for career information and Patricia A. McLagan's publication, "Training and Development Competencies."

Writing and Editing

With a pencil and a flair for words, you can set yourself up in a portable career developing fiction or nonfiction for books, newspapers, company newsletters, technical studies and reports, textbooks, trade journals, radio and television broadcasts, or advertisements. In countries with groups of English-speaking people, there are usually locally printed English-language newspapers and other publications that may welcome your contributions.

CASE IN POINT

When Uta Dietrich accompanied her husband, a doctor, on a year-long assignment to Madras, India, she kept her job of writing a garden column for a community newspaper in Connecticut. Besides her weekly columns, she began writing garden articles for publications she identified through *Writer's Market*, an annual publication.

"There are gardens all over the world," she says. "In India I wrote about tea plants and plantations, English-style gardens, and many other things. If you have an interest, it is likely to be manifested in the culture, wherever you are."

CAREERS COMPATIBLE WITH CHILDREN

If, besides repeated relocations, young children are or will be part of your life, you will be asking for trouble if you set your sights on a career characterized by 18-hour days and a clearly prescribed, rigid path to the top. Lawyers, ad executives, CPA's, and politicians are among those in such demanding and inflexible careers. Many relocators with families find it more practical instead to focus on jobs requiring skills that won't go stale during an absence and cause a severe loss in professional standing. These include, for example, graphic design, retail buying, and travel agent work, in addition to the portable careers previously mentioned. The jobs most compatible with raising children are those that allow you maximum control of your work schedule; for example, sales representative, real estate agent, and home-based jobs, such as free-lance writing and art, that enable you to take advantage of children's naps.

EXAMPLES OF FIELDS THAT ARE TRANSPORTABLE ABROAD

Accounting	Engineering	Linguistics
Administration	Family Planning	Nutrition
Anthropology	Graphic Design	Political Science
Bookkeeping	Health Care	Program Development
Community Development	Horticulture	Psychology
Economics	Law	Recreation

PICKING UP PORTABLE SKILLS

Individual skills that can be self-taught and independently updated, such as word processing and editing, are likely to be very portable. To ensure satisfying employment as you move from place to place, acquire skills that are marketable as well as transportable. Travel-related skills, including ticket sales and tour arranging, are increasingly in demand overseas. Other skills that often can be used worldwide in a variety of jobs are writing, art, photography, instructing, deaf signing, sales, interpreting, research, typing, and data processing, including programming and the ability to use computer software such as financial management packages. In addition, foreign service spouses report a high demand overseas for hair styling, dance and physical fitness instruction, and catering.

Computers represent the most widespread technical innovation of our time, since they are now used in virtually every industry. One worker in eight now uses a computer, and this number is growing rapidly, according to the *Occupational Outlook Quarterly* (Winter 1985). While some occupations require extensive computer training, others require only brief training in operating computers. Of course, programmers, systems analysts, and scientists who design computers need considerable training. Among those requiring minimal training are librarians, secretaries, travel agents, and postal clerks. Between these two extremes, other workers may need to learn how to program computers, including accountants, architects, engineers, dietitians, statisticians, and social scientists. Overseas employers often look for data processing skills.

While you may not want a high-tech career, computer literacy is likely to put you ahead of other applicants in competitive hiring situations and enable you to feel comfortable dealing with the computer hardware and software peripheral to your job.

Many spouses who have lived abroad suggest picking up a number of skills through education and experience that will fit in different places around the world. Of course, you must be competent in the language of the country to which you are moving if you hope to be employed there.

SELECTING A WORK SETTING

Since most jobs can be performed in more than one environment, evaluate a number of work settings to identify the ones that will satisfy your priorities. For example, secretaries and programmers work in banks, corporations, consulting firms, government agencies, insurance companies, and many other settings. While jobs in different settings may carry similar titles, the nature of the work often varies greatly. Personnel specialists in the Federal Government typically have a very narrow, specialized range of duties, but in a 300-employee manufacturing company, they may be responsible for all aspects of a personnel operation, from recruitment and interviewing to benefits administration, compensation, and affirmative action.

Consider the work settings listed here and the selected descriptions that follow:

EXAMPLES OF WORK SETTINGS

Academic Institutions
Catering Firms
Chambers of Commerce
Commercial Art Firms
Consulting and Contracting Firms
Corporations
Diplomatic Community
Environmental Technology Firms
Financial Institutions
Foundations
Government
Health-Care Facilities
High-Tech Firms
Home (self-employment)
Hospitals and Clinics
Hotels
Insurance Companies
International Nonprofit Organizations
Labor Unions
Law Firms
Libraries
Mental Health Agencies
Military Installations
Political Support Groups
Publishing Companies
Real Estate Firms
Research Organizations
Restaurants
Retail Stores
Schools
Scientific Laboratories
Theaters
Tour Companies
Trade and Professional Associations

Consulting and Contracting Firms

According to *Webster's Third New International Dictionary*, a consultant is one who gives professional advice or services regarding matters in the field of his or her special interest or training. Consulting and contracting firms seek out and hire such specialists to work on short-term contracts funded by outside sources. Performing every conceivable type of project in this country and abroad, these firms range in size from one or two persons up to thousands of internationally based staff members. Coopers and Lybrand is an example of a huge consulting firm. It does contract work with both public and private institutions, and maintains an international staff of 30,000 in 97 countries. The U.S. Agency for International Development (AID) is one of the largest dispensers of government contracts to consulting firms.

The Complete Guide to Public Employment by Drs. Ronald and Caryl Rae Krannich devotes a great deal of attention to consulting firms and the Agency for International Development system, which generate numerous jobs for those interested in international employment. To identify firms and job opportunities, refer to the Krannichs' book as well as the resources listed in Chapters 6 and 11 and Appendix C.

Corporations

Corporations vary according to size, location, and particular mix of products or services. The bottom line for most corporations is profit, with many firms accountable to stockholders. The corporate work environment offers a range of opportunities for financial analysts, managers, librarians, editors, engineers, clerks, graphic artists, and food service workers, to name but a few. To qualify for a job as a specialist in international business, Eric Kocher's book, *International Jobs*, suggests a technical business curriculum similar to that offered by an MBA program, consisting of five or six courses divided into two basic tracks: accounting-marketing and accounting-finance. You are not likely to get hired for your international relations background alone.

To identify specific organizations doing domestic and international business, start by reading *Business Week*, the *Wall Street Journal*, and *Fortune Magazine*. Refer also to the directories in Chapter 6 and Appendix C.

Diplomatic Community

If you relocate as a foreign service spouse to a country where you are unable to work on the local economy because of host country restrictions placed on people with diplomatic or official status, there are many things you can do within the diplomatic community, for example, financial planning, catering, clothing design, and teaching. According to a State Department spokesperson, the missions can almost always use clerical and computer skills. With the proliferation of computer hardware in missions overseas, they have difficulty finding enough people qualified in data processing.

When foreign service spouses take advantage of the functional training offered by the Foreign Service Institute in Washington, as described in Chapter 10, they may be able to find professional or clerical work in the administrative, personnel, budget and fiscal, or consular areas in embassies abroad.

Another option open to foreign service spouses is to take the highly competitive Foreign Service Exam, and, if they pass the various requirements, become officers and work at posts with their employed spouses. Keep in mind, however, that both members in such a tandem couple arrangement do not consistently get their first choices in assignments and, because nepotism or the appearance of it may sometimes be an issue, a spouse may have to spend time on leave without pay or accept an assignment at a different post.

Foundations

According to the Foundation Center, a foundation is a nongovernmental, nonprofit organization that maintains or aids educational, social, charitable, religious, or other activities primarily by making grants. Nearly 22,000 foundations exist in the United States. Examples of foundations with a domestic focus include the Bristol-Myers Fund and the Helena Rubenstein Foundation. Examples of major foundations funding international development include the Ford Foundation, the W.K. Kellogg Foundation, and the Rockefeller Foundation.

Besides a board of trustees, most foundations consist of an administrative staff with skilled professionals who manage foundation funds, review proposals, award grants, and administer programs.

Government

Nearly 18 million individuals work in federal, state, and local agencies in the executive, legislative, and judicial branches.

At the federal level, employment opportunities run the gamut from typists and teachers to lawyers and scientists. Depending on your location and qualifications, you may be eligible for federal employment opportunities that exist throughout the United States and overseas. Spouses of U.S. Government civilian and military personnel, in particular, are eligible for many extra benefits related to their mobility, including noncompetitive employment reinstatement and employment on military installations or in embassies and consulates overseas. Federal agencies that operate abroad as well as in the United States include the Agency for International Development, the Department of Agriculture, Department of State, Department of Defense, United States Information Agency, and the Central Intelligence Agency. If federal employment appeals to you, refer to Chapters 5 and 14.

While employment opportunities at the state level also run the gamut, close to half are in education. Other areas that provide work possibilities include welfare, mental health, highway maintenance and safety, and parks and recreation. For more about state government employment, refer to the resources in Appendix C.

At the local level, most jobs are tied to specific city services such as police and fire, parks and recreation, and education. Large municipalities and county governments encompassing populations numbering at least 200,000 offer the best job opportunities. Since local governments tend to be internally decentralized and fragmented, finding employment at this level poses real challenges.

Health-Care Facilities

While medical personnel traditionally perform diagnostic tests and surgery in hospitals, they soon will be more likely to do this kind of work in outpatient settings. As you search for a job in the health-care field, consider the plethora of work sites, including patients' homes, hospices, doctors. offices, corporations, community clinics, health maintenance organizations, centers for ambulatory surgery and urgent care centers, which are free-standing clinics in medical centers, office buildings, and shopping centers. Nursing homes are another work site possibility in the health-care field; with the advances in medical know-how that keep people alive longer, the number of facilities are steadily growing.

Home

Many jobs in years to come will be based at home, the futurists predict. Depending on your field and your entrepreneurial inclinations, you might convert your work into a self-run business if you find yourself in a location where your qualifications are incompatible with employers' needs. Many self-run businesses can be transported to new locations without too much difficulty.

> **CASE IN POINT**
>
> As director of Closet Assets, Jean Martin, an Air Force spouse, has made a career of teaching and creating programs for business and industry, professional associations, educational centers, and special event activities. Even though relocations have taken her from northern Italy to Denver, Washington, DC, and San Antonio in a period of seven years, she has successfully reestablished her business after each move. Jean has this to say: "I used to plan on six months before making a profit, but now that I affiliate myself with national organizations, such as J.C. Penney and the American Cancer Society, it will not matter where my business is located. To save money on the costs of reestablishment, I work from my home and keep in mind the multiple uses I can make from things I create for my business, such as note cards and stationery." Jean is also the author of several publications, which are listed in Appendix C.

For details about self-employment, including ideas for home businesses, see Chapter 4.

International Nonprofit Organizations

Often referred to as private voluntary organizations (PVO's) in the United States, and nongovernmental organizations (NGO's) abroad, international nonprofit organizations are primarily oriented toward a specific international cause or issue, such as economic or community development, health care, relief, human rights, or foreign affairs. Examples of these organizations are the American Friends Service Committee, CARE, Catholic Relief Services, Food for the Hungry, Holt International Children's Services, and Lutheran World Relief. According to one foreign service spouse, "NGO's are good groups to get consultancies with overseas. They are often very small organizations in need of special technical skills, knowledge of foreign countries, cross-cultural skills, and competency in the country's language. While I was abroad, I picked up a number of short-term jobs with these organizations by networking."

Military Installations

Relocating spouses — especially military spouses — can get a variety of positions on military installations in the United States and overseas in the following categories of employment: civil service, contract, exchange system, nonappropriated fund, bank and credit union, and Department of Dependents School (DODDS) employment.

The personnel offices at the bases where you may want to work can give you more information about employment opportunities and application procedures.

Research Organizations

Often operating on a nonprofit basis, research organizations are frequently involved in fundamental, applied, or developmental studies, as well as data gathering, analysis, and synthesis activities. Besides research institutes, this category includes laboratories, experiment stations, computation centers, statistical laboratories, information retrieval centers, and some museums. Examples of domestic research organizations include Harvard University's Fogg Art Museum, the Institute for Cancer Research, and the Urban Affairs Institute.

Special research units at universities and some consulting firms conduct research on an international scale. Among the major research firms conducting international research are the Aspen Institute, Brookings Institute, Rand Corporation, and SRI (Stanford Research Institute) International.

Trade and Professional Associations

According to the *National Trade and Professional Associations* directory, both trade and professional associations are nonprofit, cooperative, voluntary organizations. While a trade association's ultimate goal is to help its members increase income from a product or service, a professional society is oriented more toward the expansion of knowledge or the establishment of professional standards. Examples of major trade associations are the Chamber of Commerce of the United States, the National Association of Manufacturers, and the Direct Marketing Association. Examples of professional societies are the American Library Association, the American Psychological Association, and the American Association for Training and Development.

Besides the many U.S.-based associations that promote members' interests among organizations and governments abroad, thousands of trade and professional associations are international in scope and headquartered outside the United States. Examples include the International Association for Community Development, the International Society for Human Rights, and the International Federation of Health Professionals.

Depending on their size and orientation, associations may be involved in the following functions, all of which create job opportunities:

- issue periodicals, including journals and newsletters
- put on meetings, conferences, and conventions
- sponsor exhibits, contests, and awards
- inform members about impending government regulations and legislation that may affect them
- communicate views of membership to government officials
- publish pamphlets, yearbooks, and articles about their industry
- develop market statistics
- draw up news releases

ALTERNATIVE WORK ARRANGEMENTS

Workers and employers have become increasingly creative when it comes to work arrangements and schedules, and now there are many routes to fulfilling work other than permanent, full-time employment. If you view your work as secondary to your spouse's career because of your parenting responsibilities or other obligations, you may want to consider a few of the inviting alternatives that allow professionalism as well as time for outside commitments.

Contract Work

As a contract worker you are employed under a contract by an organization, usually for the duration of a specific project. Typically, you are paid a certain amount to complete the work, and you receive no fringe benefits. The skills used in contract work are almost unlimited, including writing, programming, training, engineering, health care, program development, project management, and meeting planning. Contract workers are employed in consulting firms, private volunteer organizations, and some of the other work settings described earlier in this chapter.

Overseas, contract jobs are plentiful. For example, in Saudi Arabia, you can teach ESOL classes on a contract basis. In Japan, you can earn $30 an hour by teaching English, and in Korea the rates are not far behind. Since computer programming skills are scarce in many countries, some U.S. firms hire programmers to work abroad under contract. If you can write, consider free-lancing for a U.S. publication or a textbook company. In Third World countries, the most sought-after skills are those that contribute to a country's development, such as agricultural economics, finance, population planning, and health care. If you are interested in doing contract work overseas, it is often to your advantage to make your arrangements before relocating. For more information about contract work, refer to Chapters 5 and 11.

Part-Time Work

Part-time work implies an abbreviated yet permanent, year-round work schedule of fewer than 35 hours a week. Part-time jobs are found most often in the clerical, sales, and food service areas. A limited number of professional-level jobs, such as those for teachers, librarians, and nurses, are available on a part-time basis. If you are looking for a challenge, consider working two part-time jobs rather than one full-time job. Some studies have predicted that by the year 2000, half of all jobs will be part-time.

Temporary Work

With temporary work you can work regular hours when you want to work, usually on short-term assignments ranging from one day to several months. In contrast to part-time work, temporary work does not commit you to a steady, long-term job.

Temporary jobs are diverse. Examples include product demonstrating, hosting, tour guiding, word processing, bookkeeping, survey interviewing, waitressing, nursing, and editing. The majority of the temporary jobs now are in the office clerical areas, although this is changing with time.

You may be persuaded to work on a temporary basis for some of these reasons:

- to test the waters before plunging into full-time work
- to sample, on a short-term basis, a variety of work environments

and jobs before making a commitment
- to get a foot in the door for work that might lead to permanent employment
- to acquire recent work experience and references for when you apply for permanent positions.
- to update old skills and develop new ones relevant to your job target
- to get in to talk with people during your exploration of career options (see Chapter 6)

Job Sharing

In a job sharing arrangement, two or more employees jointly perform responsibilities equivalent to one full-time job, and the full-time salary and benefits are prorated. Having worked out the details ahead, applicants interested in job sharing typically present themselves to employers as one unit.

Flextime

While maintaining a required work period — for example, from 10 a.m. to 3 p.m. — many organizations allow employees to select their preferred hours of employment but work a set number of hours each day, week, or month. For example, employees may work from 7 a.m. to 3 p.m., 8 a.m. to 4 p.m., or 10 a.m. to 6 p.m. five days a week. Flextime offers advantages to both employers and employees and has been well received by both groups. As an employee using this work arrangement, you may reap these benefits: faster commutes during hours of low traffic congestion, working during your hours of highest productivity, more time for leisure, and more availability for family responsibilities.

Compressed Workweek

Under this plan, employees *average* 40 hours a week over fewer than five days; for example, four 10-hour days a week, three 12-hour or 13-hour days a week, or four 10-hour days in one week and five eight-hour days in the following week. One solution for a couple with two full-time jobs, parenting responsibilities, and a desire to retain most of the child care themselves: both parents could work three 13-hour days with only one workday overlap between them.

Overseas Academics

Since many countries reserve employment opportunities for their own citizens, you may not always be able to work overseas. When this is the case, you might consider using your time to go to school.

CASE IN POINT

Even before Gretchen Bloom relocated to India, she knew it was a country where she would not be able to locate work readily on the local economy. She was also aware that child care and education overseas are inexpensive, so she used the time to her advantage. Summarizing her experience at Nehru University in New Delhi, Gretchen says, "I went to school full time for three years, and got two master's degrees for a total of only $250, due to India's government subsidies for education for all students. My sociology and community health degrees have always been fully accepted by employers back here in the United States."

Gretchen found her academic involvement to be an excellent entree into the community in India and, later, in a developing country in Africa: "My thesis work allowed me opportunities I might otherwise not have had. With government clearance to do research, I was able to talk with a variety of people in the community."

Volunteering

Volunteering is an ideal way to maintain your credentials in your field, and it may be your only means of working in some locations. Challenging volunteer opportunities exist in a variety of membership organizations, including professional, community, civic, religious, and alumni groups.

Consider the many reasons for making a commitment to a volunteer job:

- to sample a variety of fields of work in order to learn about training requirements, before making a commitment
- to get recent, relevant, documented work experience for a resume
- to get free training and develop the necessary skills for a new field of work

- to develop contacts and current references in an area of interest
- to ease the transition from homemaker to paid employee
- to hear about paid jobs from within the organization before they are publicized to outsiders
- to have a worthwhile involvement while searching for the perfect job

---

CASE IN POINT

During his first eight years of marriage, Michael Lingard had moved three times, and he knew there would be more moves throughout the world because of his wife's career. Currently the administrator of a drug treatment program for adolescents, Michael tells about following his wife on an assignment to a developing country where he believed he would not be able to work in his field: "Of course I was frustrated and angry about playing househusband and not being able to get paid for what I had spent time and money training for. But after getting through that stage, I was able to look at my dilemma and creatively analyze what I could develop from what little was available."

At that point in his life, Michael had two priorities that were more important than salary: (1) to avoid having gaps in his employment history, and (2) to keep current in his field — administration and development of programs with youth. After writing an impressive proposal for a year-long, curriculum-related enrichment program, Michael convinced the community school's staff of the program's merits. In preparation for returning to the States, Michael developed a resume and included his experience:

<u>Enrichment Center Director</u>, Southway School, Ibadin, Nigeria. 1980 to 1981.

> Assessed academic and extracurricular needs of a diverse student population. Planned, implemented, and supervised a school-wide, curriculum-related enrichment program for 285 youth. Recruited and trained more than 100 persons to staff the program. Conducted meetings, wrote recruitment literature and program catalog, and supervised budgetary matters. Developed a 20-page instructional guide for future directors of the center.

That was several years ago, and today Michael has this to say about his work in Nigeria: "I put as much effort into that volunteer job as I ever put into any paid job, but it was worth every minute because the experience contributed substantially to my professional background and enabled me to get the job I have today. What's more, I think I really made a difference to those kids."

OPTIONS FOR A RELOCATING SPOUSE

For more information about the often-missed value of volunteering, refer to Chapter 10.

For additional options, read the next three chapters. Chapter 6 is especially useful because it outlines the ways to investigate the alternatives you are considering. During this process, keep your mind open to designing your own unique job, which more and more people are successfully doing in this age of rapid change.

4

Is Self-Employment for You?

A recent article in a popular magazine was subtitled, "If you need an employer, why not become one?" Rather than trying to fit into an employer's niche, you may find that your opportunities for satisfying employment are greater with a small self-run business that can be easily moved and reestablished in new communities. To see if business ownership is a viable option for you, answer the questions in the accompanying quiz.

ENTREPRENEURIAL QUIZ

Answer Yes or No:

1. I have good physical and emotional stamina.
2. I am apt to stay up late at night in order to finish a project.
3. There are a lot of things about which I feel very strongly.
4. I usually feel confident about my decisions.
5. I can say no firmly.
6. Things that happen to me, good or bad, are generally things I make happen rather than due to luck.
7. I prefer doing things to planning things.
8. I am organized and efficient.

IS SELF-EMPLOYMENT FOR YOU?   51

9. I work effectively alone rather than requiring the presence of others as motivation to get started.
10. I do not mind the isolation of working alone.
11. I get along well with people.
12. As a child I engaged in money-making activities such as delivering newspapers and selling produce.
13. If I had to decide between working for an organization I did not own or running my own business, I would choose to start my own business even if it meant receiving considerably less compensation.
14. Job security is not that important to me. In fact, I enjoy a certain amount of ambiguity and have a willingness to risk.
15. My spouse and family would be supportive of my decision to start a business and would be helpful during the possibly difficult period of start-up.

The answers and scoring for this quiz are at the end of this chapter. While you can turn there now, you will have a better understanding if you first read the following section.

ADVANTAGES AND DISADVANTAGES

The advantages of business ownership are numerous. Self-employment offers independence in that you can make your own decisions and do what you want to do. You can choose where you want to work and set the pace in terms of the number of hours worked and the amount earned. Self-employment often provides a variety of assignments and contacts and may be intellectually stimulating. You are likely to have immediate and obvious rewards from producing quality products or services. There are tax benefits and, if you make it, personal and financial rewards.

Running a business from your home provides additional benefits. In many cases, you can test a business idea with a minimal investment of money and time because the cost of office or work space, telephone, and utilities is already covered, at least partially. You have freedom from commuting and, in general, more time-freedom because you are better able to work according to your own schedule. You can wear comfortable clothing. And, finally, a home-based business can be an integrating force in the life of the family and enable you to better manage both work and family responsibilities.

> **CASE IN POINT**
>
> Evelyn Davis runs a booming computer services business in the basement of her upstate New York home. She does billing and word processing for small businesses, labels and membership lists for organizations, typesetting for printers, and resumes for job hunters.
>
> With two small children, Evelyn finds working at home idyllic. To attend to her family's needs, she sometimes must schedule her work late at night, but that does not bother her. She says, "Since I'm not constrained by an employer's eight-hour workday, I can work from 9 p.m. to 2 a.m. one night and 10 a.m. to 3 p.m. the next day, and the following day not work at all if that is what I want to do." By working at home, Evelyn has saved a considerable amount on rent, clothing, child care, and transportation, and she has invested that money in hardware and software for her business.
>
> Looking toward a relocation to San Diego when her husband is transferred, Evelyn says, "Because of the portability of my career, I won't have to hunt for a new job. While I plan to develop new customers on the West Coast, the nature of my business allows me to retain an ongoing relationship with many of my present clients. With overnight courier service, it won't matter that I'm thousands of miles away from my contacts."

Business ownership has its down side, too. It's true that this is the one area where you can *hire* yourself rather than waiting to be selected by an employer. Yet this self-selection process is often the very reason for the high rate of business failures. The chance of a new business closing within seven years is about 50 percent according to David Birch, a researcher in Cambridge, MA, who is known for his studies of job creation. Although not all business closings are business failures, Birch says 85 percent of businesses that fail are small ones. Other experts quote even higher failure rates for small businesses. Among the top reasons for business failure is poor management by the owner. Too often, prospective business owners look at the advantages of self-employment without also considering the disadvantages.

The drawbacks of self-employment include long hours, financial and career risks, uneven and low income to start, no security or fringe benefits, lots of responsibility, anxiety with each new project, and lack of support help. If you relocate repeatedly, you have to start over with each move, which requires ongoing promotional activities, attracting new clientele, reestablishing credit, and possibly moving inventory and finding new suppliers.

When you work from your home, self-employment has additional disadvantages. Since others may not recognize your privacy to work or not to work, you may receive social calls during business hours and business calls during personal time. The demands from family, lack of structure, and proximity to diversions — television, refrigerator, vacuum cleaner — may keep you from your work. If it is important to you to work around others, you may find the isolation of a home-based business too lonely. Finally, depending on the kind of business you have in mind, your housing may not provide adequate space.

CASE IN POINT

Eric Seidler has had little trouble transferring his writing skills from one locale to the next, but his home-based endeavors have not always been problem-free. While he and his wife were childless, Eric could not imagine any better set-up than working at home. His rigid self-discipline and assertive response to outside interruptions enabled him to produce many free-lance pieces for magazines and newspapers. Typically, he worked at his typewriter from 8 a.m., when his wife left for work, until 6 p.m., when she returned home. However, their lives changed when they produced twins.

Even though the couple relied on outside help during the day, Eric found he could not be as productive at home as he once was. He says, "I felt cramped because my office had been converted to a nursery, and I had to work in a corner of our bedroom. What's more, I was easily distracted; with twins, there is always so much to do, and I felt compelled to help out." Renting inexpensive office space near his home, Eric resumed his former level of productivity.

Years later, after the family moved to larger quarters in Burlington, VT, and the children were older, Eric returned his office to his home. He reports that his writing career is flourishing.

Now, if you haven't already done so, refer to the end of the chapter to compare your responses to the quiz with what research reveals are the attributes of the successful business owner. You may be ready to consider what type of business to start if your score indicates your potential for entrepreneurship.

For a business to succeed, there are three requirements:

- the right idea in the marketplace at the right time
- the right person to implement the idea
- the right time in that person's life to implement the idea.

Perhaps you already know whether or not you fit the second and third requirements. The following may help you determine how to meet the first.

HOW TO DECIDE ON A BUSINESS

Focus on your priorities and qualifications as revealed by the self-assessment exercises in Part I. While it is important to consider your interests and work values as you choose a business, don't overlook your actual skills. Thousands of businesses fail annually because the owners are not qualified in the area of their new ventures. Equally important, evaluate whether your personal values and preferred lifestyle line up with what your proposed business would provide.

To increase your odds for success, a self-run business should meet all three of these criteria:

- relatively simple and inexpensive to start
- portable
- increasingly in demand.

Most businesses fit into one of four categories as described here:

Manufacturing: requires converting raw materials into finished goods, and is the most expensive type of business to start.

Wholesaling: consists of the middlemen for businesses, serving as distribution links to stores/businesses that sell to the end users.

Retailing: entails selling goods, products, and commodities to consumers by mail, by telephone, over the counter, by machine, or by a sales force.

Service: involves offering personal/professional assistance on tasks customers cannot or do not want to do for themselves; examples include financial planning, tutoring, catering, child care, and hospitality services.

IS SELF-EMPLOYMENT FOR YOU?

For a relocating spouse, the business-most-likely-to-succeed will fall in the category of *service*. The technological revolution, increase in dual-career families, and trend toward a leisure-oriented society all contribute to the increased demand for experts and for help from others outside the home. For specific ideas, examine the accompanying list of business ideas for the relocating spouse. If you can think of other portable businesses, add them to the list.

BUSINESS IDEAS FOR A RELOCATING SPOUSE

accountant or bookkeeper
answering service owner
antique furniture restorer
arts and crafts instructor
bridal consultant
cake decorator
calligrapher
camera repairperson
career consultant
caterer
child care specialist
children's entertainer
color consultant
cooking instructor
counselor/therapist
dance instructor
diet counselor
doll maker
dressmaker
elderly care specialist
fashion consultant
flower arranger
gardener
green plant maintainer
home and business organizer
interior decorator
investment counselor

maid service owner
mail order business owner
make-up consultant
messenger service owner
music teacher
newsletter publisher
party planner
pet groomer
photographer
piano technician
picture framer
programmer
quilt maker
real estate agent
researcher
seminar leader
tax preparer
teacher
translator
tutoring service owner
typist
upholsterer
video producer
wake-up service owner
weaver
word processor
writer

To ensure that your business venture can be operated at most locations, research the regulations you may encounter with each new relocation; for example, policies affecting housing at some military installations or foreign service posts may make it difficult for spouses wanting to make home sales; and, regarding overseas assignments, postal regulations prohibit the mailing of items for resale through APO or FPO. Be aware of local licensing and other restrictions such as neighborhood zoning rules. Although regulations vary from place to place, you can gain an understanding of obstacles you might encounter by checking with licensing and zoning offices in county or town government agencies.

Check Out the Market for Your Idea

Don't let your love for an idea cloud your vision to the point where you are unrealistic about its business potential. The variety of ways to check out the market include:

1. Refer to the *Yellow Pages* in your new area to see how many similar businesses already exist.
2. Contact your potential competition to see how well they are doing and how big a market they think there is. Identify yourself as a future business owner, or say you are gathering data for a research project. (While confident business owners are often willing to share information, you may want to contact related businesses or businesses outside of your location if these approaches make you uncomfortable.)
3. Locate suppliers who serve these businesses and ask them questions about the market.
4. Contact the following:

- individuals and organizations that have used businesses related to yours
- local government agencies that regulate businesses
- chambers of commerce
- trade or professional associations in the field.

5. Decide on the range of your market — local, national, or international — and, if your business idea will involve markets beyond your community, consult regional or national trade associations, the U.S. Chamber of Commerce, the Department of Commerce and Census Bureau, the American Marketing Association (for leads to sources of specific market research information), and trade journals in the field.
6. Work part-time in the field — one of the very best ways to

learn about a business before committing yourself to it! The information you get from this apprenticeship experience may well mean the difference between success and failure.

WHY YOU NEED A BUSINESS PLAN

If you plan to seek financing for your venture, a well-thought-out, written business plan is essential. In any case, it is a valuable tool for clarifying and scheduling the tasks needed to start your business. A business plan forces you to figure out your costs and potential profits and take an objective look at your future business to judge whether the risks and hard work are worth the rewards offered. For details on how to create a business plan, check the resources in Appendix C and the Small Business Administration publications, as described in this chapter.

THE LEGAL AND TAX SIDE

While businesses can take one of three basic forms — sole proprietorship, partnership, or corporation — most home-based businesses and other small ventures start out as sole proprietorships. You may want to avoid a partnership arrangement because, as some former partners complain, they are like marriages — easy to get into but difficult to get out of. As for incorporation, the paperwork and expense may prevent you from focusing on other more important areas during the startup phase of your business. You can change the form of your business later if growth or other factors warrant it.

As a small-business owner you are allowed many tax deductions, but you must keep very accurate and detailed records on all your business-related expenses.

Unless experience enables you to handle the details of business start-up alone, you may need some expert assistance:

Accountants: The best source of help is probably an accountant experienced in dealing with small business start-ups. This kind of expert can advise you on the legal form and tax status of your business, your cost and profit projections, how to set up a record-keeping system, and, perhaps, what kind and how much insurance to carry.

> **CASE IN POINT**
>
> Forty-five and energetic, Sonya Hillman runs a successful catering business and cooking school despite her nomadic life. To quickly re-establish herself after moving, Sonya begins by locating an accountant there. She does this by contacting independent consultants, the chamber of commerce, and professional societies for small businesses.
>
> Explaining how she uses an accountant, Sonya says, "After moving to a new region of the country, I meet with a small-business-oriented accountant who alerts me to the local scene. While I can handle business start-up and day-to-day accounting tasks, an accountant can tell me about local zoning and licensing regulations or refer me to the proper sources for that information." Early in the life of her business, it was an accountant who taught Sonya how to price her services to make an adequate profit and informed her that she could save taxes by employing her children to handle the small jobs in her enterprise.
>
> As her business grows, Sonya looks to her accountant for advice about tax savings, incorporation, and the need for additional insurance.

Internal Revenue Service: A variety of free publications on taxes are recommended in IRS Publication 17, for sole proprietors, including the following:

- # 334 Tax Guide for Small Business
- # 533 Self-Employment Tax
- # 534 Depreciation
- # 535 Business Expenses
- # 538 Accounting Periods and Methods
- # 552 Recordkeeping for Individuals and a List of Tax Publications
- # 583 Information for Business Taxpayers — Business Taxes, Identification Numbers, Recordkeeping
- # 587 Business Use of Your Home

IRS Publication 17 and the aforementioned publications are available from your state's Internal Revenue Service office, or you can make copies from publications on file at your local library.

Lawyers: A lawyer can steer you through many of the complexities that accompany business start-up, such as local licensing and zoning regulations. But if, for whatever reason, you choose to seek the advice of only one professional, go to an accountant and find the legal information on your own.

Small Business Administration (SBA): A variety of publications are available from SBA, including: (1) "Starting and Managing a Small Business From Your Home," available for $1.75 from the Government Printing Office, Washington, DC 20402, and (2) "The Business Plan for Home-Based Businesses," available from SBA, PO Box 15434, Ft. Worth, TX 76119. SBA's Service Corps of Retired Executives (SCORE) offers general management assistance to potential or new business owners. For publications or management assistance, check with your nearest SBA office or, as a last resort, write SBA, 1441 L St., N.W., Washington, DC 20416.

GROUPS THAT CAN ASSIST YOU

The American Woman's Economic Development Corporation or AWED (The Lincoln Building, 60 East 42nd St., New York, NY 10165; hotline 1-800-222-AWED; 1-800-442-AWED in New York State; 212-692-9100 in Alaska and Hawaii) offers training programs to any woman, in any business, at any stage, and provides two reasonably priced telephone counseling services: (1) intensive business counseling, and (2) the hotline, for women who require a quick answer to an immediate business question.

The National Association for the Cottage Industry (PO Box 14850, Chicago, IL 60614; 312-472-8116) is an advocacy group for home-based workers, which provides information on topics, including zoning, licensing, accounting procedures, and legal questions. This group publishes a bimonthly and a quarterly publication and puts on two to three national trade shows annually. As a side benefit, insurance is offered to members.

HOW TO PROMOTE YOUR BUSINESS

Once you have identified your market, you need to reach it. Many a business fails not because of a poor service or product but because the business owner did not make contact with potential clients and customers. By talking with owners of businesses similar to yours, you will learn some of the best ways to reach your market.

Although you must promote your product or service in order to sell it, not all promotion costs a lot of money. Examples of free promotion:

- word of mouth
- participation on panels
- press releases and stories about your business in local media
- notices on bulletin boards
- offering noncredit workshops relevant to your business through established groups.

CASE IN POINT

Shirley Gabron, a self-employed financial planner now living in Seattle, WA, lays the groundwork for her business before she relocates. "I learned the hard way," she says, "that clients don't just come your way. After my first relocation, I rented office space, invested in new stationery and business cards, and sat back waiting for the phone to ring. To make a long story short, my phone rarely rang, and I lost months of income."

Now, three months prior to moving, Shirley looks for opportunities to increase her visibility in her new location. Since many of her clients result from personal contacts, she joins the chamber of commerce, other community organizations in line with her interests, and the local chapter of her professional society. Through public libraries, she arranges to offer free one-evening financial planning workshops. For further visibility and some remuneration, Shirley gives short seminars through adult education programs.

"To determine the need for financial planning seminars," she says, "I analyze past catalogs from educational institutions, then contact the program directors and submit detailed proposals. With this approach, I am able to be in front of audiences full of potential clients soon after I move." Shirley doesn't get rich from her seminars, but her curriculum attracts the participants to her financial planning services.

Soon after she moves, Shirley throws a huge party at which she distributes her business brochures and displays other promotional material. News about her enterprise spreads quickly because she invites people throughout the community, including her dentist, minister, neighbors, husband's colleagues and their spouses.

While Shirley still doesn't look forward to relocation, she is able to avoid the professional setbacks that characterized her past.

A WORD OF CAUTION . . . AND OF CONFIDENCE

While most of the self-employed tend to be older, white males, since 1979 the number of self-employed women has increased five times faster than the number of self-employed men and more than three times as fast as female wage and salary workers (World of Work Report). But if you are considering joining the ranks of the self-employed, don't do it as a way to escape job hunting, and do be realistic about what is involved. Remember the statistics on business failures. It is one thing to have an exciting business idea; it is something altogether different to have to do recordkeeping and marketing, and to be isolated from others day after day.

However, ownership of a small portable business is an attractive option for a relocating spouse and should be given careful consideration. Even if you have a mobile lifestyle and must reestablish yourself repeatedly, this will become easier with time. Furthermore, you will become more and more adept at providing your business service or product, and your reputation will grow along with your confidence.

SCORING THE ENTREPRENEURIAL QUIZ

To see if self-employment is for you, count your "yes" answers to the quiz at the beginning of the chapter, and then refer to the scoring that follows:

Scoring:
- 13 to 15 "yes" answers: You probably would be successful at business ownership and find it satisfying.
- 9 to 12 "yes" answers: Before choosing self-employment as a work option, give it careful consideration — it may not be for you.
- 0 to 8 "yes" answers: Eliminate self-employment from your list of work options. You will find other work more fulfilling.

The answers to the Entrepreneurial Quiz are interpreted below. The numbers correspond to those on the quiz at the beginning of this chapter.

1 and 2. The successful entrepreneur is energetic and is able to work for long hours with relatively little sleep. She/he is persistent at problem-solving — has an intensive desire to complete tasks and projects.

3, 4, and 5. Decisiveness is essential for successful entrepreneurship because running a business involves a constant stream of decisions.

6. Successful business owners have what's called an "internal locus of control," meaning they believe that both their accomplishments and their failures are within their control rather than being determined by external circumstances or luck.

7. Successful entrepreneurs are people of action and prefer doing things to reading, writing, thinking, or planning.

8. To keep track of all the details that running a small business entails, you must be organized and efficient. Otherwise, you will have trouble meeting deadlines, providing services, and satisfying clients or customers.

9 and 10. Self-employment frequently means isolation from others. Some people find it difficult to get started without the structure of a time schedule provided by working for or with others.

11. Even though successful business owners are described as "doers," they often must get things done through other people as well.

12. Since personality traits may develop early in life, entrepreneurial pursuits in your youth may indicate your probable success and interest in business ownership. Many, but not all, successful entrepreneurs had independent ventures long before starting their own businesses.

13. Although most entrepreneurs start their businesses with the expectation of eventually making more money, this is not the dominant motive. Instead, most of them seek the independence of self-employment at the expense of financial security. Furthermore, it normally takes several years to show a profit.

14. Business owners are able to tolerate continuous uncertainty regarding their work. Because of their self-confidence, job security is not a priority for them, and they enjoy taking moderate risks.

15. Because the financial and time demands of business start-up can be great, it is important that your entire family is in agreement with your decision to go into business for yourself. Consider the ages of your children and the emotional and physical well-being of all family members before making a decision for business start-up.

5

Working for the Federal Government

More than 1,000 different federal occupations exist in fields ranging from art to zoology in environments that include offices, laboratories, national parks, shipyards, military installations, consulates and many other settings across the United States and around the world.

Contrary to popular belief, only about 12 percent of all federal jobs are in Washington, DC. Outside of Washington, each of the federal agencies is represented throughout the United States in 10 *regions:* Boston, New York City, Philadelphia, Atlanta, Chicago, St. Louis, Dallas, Denver, San Francisco, and Seattle. These regions are divided into *areas*, where, depending on the need, agency offices are located. Cities with more than 25,000 federal employees, besides those already mentioned, include Baltimore, Norfolk-Virginia Beach, San Antonio, Detroit, Los Angeles-Long Beach, and Oklahoma City. Overseas, about 55,000 civilians and 500,000 military personnel work in federal jobs.

THE UP SIDE

ay rates for many federal jobs are competitive
or similar work outside the government. However,
al jobs, the rates have not kept pace with inflation.

Vacations: The paid vacation time extended to government employees goes beyond that offered in most other work settings. New federal employees earn 13 days' annual leave each year until they have completed three years of federal service, at which time they begin to earn 20 days per year.

Pension: Although federal pension benefits for retired employees are being reevaluated, they currently exceed those offered by many other employers.

Fair treatment: Numerous federal regulations and laws guarantee that federal employees and job applicants receive fair treatment, including no employment discrimination.

Mobility: The mobility factor associated with federal jobs is a special benefit for the relocating spouse. Spouses of U.S. Government civilian and military personnel, in particular, are extended many extra benefits related to their mobility, including eligibility for many government jobs on military installations or in embassies and consulates overseas and eligibility for noncompetitive employment reinstatement.

THE DOWN SIDE

Red tape: A huge, disjointed institution, the Federal Government has developed numerous confusing regulations that often delay work schedules and frustrate employees as they try to do their jobs.

Criticism: Politicians and often the general public use federal employees as "whipping boys" by attacking them for being overpaid and for doing poor and unnecessary work.

Few incentives: Good performance may not be as well rewarded in government as it is in nongovernment employment.

Incompetent employees: While many very competent individuals work for the Federal Government, it is difficult to get rid of incompetent employees because of the personnel policies that protect workers' rights.

Even with its disadvantages, federal employment is an attractive work option for the mobile spouse because federal employees who want to relocate may apply for jobs at agencies in new locations and, if they are hired, continue their benefits and federal service seniority.

CASE IN POINT

A career-minded couple in their mid-30s, Bill and Nora Lombard both work for the U.S. Government.

Nora explains why she decided to join her husband as a federal employee: "When Bill took a new job with the Department of Defense, it meant he would be periodically transferred throughout the United States and abroad. Until that time, I had enjoyed working for large corporations and consulting firms, but I decided that repeated relocations would affect my work record less in the Federal Government than elsewhere."

Nora's career, if measured by her salary and level of responsibility, has not gone continuously upward, but she has consistently been able to find work whenever she has wanted to work. Given some of the places to which her husband has been transferred, Nora is convinced she would have had fewer opportunities outside the Federal Government.

SEEKING OUT THE OPPORTUNITIES

- Visit a federal job information/testing (FJI/T) center, listed in Appendix A, to see resources and get information about federal employment. Refer to the posted listings of current positions, for example, "OPM Federal Job Opportunities Listing — Nationwide" and "OPM Senior Executive Service Opportunities Listing."
- Determine under which Office of Personnel Management (OPM) announcements to apply by reading information from FJI/T centers. Examples of announcements include "Stenographers/Typists," "Professional and Administrative Career (PAC) Positions," "Administrative Careers in Washington" (Announcement No. WA-5-07), and Social Worker, GS-9 to GS-11" (Announcement No. VA-0185).
- Identify offices and individuals doing work relevant to your interests by referring to the *United States Government Manual*. Write or call an agency about its functions and activities, and you may receive a wealth of information. You may be able to examine in-house journals and newsletters if you visit agency personnel offices, libraries, or public affairs offices.
- To locate specific agency vacancy announcements, refer to

bulletin boards and reference books in agency personnel offices. Regularly read commercially produced publications such as the *Federal Times* and *Federal Career Opportunities* that list domestic and overseas job openings. For the jobs you are interested in, telephone the listed officials to request vacancy announcements.
- Make a list of all your contacts in government agencies, and enlist their help in checking on job openings. Give them copies of your SF171 — the application for federal employment — to take to their agencies. Arrange opportunities to talk with people to explore your options and to increase your contacts. For their telephone numbers and mailing addresses, refer to the *Federal Yellow Book*, the *Federal Executive Telephone Directory*, or individual agency directories.

CASE IN POINT

When Jeanne Fitzpatrick left Columbia, SC, for Washington, DC, she decided to leave teaching as well. Before finding permanent employment as an educational specialist with the Department of Labor, Jeanne worked in a temporary job with the Department of Commerce. She says, "My temporary job in personnel helped me realize I wasn't interested in that field, but it gave me some contacts and opened some doors, which are crucial for any career transition. I knocked on people's doors, sent out my SF171s, and followed up after I had sent them. Every time I went on an interview, I asked my interviewer for additional contacts. I obtained the job I have now through four layers of contacts — four layers removed from the first person I had chatted with."

HOW TO GET A FEDERAL JOB IN THE UNITED STATES

Hiring procedures for federal jobs in the United States vary depending on whether or not you have previously worked for the Federal Government.

If you've never worked for the U.S. Government, contact an FJI/T Center, which is part of the Office of Personnel Management (OPM). As the federal government's personnel agency for positions in the *competitive civil service*, OPM provides information about local application procedures and federal employment opportunities, examines applicants' qualifications and determines their eligibility, and refers them to agencies for employment consideration from *registers,* which are centralized inventories of applicants.

While most federal jobs are part of the competitive civil service, some federal organizations are excluded from it. These organizations, in the *excepted service*, can fill jobs through their own hiring systems, and applicants do not have to first pass an OPM examination. Examples of organizations in the excepted service include the U.S. Postal Service, the Library of Congress, the Federal Bureau of Investigation, and the Central Intelligence Agency. For a complete listing, read OPM pamphlet BRE-84, "U.S. Government Establishments with Positions Outside the Competitive Service." If you are interested in an excepted service position, contact the organizations directly to learn about their application procedures.

The OPM Application Process

After you apply for a competitive civil service position, OPM examines your qualifications to determine if you meet the necessary requirements to be considered for the position categories you specify. An examination involves evaluating your experience and training as described on your application along with supplemental information you are requested to provide. For this reason, the content and quality of your SF171 are extremely important. For detailed information on where to get and how to complete this important document, refer to Chapter 14. For some positions — for example, in the general administrative and clerical areas — an examination requires a written test in addition to an application.

After OPM examines your qualifications, you will be notified whether you are eligible to be considered for the category of positions you specified. Depending on the type of examination, this notification could be in the form of a GS rating, a test score, or other indicator.

Most federal white-collar jobs are classified according to the General Schedule (GS) pay system. Starting with GS-1 and going up to GS-18, positions are graded according to the level of difficulty of the work. The higher the grade, the higher the salary and, therefore, the more complex the duties, responsibilities, and qualifications required. For example, GS-9 to GS-12 are mid-level grades, GS-13 to GS-15 are senior grades, and GS-16 to GS-18 are often referred to as the super grades.

Most federal blue-collar positions are classified according to the Wage Grade pay system. Rates under this system vary according to location and are periodically adjusted to ensure comparability with the rates paid in private industry for similar work.

While OPM examines applicants and provides names of qualified applicants to agencies upon their request, OPM is not responsible for locating jobs for applicants. Applicants should take initiative to seek out their own jobs.

When OPM has enough candidates to fill projected vacancies, it closes the appropriate register and does not accept applications for it. However, if you held any type of federal employment while overseas and missed the opportunity to apply because of a recent overseas tour of duty, OPM will accept your application providing you apply within 120 days of your return to the United States, so long as you are a U.S. citizen and have proof of your overseas federal employment. Those with veterans' preference can also take advantage of this privilege. If you think you qualify for this provision, alert the OPM staff so they can advise you on how to apply.

The Selection Process for a Specific Agency Vacancy

After receiving a request from an agency to fill a position, OPM forwards the names of people highest on the register who meet the requirements, and the agency's hiring official chooses from among the top three available applicants. The names of applicants not selected are returned to the OPM register until they are hired, their eligibility expires, or the register is terminated. Agencies have direct hiring authority for some specialized and temporary positions; for example, secretaries and engineers can apply directly to agencies without first going through OPM.

When you are considered for a specific agency vacancy, examiners determine your eligibility based on the information you present to them on your SF171. To qualify for most federal positions, you must be a U.S. citizen and have the education and/or experience required for the grade level you choose. However, for some jobs, instead of a specific number of years of education or experience, you must describe your qualifications in a manner that clearly shows you have the knowledge, skills, and abilities to do the work specified in the agency's vacancy announcement.

Your chances for being hired depend on your qualifications (including how well you describe them and relate them to an agency's requirements), the frequency of vacancies in the area where you want to work, and the number of qualified applicants who want the same kind of job and level you have requested.

Types of Appointments

When you are hired by the Federal Government, you are offered an *appointment*. Most civil service appointments in the United States are either career-conditional, temporary, or term, with the following conditions:

Career-conditional: With this type of appointment, you are eligible for all fringe benefits, as well as transfer and promotion privileges. A career-conditional employee must complete a one-year probationary period, and after three years' service receives a *career appointment* and permanent civil service status or tenure. With a career conditional appointment, you may leave federal service for a period of up to three years and be reinstated by any federal agency without going through the competitive appointment procedures. If you leave for longer than three years, you must either be reevaluated by OPM or take a written test depending on the type of position for which you apply. Liberal exceptions to this limitation are granted spouses of U.S. Government employees.

Temporary: Temporary workers are appointed for one year or less, and cannot transfer or be promoted or automatically move to a career-conditional appointment without recompeting with candidates on a civil service register.

Term: Lasting more than one year but less than four, a term appointment is for work on a specific project. While term employees can be promoted or reassigned to other positions within the project they were hired for, they cannot transfer to outside positions or automatically move to career-conditional appointments without recompeting with candidates on a civil service register.

For more information on the federal government application and selection process, refer to David Waelde's excellent book, *How To Get A Federal Job* (see Appendix C).

Reinstatement Eligibility

Reinstatement refers to the noncompetitive reemployment of a former federal career or career-conditional employee. With reinstatement eligibility you can be hired by agencies directly, without going through OPM and its competitive selection procedures. Some job announcements specify *civil service status required* because applicants with reinstatement eligibility can be hired more quickly than those without previous federal experience.

Your reinstatement eligibility does not necessarily limit you to the same type of job or grade level you held previously. At the same time, reinstatement eligibility is not a right to return to a specific job, and an agency has no obligation to hire you.

Normally, to be eligible for reinstatement, you must either have completed three years of essentially continuous service as a career-conditional employee, or, unless you are a veteran, have been separated no longer than three years from a career-conditional appointment when you are reinstated. However, these time requirements for reinstatement have been modified to accommodate spouses who must leave career-conditional appointments to accompany U.S. Government personnel on overseas duty assignments. In such cases, a period of overseas residence does not count against the three-year limit on reinstatement eligibility. For example, if you must leave your career-conditional appointment to depart immediately for your spouse's overseas tour, you will have a full three years of reinstatement eligibility upon your return home. If you terminated your appointment and waited six months before moving overseas, you will have two and a half years of reinstatement eligibility upon your return.

CASE IN POINT

Karl Williamson had been working 19 months as a programmer with a federal agency in the Midwest when his wife was transferred to Europe by the military. While Karl loved his job, he did not want to live apart from his spouse while she was stationed abroad, so he terminated his federal employment.

During his two and half years overseas, Karl was able to pick up a number of consulting jobs, which he attributed to his technical skills and his foresight; before relocating, he had contacted organizations doing business abroad, including corporations, private development agencies, and international organizations.

When Karl returned to the United States with his wife, he took advantage of the noncompetitive reinstatement eligibility he had earned as a military spouse. He says, "Even though I had less than the standard three-year requirement for civil service status, I was able to bypass OPM and apply directly for positions in a number of federal agencies in different locations. An additional benefit — I reentered federal employment at a

WORKING FOR THE FEDERAL GOVERNMENT

> higher grade than the one I previously held, because of the quality of my overseas programming experience."

After reinstatement, you usually have to begin a new three-year waiting period before acquiring career status, but check with the personnel office to see if previous service can be counted.

An additional benefit for career or career-conditional employees whose spouses are being reassigned is the possibility of converting to a brief period of leave without pay rather than terminating when the formal employment period ends. This transitional period provides for relocation and reemployment without a break in federal service. If the employee cannot find a federal job by the end of the transitional period, the appointment is terminated. The Department of Defense's policy allows 90 days of transitional leave.

Direct Appointment Eligibility for Spouses of U.S. Government Personnel

Even without reinstatement eligibility, you can bypass OPM and get direct appointments with federal agencies in the United States if you meet the provisions of Executive Order 12585 (EO 12362 as amended). With direct appointment eligibility, your attractiveness as a potential employee may be enhanced because you can be hired more quickly than other applicants. If you have a current or recently lapsed security clearance, the hiring process is even more rapid for positions requiring clearances.

To be eligible for appointment under EO 12585, you must meet certain conditions:

- You must be a United States citizen *when* you apply for employment in the United States. Even if you were not a citizen while working overseas, you may be eligible as long as you become a citizen by the time you apply for employment in the United States.
- While working in the overseas position(s), you must have been a family member of one of the following serving in an overseas position:

  1. a civilian employee
  2. a nonappropriated fund employee
  3. a member of a uniformed service

To qualify, you need not be a *current* dependent of an active duty or civilian U.S. Government employee, as defined above, as long as you were in official dependent status while working overseas.

- As this book returns to press, you must have served a total of 18 months in positions funded by congressional appropriation under a nonpermanent local hire appointment *after* January 1, 1980. Time worked prior to this date does not count toward the 18 months. Regularly scheduled part-time work is counted as if it were full-time service, and intermittent employment is counted for each day actually worked. Furthermore, time spent on leave without pay, including maternity leave, can be counted if it does not exceed six months in each calendar year, the employee remains on the agency's employment rolls during the period, and the employee continues to live overseas as a family member of the federal government employee. Employees can combine service earned during several tours to meet the 18-month requirement as long as all creditable service has been earned within a 10-year period.

CASE IN POINT

Following her husband between Washington, DC, and foreign service posts in the Middle East, Meredith Cutler has been able to maintain a steady career with the Federal Government. During the early years of her marriage, she lived abroad and often worked in part-time or temporary clerical jobs in the U.S. Embassy.

While Meredith was somewhat resentful at the time about not having access to the higher-level jobs for which she felt qualified, she now says, "When I returned to the States last year, I discovered that my time in all those little overseas jobs allowed me to bypass the bureaucratic application process for a federal job in Washington, DC. Besides direct appointment eligibility, I had a current security clearance that enabled federal employers to hire me more rapidly than other applicants. Knowing what I know now, I would choose a clerical job in an embassy before accepting an outside job with more responsibility, because the benefits of federal service are very important to me."

- You must meet all the qualifications required for the position in the United States for which you apply, and have received a

WORKING FOR THE FEDERAL GOVERNMENT

successful performance rating for your overseas service. To show that you served in appropriated positions, you must have an SF50 (Notification of Personnel Action) or other official documentation of your previous service.
- As a result of the reversed executive order, you now have up to three years before you must exercise your eligibility for a noncompetitive appointment after returning from your overseas tour. In particular hardship cases, OPM may approve a longer time period.

Although personnel in OPM field offices and civilian personnel offices will be able to answer your questions on job availability and qualification requirements, they may, in some case, be uninformed about EO 12585 and other provisions favoring spouses. Therefore, go armed with this book and information relating to your personal employment status or eligibility.

WORKING FOR THE FEDERAL GOVERNMENT OVERSEAS

U.S. citizens are employed in foreign countries in a variety of competitive service positions with many different federal agencies and the U.S. military. Representative agencies include the following:

Economic-Assistance Agencies: Agency for International Development, Peace Corps, Department of Defense, African Development Foundation, Overseas Private Investment Corporation, and Export-Import Bank.

Agencies Representing the United States Diplomatically: Department of State, and United States Information Agency.

Other Agencies with Staff in Developing Countries: Department of Agriculture, Federal Highway Administration, National Oceanic and Atmospheric Administration, United States Travel and Tourism Administration, and Central Intelligence Agency.

For more information about federal agencies that employ U.S. citizens overseas, refer to the resources listed earlier in this chapter and three books, in particular, from Appendix C: *Careers in International Affairs, The Overseas List,* and *The Complete Guide to Public Employment.*

For specific information about federal job openings overseas, write:

For Pacific area: San Francisco Area Office, U.S. Office of Personnel Management, PO Box 7405 (located at 211 Main St., Rm. 235), San Francisco, CA 94120.

For Atlantic area: Washington Area Office, U.S. Office of Personnel Management, 1900 E St., N.W., Washington DC 20415.

The federal employment system overseas is very different from the civil service system within the United States. Since OPM does not have offices overseas, many of its functions are handled by local civilian personnel offices.

In many cases, Federal Government employees are transferred overseas from the United States as the vacancies occur. When a determination has been made to fill a federal vacancy in a foreign country locally, the appointee may be a U.S. citizen residing or traveling in the area, the spouse or dependent of a citizen employed or stationed in the area, or a native resident. However, many positions at U.S. posts and installations in foreign countries are not open to spouses because of agreements designed to ensure that, wherever possible, native residents will be employed.

In some countries, by special agreement with the host country, positions normally reserved for native residents can be offered to dependents of U.S. Government employees. Most overseas federal jobs currently available to the dependents are nonpermanent appointments, which can be used to earn eligibility for direct career appointments.

How to Get A Federal Job Overseas . . . When Your Spouse Already Has One

Information on employment opportunities may be available in the area where your spouse is assigned, through civilian personnel offices, community liaison offices or service centers, and local post newsletters. However, many overseas jobs available to spouses of U.S. Government personnel are "local hire" positions, for which your employment application usually will not be considered until after you relocate overseas.

Establish your employment eligibility with the local civilian personnel office as soon as you arrive overseas, because qualified applicants are often considered in order of their application dates.

While local procedures vary, civilian personnel offices generally inform applicants of the type and grade level of positions for which they qualify and enter their names on a list of eligible candidates.

Types of Overseas Appointments

Dependent Hire Appointment: The majority of U.S. Government spouses employed by the Defense Department overseas are hired under this type of appointment, and it can be used to acquire eligibility for direct hire appointments under Executive Order 12585, as described previously.

Part-time/Intermittent/Temporary (PIT) and American Family Member (AFM) Appointments: Similar to dependent hire appointments, PIT and AFM appointments are used in U.S. diplomatic and consular establishments and contribute to eligibility under EO 12585. PIT appointments are often used to handle seasonal workload surges, fill in gaps between assignments of regular foreign service personnel, and deal with unusual or unpredictable circumstances. AFM appointments were created originally for staffing by foreign service national employees but, with certain restrictions, have been made available to American family members. American citizens who are family members of U.S. Government personnel are eligible for PIT and AFM appointments. Citizens who are not family members may be considered for PIT appointments.

While PIT positions tend to be clerical, this varies according to location. For example, since a low level of education prevails in Africa, qualified foreign nationals may be difficult to find, a situation that would cause higher-level openings to be more available to spouses.

Nonappropriated Fund (NAF) Appointments: Instead of being funded by congressional appropriation, NAF jobs are funded by membership fees, club proceeds, and the like. Since NAF jobs are not considered federal jobs, work under this type of arrangement does not count toward eligibility for a direct appointment under EO 12585.

Department of Defense Dependents School (DODDS) Appointments: Spouses can qualify for two types of appointments in DODDS schools: (1) as support personnel under an arrangement similar to the dependent hire appointment previously described, and (2) as professional educators who are initially hired overseas on a nonpermanent basis for a period not to exceed the current school year. While these educators may be subsequently appointed on permanent appointments for future school years, only their nonpermanent or dependent hire employment can be used to acquire eligibility for direct hire appointments under EO 12585.

Overseas Limited Appointments: Used primarily to fill nonpermanent overseas positions above grade level GS-8, these time-limited appointments are made from among residents of the overseas area. While not providing civil service status, time in such an appointment can be credited toward the EO 12585 eligibility requirements.

Berlin Tariff Agreements: Local-hire employment under this special employment system (used in the territory of Berlin by Allied Forces) can be credited toward the EO 12585 eligibility requirements.

Employment Contracts: A number of federal agencies, besides the Departments of State and Defense, employ workers overseas under employment contracts. Jobs under employment contracts are real possibilities for spouses, especially in developing countries, where the Agency for International Development (AID) is represented. Because of the attractiveness of hiring someone local with a full set of allowances already paid for, AID hires many spouses whether or not they are dependents of U.S. Government employees. Since service under this arrangement is not considered federal employment, the time spent on employment contracts cannot be credited toward the EO 12585 eligibility requirements. For more about contract work, refer to Chapters 3 and 11.

Other Employment Arrangements: Other agencies hire workers on arrangements peculiar to them, and employment under these arrangements can be credited toward the EO 12585 eligibility requirements if:

1. it involves a nonpermanent appointment to a federal position,
2. the appointment is local hire (made from among applicants residing in the overseas area), and
3. the funds to support the position are appropriated by the U.S. Congress.

Returning to the United States From Overseas

In preparation for returning to the United States, make sure you have copies of all records pertaining to your overseas employment so personnel offices in the United States can verify your service.

If you meet the EO 12585 direct appointment eligibility requirements, you can bypass OPM and apply directly to personnel offices in agencies of your choice. Federal agencies in the United States can offer you direct career-conditional appointments. Then, to get a career appointment or status, you must serve a three-year period that includes a one-year probationary period toward which your overseas service cannot be counted.

If you do not meet the EO 12585 eligibility criteria or do not have civil service status, you will have to go through OPM and the regular competitive hiring process for civil service positions as described earlier in this chapter.

Some of the information in this chapter was adapted by permission from an unpublished (Office of Personnel Management) report by Ed McHugh, Dana Emery, and Dorothy Longo entitled *Civil Service Employment: A Guide for Spouses of United States Government Military and Civilian Personnel* (1984).

6
Exploring Your Options

Now that you have read about a variety of work options, you are ready to investigate those that appeal to you. You may even discover additional possibilities as you explore fields of work, specific jobs, and work settings. To avoid wasting time in an incompatible situation — a career, a place to work, a college major, or any other endeavor — thoroughly evaluate and compare its attributes to your priorities and qualifications from Part I.

As a job seeker, you will be better able to impress employers if you research their organizations and the skills required for specific jobs before submitting applications and going on interviews.

CASE IN POINT

After teaching for 12 years in three different cities, Lindsay Milton was ready for a career change. Looking to her forthcoming relocation from Detroit to Cleveland as a time to move into a new field, Lindsay fantasized about working in a corporate personnel position. Personnel appealed to her because it provided more opportunities to work with adults, a higher salary, and more prestige. While she wanted nothing more to do with education, she credited that experience for her superior communication and interpersonal skills and her attention to detail.

Lindsay knew little about what *personnel* entailed outside of an educational setting, but she wasted no time in sending resumes to the personnel directors of 23 large corporations listed in a publication from Cleveland's

EXPLORING YOUR OPTIONS

Economic Development Commission.

Six weeks later, as she packed for her move, Lindsay pondered the results of her efforts: "Although my resume was excellent and I was enthusiastic about my interviews, I got 15 rejection letters, no response from five companies, and only two interviews. I wonder where I went wrong?"

Now happily employed as the coordinator of college relations in the personnel department of a large corporation, Lindsay says, "I learned the hard way it is important to do your homework before applying for jobs. I destroyed my chances for finding employment with 23 excellent organizations because of my ignorance about the personnel field and the organizations to which I was applying. I should have postponed my job search until I had investigated my options."

To investigate your options, here are six effective methods to use. While each is described separately, they work best when used in combination.

- reading
- talking with people
- observing people at work
- sampling
- taking courses
- using computerized guidance and information systems

Even though this chapter focuses on gathering information to make well-thought-out decisions about employment, these methods are effective for helping with other decisions, including where to go to school, volunteer, vacation, or retire.

To keep track of the information you accumulate, use a form like the accompanying Work Research Information Sheet.

Field of Work	Job Title	Required Skills	Work Setting	Organization Name

WORK RESEARCH INFORMATION SHEET

READ ALL ABOUT IT

To learn about your alternatives, take advantage of the wealth of written material available through a variety of sources.

For starters, the following four *Department of Labor publications*, beneficial to anyone deciding about a career, are available in reference rooms of public libraries and most other centers housing career information:

- The *Guide for Occupational Exploration* (GOE) groups thousands of occupations by interests and by abilities and traits required for successful performance. For each work group, the GOE provides descriptive information, so individuals can evaluate their interests and relate them to fields of work. An updated and more comprehensive version of this resource is available from American Guidance Service (see Appendix C).
- The *Dictionary of Occupational Titles* (DOT) provides brief descriptions of 20,000 occupations – nearly all the jobs in the U.S. economy. Effective for generating alternative employment options, this 1,371-page resource enables you to locate jobs by physical demands, working conditions, interests, skills, educational requirements, etc.
- The *Occupational Outlook Handbook* (OOH) provides information on approximately 200 occupations, including job duties, working conditions, places of employment, education and training requirements, advancement possibilities, job outlook, earnings, and sources of additional career information. Published every other year, this excellent resource should not be missed.
- The *Occupational Outlook Quarterly* (OOQ) is issued four times a year and carries articles on new occupations, labor force trends, and unusual jobs.

Books about work provide specific and detailed information. Two examples of books from Appendix C are *Teachers in New Careers: Stories of Successful Transitions* and *Opportunities in Paralegal Careers*.

Pamphlets and articles are less likely to become dated than books and are superb resources about employment. The best sources are trade and professional associations. Examples of pamphlets include "Your Career in Human Resource Development: A Guide to Information and Decision Making" published by the American Society for

Training and Development, "Zoo and Aquarium Careers" by the American Association of Zoological Parks and Aquariums, and "What's It Like to Work With Computers?" by General Electric. As you might suspect, pamphlets and articles sometimes reflect the biases of the organizations that publish them.

Directories enable you to identify employers you may not otherwise consider and to connect with the work settings described in Chapter 3. Besides providing contact information for organizations, directories sometimes give names of key staff members and describe an organization's activities, publications, budget, and future plans. The following are examples of directories and other resources about organizations:

- *Careers in the Nonprofit Sector: Doing Well By Doing Good*
- *The Consultants and Consulting Organizations Directory*
- *Encyclopedia of Associations*
- *Foundation Directory*
- *National Trade and Professional Associations*
- *Research Centers Directory*
- *Standard and Poors Register of Corporations*
- *Thomas Register of American Manufacturers*
- *The United States Government Manual*
- *Washington Information Directory*

The following resources, as well as many of those previously listed, provide information about organizations doing work overseas (also refer to Appendix C):

- *American Register of Exporters and Importers*
- *Careers in International Affairs*
- *Current Technical Services Contracts and Grants* (a publication of the U.S. Agency of International Development or AID)
- *Directory of AID Indefinite Quantity Contracts*
- *Directory of American Firms Operating in Foreign Countries*
- *Directory of U.S. Based Agencies Involved in International Health Assistance*
- *Europa Year Book*
- *Major Companies of Europe*
- *Overseas Development Network Opportunities Catalog*
- *The Overseas List: Opportunities for Living and Working in Developing Countries*
- *U.S. Nonprofit Organizations in Development Assistance*

Abroad (Known as the *TAICH Directory*)
- Voluntary Foreign Aid Programs
- Yearbook of International Organizations

Many of the preceding directories and additional ones are listed and described in detail in the context of job search skills and strategies in Ronald and Caryl Rae Krannich's outstanding book, *The Complete Guide to Public Employment: Opportunities and Strategies With Federal, State, Local, and International Careers* (see Appendix C). For the names of other directories in your areas of interest, check with reference librarians, *The Directory of Directories,* and the *Guide to American Directories.*

Sources of Written Information

Besides public libraries and bookstores, there are many other sources of written information about work and organizations as shown in the accompanying lists. To get access to this information, you may need to write, call, or visit your new location prior to relocation.

An increased demand for information has prompted many large public library systems to institute telephone reference services. With this recent development, researchers — including job seekers — can remain in the comfort of their own homes and phone questions to the experts. For example, a writer relocating to Montgomery County, Maryland, who dials 217-INFO for help in identifying the area's newspapers would be told about *Hudson's Washington News Media Contacts Directory.*

An excellent collection of international documents and other resources for identifying and researching consulting firms is at the central library of the Agency for International Development (AID) — 1601 North Kent, Rosslyn, VA, 703-875-4818. For example, they have the previously mentioned *TAICH Directory* and *Voluntary Foreign Aid Programs.*

Unless you are in the Washington, DC area, you may want to order the AID resources in either microfiche or hard copy. For a free listing of order numbers for specific titles, write AID Library, Room 105, SA 18, Agency for International Development, Washington, DC 20523-1801, Attention: Reference. Once you have the numbers for your selected documents, order them by writing User Services, AID Document and Information Handling Facility, 7222 47th Street, Chevy Chase, MD 20815. You can also reach them by telephoning 301-951-7191.

SOURCES OF WRITTEN INFORMATION

About Work
- career centers in high schools, colleges, and independent organizations
- business divisions in large public library systems
- career centers for special groups, including women, veterans, youth, handicapped persons — often independent, nonprofit groups or part of county agencies
- libraries in colleges and universities — an excellent source for trade and professional journals
- local, area-wide, and national newspapers
- state and local employment offices
- national trade and professional associations (for referrals to the appropriate associations, contact the information-central office of The American Society of Association Executives at 202-626-ASAE)

About Specific Organizations
- public relations or public affairs departments of organizations
- company newsletters, annual reports, and brochures (write, call, or drop by organizations to get these)
- chambers of commerce — national and local
- business sections of large newspapers
- economic development commissions, in county government agencies
- job fairs
- federal civilian personnel offices
- federal job information and testing centers
- directories of organizations

ASK AROUND

As you make decisions about employment or other endeavors, take at least some time to talk with people who are directly involved in your areas of interest to get up-to-date and realistic facts. Otherwise, you may waste valuable weeks or even months pursuing fantasies that may not exist or be compatible with your qualifications or priorities. To get information about work, aim at people on your employment level or one level higher and avoid personnel departments. If you are exploring options prior to relocation, talk with people in similar circumstances with interests related to yours so you can learn from their experiences. Also apply some of the long-distance approaches described in Chapter 11.

Even though most people will spend time with you if you ask them to talk about subjects that really interest them, this method of gathering information may seem frightening. As a way to get comfortable at it, ask people questions in low-stress situations on subjects of your choice — an issue, a leisure activity, a place, a problem, a hobby, or whatever fascinates you. Your new community provides many sources of information, including reference librarians, the *Yellow Pages*, the chamber of commerce, neighbors, and your spouse's colleagues. Visit people you are referred to, and ask a few basic questions until you feel comfortable. Then, proceed with the process of talking with people about the more serious job or non-job options you are considering.

CASE IN POINT

When Margaret Sampson relocated to Santa Fe, NM, she decided to make a transition from real estate into a new career field. To discover where there was a match between her skills and jobs in Santa Fe, Margaret talked with everybody she met who was doing a job she knew nothing about. She says, "I simply asked, 'What do you do every day?' 'What skills do you need to do that job?' 'What particular function are you in?' " Through that process, Margaret decided to go into marketing research in a corporate environment. She reports, "When I interviewed with companies, I was able to say, 'I know you have employees doing research. That's the kind of position I could go into.' I wouldn't have known that if I hadn't asked questions about jobs."

Making Contacts

As a relocating spouse, you may know fewer local people than others know, but you probably know more than you think you know, and you can meet new people quickly. Try this exercise:

Get several sheets of lined paper and make two to three columns per page with the following headings according to your situation:

- relatives
- friends
- acquaintances
- neighbors
- co-workers — yours and your spouse's

EXPLORING YOUR OPTIONS 85

- community/church/synagogue contacts
- classmates — past and current
- others

Now, set aside an hour to brainstorm and write down the names of all the people you know who fit in these categories. Another way to get names of people to talk with is to use directories such as those listed in this chapter and Appendix C. Call selected firms and tactfully quiz switchboard operators to learn the names of department heads. Other ways to get names include reviewing membership directories and class reunion and meeting lists.

The people whose names you have identified to this point are your *direct contacts*. Talk with them about the information you are seeking. Whether or not they can provide the information, they may be able to refer you to others who can help you. Counting these *indirect contacts* — people who are two or more "levels" away — each of us has hundreds of contacts and access to unlimited information as shown in the accompanying diagram.

YOUR DIRECT AND INDIRECT CONTACTS

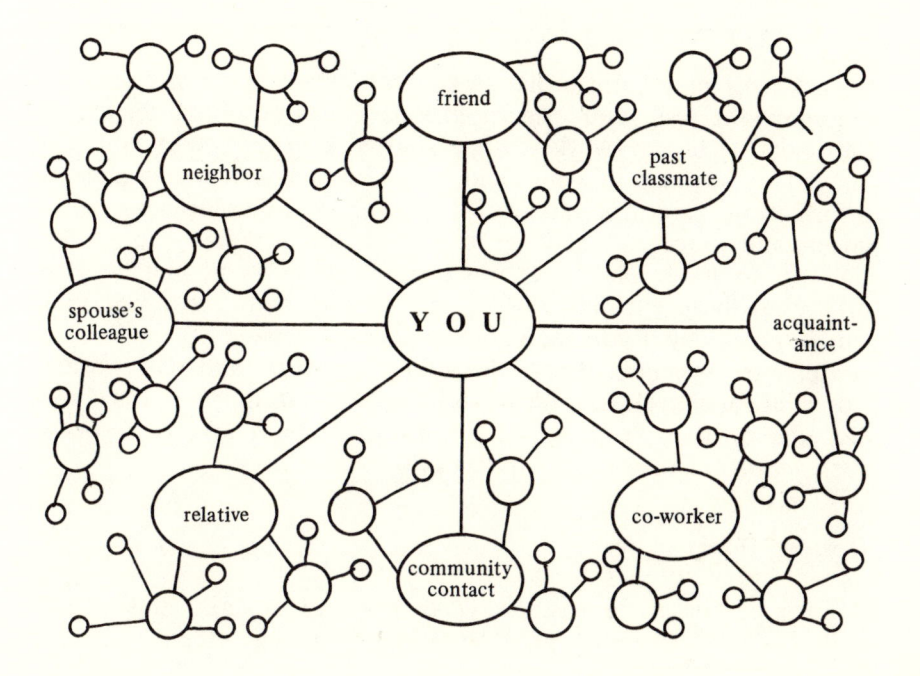

The process of developing and using your contacts for information, advice, and support is called *networking*. Since you leave behind many of your networks when you move, take advantage of all opportunities for developing new ones in your new location — social settings, alumni associations, and even when you are riding a bus or standing in line at a supermarket.

CASE IN POINT

Salvadore Montebono discovered that neighbors can provide an invaluable link to businesses and industry in a new community. He says, "Shortly after we relocated, a family in our new neighborhood invited 22 couples to a backyard barbecue to welcome us. While the guests were surprised that we had moved because of my wife's employment rather than mine, they were interested in my career goals and extremely generous about putting me in touch with their business colleagues. Several neighbors became quite committed to my reemployment and spent a considerable amount of time generating ideas for me."

As a result of being open with his new neighbors about his employment situation, Salvadore quickly made connections with people in his field and identified the organizations on which to focus his job search. His reemployment took considerably less time than he expected.

Networks may be informal groups, whose members often share a common interest, and formal groups or associations related to particular fields of work. Formal network groups help you stay current or advance in your field by offering business tips and job information, meetings and workshops for skill development, newsletters and journals, and information on how to keep your credentials up to date. The long-term benefits of network memberships may contribute substantially to maintaining and developing your career, especially if you are in a rural area or overseas.

Refer to Appendix B for a list of 131 networks and other groups. For additional groups, refer to *A Woman's Yellow Pages*, the *Encyclopedia of Associations*, and the *National Trade and Professional Associations* directory (see Appendix C).

Opening Doors

Each of the three basic ways to get into organizations to talk with people — walking in, telephoning, sending letters — has its advantages and disadvantages. Whatever method you use, offer assurance that you will only take about 20 minutes of the person's time, and then stick to that.

Walking in: This time-saving method is acceptable in some informal work settings, but it would not work in formal corporations like IBM. However, you can walk into most organizations to pick up written material, and, at the same time, get a feeling for the work environment.

Telephoning: This method is fast and direct, and is especially effective in informal situations or when the person you are calling is expecting to hear from you. However, if he or she knows nothing about you, you may not even get past the secretary. When telephoning, you have no way to know if you are interrupting the individual you want to contact.

Do not leave a message for your contacts to return your call because they probably won't bother. Instead, ask, "When can I reach _____?" or "What is a good time to call?" Other ways to get through to the employee you hope to reach include:

- Calling at times the support staff may not be on the job — for example, before 8:30 a.m. or after 5:30 p.m.
- Saying, for example, "May I speak with _____? This is _____." By giving your name without being asked for it, you may be taken for a friend or colleague.
- Naming a technical problem the support staff cannot respond to — for example, "I need to talk with Ms. Tittlebaum because I am researching the employment projections for medical laboratory personnel through the mid-1990s in the northeastern United States."

Since you may not be able to secure a face-to-face meeting with your contact, be prepared to ask your questions over the telephone. If you are told to send a resume, respond that you are interested in information, not a job.

Sending letters: While this method of getting time with people is the slowest and most time consuming, it often yields the best results. A person who is familiar with you because of your prior communication is not as likely to refuse your request for time and advice when you telephone. If your letter specifies a date when you will be calling, you may be more motivated to follow through. And you increase your chances of getting an appointment when you mention a mutual contact in your letter. Even though it is important for your letter to be brief and to the point, you could list a few questions you hope to ask when you meet with the person; for example, "What are the advantages of getting a computer sciences degree compared to taking four or five computer programming courses?"

Use the sample letters on pages 89 and 90 as guides when you write to request time with people.

Note that the second letter mentions an enclosed resume. You can develop a general, unfocused resume to use as you talk with people to explore your options. Then, when you settle on what it is you want to do, create a focused resume, as described in Chapter 12.

What to Talk About

Before meeting with people, find out as much as possible about them, their fields of work, and their organizations. To become knowledgeable and to develop suitable questions, use the resources in Appendix C as well as publications issued by organizations. Refer to the following lists as you develop your questions.

Fields of Work

- Do you foresee big changes or developments occurring in this field in the future, and how will they affect opportunities?
- At present is there an oversupply or undersupply of people in your field? Will this situation continue?
- What educational preparation is desirable for advancement?
- What other fields of work could one enter for which this experience would be valuable?
- How much can one expect to earn in an entry-level position in your field of work? (or after 5, 10 years, or at top of the ladder?)
- What are the opportunities for self-employment in this field?
- Are there opportunities for promotion within this field? Would it be necessary to change occupations to advance?
- If I chose this field, what suggestions for advancement would you have for me?
- Who else could you refer me to for more information on this?
- Do you mind if I keep in touch with you as I narrow down the field in which I want to work?

Letter Requesting Time to Explore a Field of Work

```
                              2468 Acorn Way
                              St. Louis, Missouri  63116
                              August 18, 198_
```

Mr. John Witte, Assistant Manager
Computer Systems Section
Fargo Data Development Corporation
132 Ashton Boulevard
St. Louis, Missouri 63178

Dear Mr. Witte:

I read in the <u>St. Louis Tribune</u> about your recent promotion to Assistant Manager of Computer Systems. Congratulations! I have been following the progress of Fargo and know that it is a superior organization in the data processing field.

I am very interested in working in the field of data processing and have considered training in programming. I am currently exploring ways to develop appropriate skills to support my career interests. However, I am new to the St. Louis area and am unsure of what approach to take. I am trying to decide whether to return to school or take an entry-level position to acquire on-the-job training. I am also concerned about the outlook for continued growth in the data processing field. I know that you are very busy with your new responsibilities, but hope you can share some of your expertise on these issues. At this time, I am only looking for information and advice, not employment.

I will telephone you on Tuesday, August 26, to schedule a brief meeting of no more than 20 minutes. I could arrange to come before or after your working hours or during your lunch break if those times would be most convenient. I appreciate your consideration.

```
                              Sincerely,


                              Janet T. Brown
```

Letter Requesting Time to Explore Specific Jobs

801 Ninth Street
El Paso, Texas 79949
June 14, 198_

Ms. Jessie Parker
Supervisor, Accounting Department
The Analog Company
6210 42nd Avenue
El Paso, Texas 79952

Dear Ms. Parker:

    When I met with Abigale Jones at the Beta Corporation earlier this week, she suggested I contact you.

    I am an experienced accounts receivable clerk who is interested in making a career change. I would like an opportunity to talk with you regarding some information and advice on how to become qualified as an accounting assistant or for related jobs. Your knowledge of this work could be very useful to my planning efforts. To give you an idea of my background, I have enclosed my resume. Be assured that I am not requesting an interview for a job at this time.

    I will telephone you on Wednesday, June 21, to arrange for a brief meeting. I realize that you are quite busy and will, therefore, take only a few minutes of your time. Thank you for your consideration.

Sincerely,

Francis A. Rathbun

Enclosure

Jobs

- What is your job title? Are there other titles that a person in your job might hold?
- What is the nature of your work? (typical day or week, responsibilities, variety, problems, decisions)
- What skills do you need to do this job?
- What do you like most about your job? What are the major frustrations in this job?
- What type of person would enjoy your job?
- From what you know of my qualifications, would you please describe my deficiencies in terms of this job? What would you recommend I do to become qualified?
- What other organizations or individuals could you recommend I contact to discuss this kind of work?

Work Settings and Specific Organizations

- How is your organization structured?
- What are the typical entry-level jobs in your organization?
- Where might my skills and interests fit into this structure?
- Are there many advancement opportunities for entry-level employees who do well?
- What job search strategies are most effective for securing employment in this type of work setting?
- What are the hiring procedures?
- What types of people does your organization like to recruit?
- What skills or talents would be most valuable for someone wanting to work here?
- What salary might an entry-level employee in this organization expect?
- Are salaries in this organization in line with comparable jobs in similar organizations?
- What other organizations are similar to this one?
- Who else could you refer me to, either in this company or in a similar organization, who could give me more information?

Make the Most of Your Meeting

Structure this time for success. Provide enough information on your background — including your skills, values, and interests — to get good advice. Never forget that *you* are the interviewer. Ask the questions you brought with you; don't shoot the breeze!

Most important of all, do not have hidden agendas. If you know exactly what work you want to do and where you want to do it, you should be going on job interviews rather than visiting employers under the pretense of seeking information. If you use this guise to get a job, it may backfire on you and will surely ruin others' chances of getting time with people for the purpose of exploring options.

It is acceptable to ask for advice about your resume; for example, "Is it appropriate for this field?" "Does it adequately reflect my background?" or "Should anything be added or deleted?" It is important to lay groundwork for future contacts, and you can do this by asking if you could send your revised resume or keep in touch as you continue to narrow your options.

Near the end of your meeting, try to get approximately three referrals to others.

How to Maintain Your Contacts

Develop a small card file for keeping track of details about the people you talk with, including where and when you met them and key words about them. Then, keep in touch with your contacts, and eventually you may get a job through this route.

As a first step in keeping your name in front of those with the authority to hire, always send thank-you letters to the people you meet. Besides thanking them for their time, you could say, for example, "As you suggested, I contacted. . . ," or "I'll keep you informed on. . ."

CASE IN POINT

Soon after moving to Syracuse, NY, while investigating the field of marketing research, Joan Fogerty met with a major employer who described future possibilities in the company's marketing department. The employer urged Joan to keep in touch, and she did just that. Every two months, to keep her name coming across his desk, Joan wrote her contact a short letter informing him of her career research and the relevant background she was acquiring through a temporary job and a self-directed reading program. She says, "Nine months later, out of the blue, he called me about two very attractive positions. I interviewed with staff in the marketing department, was hired, and love my job." Keeping in touch does pay dividends.

EXPLORING YOUR OPTIONS

Thus far, this chapter has concentrated on two ways to explore options, reading and talking with people. The remaining four ways — observation, sampling, course work, and computerized guidance — will now be covered briefly.

LOOK AROUND

Ask your contacts who are doing things that appeal to you if you could spend a day, or even a few hours, with them in their work settings. Meet other employees; have lunch in their cafeterias to hear what they talk about. Your firsthand impressions may clarify possible misconceptions and save you the time and expense of making wrong decisions.

CASE IN POINT

Sondra Morrison had spent five years as a medical research technician for a large government laboratory in Oak Ridge, TN, before leaving to raise her two children. Years later while living in Boulder, CO, with teenagers about to enter high school, Sondra decided to return to the world of paid employment in a field where she could work more directly with people.

Uninterested in extensive retraining, Sondra settled on residential real estate sales. She took the required courses for licensing, and aligned herself with a recognized real estate firm in her community. It wasn't long before she regretted her choice of a new career. Somewhat embarrassed, Sondra explains, "Although I like working with people, I discovered I don't like selling things to them — especially expensive things like houses. Coupled with this, I hated the hours and constant demands that go with real estate selling."

Now in a career she really enjoys, Sondra has this to say in retrospect: "Now that the damage is done, I realize I could have saved myself a lot of money and frustration by asking several agents if I could have accompanied them with one or two of their clients to learn what real estate involved on a day-to-day basis."

TRY IT ON FOR SIZE

You can "sample" different work settings and jobs through temporary and volunteer work, internships, and apprenticeships, as described in Chapters 3 and 10. Sampling allows you to test your interests and learn about training requirements in a variety of situations before making a full-time commitment.

CAREER-RELATED COURSE WORK

Course work is typically associated with skill development (as described in Chapter 10), but it can also be used to explore career options. Besides traditional degree programs, course work includes individual credit and noncredit course, professional development programs, university-sponsored conferences and workshops, correspondence courses, external degree programs, and learning via audio and video cassettes.

COMPUTERIZED GUIDANCE

A number of college and university career centers are acquiring computerized guidance and information systems that allow users to do career planning at their own pace.

Highly recommended by is users, DISCOVER for Adult Learners was developed by the American College Testing Program (Iowa City, IA). The system consists of a group of computer-delivered experiences that help adults assess themselves, explore educational pathways and occupations, prepare for employment or self-improvement, get a job, and cope with career changes and transitions. DISCOVER is available to the public at no cost or for a minimal charge through an increasing number of sites — currently more than 2,000 — throughout the United States. To see where you can use DISCOVER in your area, write to The DISCOVER Center, 230 Chilling Circle, Hunt Valley, MD 21031, or call 301-584-8000.

The other computerized system for adults is SIGI (System of Interactive Guidance and Information). Developed by the Educational Testing Service, SIGI is available at more than 800 sites in colleges, universities, and private counseling centers. Users make informed career decisions by assessing their values, interests, and skills; acquiring individualized lists of occupations and up-to-date occupational information; reviewing the skills necessary for occupations; and identifying needed preparation. For information about SIGI, write The SIGI Office, Educational Testing Service, Princeton, NJ 08541, or call 1-800-524-0491.

III

CHOOSING

The man who insists on perfect clearness before he decides, never decides. Accept life, and you must accept regret.

Frederic Amiel

7

The Job Market and Employment Trends

After exploring a variety of alternatives, you are prepared to specify an employment goal by matching the options to your priorities and qualifications. First, however, to ensure that the type of work you *want* to do is compatible with what you will be *able* to do in your new location, investigate the job market and employment trends where you will be working.

Unfortunately, the job market is not centralized like a stock market. There is not just one job market, there are many – the job market for social workers, the job market for food service workers, and the job market for fund raisers, to name but a few. To complicate things even more, especially for the relocating spouse, the market for different jobs varies geographically. The demand for your field is influenced by factors such as a region's economic conditions, population density, residents' education level, and marketplace orientation – for example, agriculture, manufacturing, or services.

LOOK BEFORE YOU LEAP: INVESTIGATING YOUR NEW LOCATION

There are several things you can do before relocating to simplify your job search. First, using the information sources listed in this chapter, acquaint yourself with how the job market in the new location is divided. For an example of this, see the accompanying diagram.

EXAMPLE OF HOW A JOB MARKET IS DIVIDED

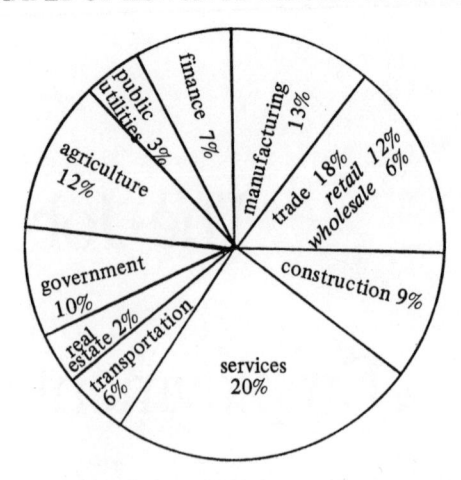

- public utilities 3%
- finance 7%
- manufacturing 13%
- trade 18%
- retail 12%
- wholesale 6%
- construction 9%
- services 20%
- transportation 6%
- real estate 2%
- government 10%
- agriculture 12%

Next, within the category and specific field in which you hope to work, investigate how job openings are likely to occur. The two primary ways of creating openings are: (1) turnover — the replacement of people in *existing* jobs because of termination (for example, retirement, pregnancy, and relocation), and (2) expansion — the creation of *new* jobs through economic growth and development. Expansion may be a more favorable indicator of future opportunities. To determine the trends in the job market where you will be seeking employment, look for patterns of growth and decline over the past several years.

--- CASE IN POINT ---

Sally Abrams, now working part-time as a Spanish translator in Atlanta, has gone through one relocation during her seven years of marriage because of her spouse's career, and anticipates as many as three more moves during her marriage.

Besides being a wrenching experience personally, the move from New York City was a professional setback for Sally. After leaving her position as a translator with the United Nations, she spent nearly a year searching for a job. With a trace of bitterness, Sally tells how that experience affected her: "Eleven months of unemployment gives you a lot of time to think! Given the job markets where I am likely to move, I now realize I'm in the wrong career. While I plan to continue doing translating on a freelance basis, I have been taking some definite steps to become qualified as a high school Spanish teacher — an occupation in which I can more

THE JOB MARKET AND EMPLOYMENT TRENDS

> readily be reemployed full-time."
>
> Taking education courses at night, Sally has a busy schedule, but is confident her foresight will pay off when her husband next announces, "Well, the boss tells me I'm needed at a plant in Akron (or Omaha, or Detroit, or Richmond)."

Relocating spouses will be able to locate job market information from several sources. For city profiles, refer to the *Encyclopedia of American Cities, Encyclopedia America, The Editor and Publisher Market Guide,* and the *Moving To* series, which are available in reference rooms of public libraries. For more information on the job market and employment trends, refer to the sources listed here:

- state or local government economic development and employment offices
- chambers of commerce
- employment and business sections in local and national newspapers
- annual or semiannual job market inserts in large city newspapers
- books about fields of work
- large city magazines
- television and radio
- U.S. Department of Labor, the Bureau of Labor Statistics
- local Department of Labor offices
- trade and professional associations
- trade and professional journals and newsletters
- The U.S. Industrial Outlook Division of the International Trade Administration (202-377-4356), which supplies information about industries.

HIGH-GROWTH FIELDS IN AN ERA OF CHANGE

The U.S. economy will add 10 million to 20 million jobs in the next decade, and nine out of 10 of those new jobs will be in the service industries, according to the Bureau of Labor Statistics. Trend forecasters John Naisbitt and Patricia Aburdene, authors of *Reinventing the Corporation*, predict that high growth for jobs will be in the following areas: the computer industry, health care, travel, entertainment, retailing, financial services, human resources, law, and accounting.

In the years ahead, more jobs are likely to surface in growing technologies such as communications, computers, robotics, biotechnology, and electric power generation. The six occupations projected by the Bureau of Labor Statistics to have the fastest percentage of growth through 1995 are:

- computer operator
- computer programmer
- computer service technician
- computer systems analyst
- legal assistant (paralegal)
- office machine operator

Of course, no one can predict the future conclusively. What *is* conclusive is that we have entered an age of rapid change. Consider the technological changes that have occurred in recent years in the world of work — automated teller machines, word processing, telemarketing, video. Even relatively nontechnical fields, such as library science and secretarial work, have been revolutionized by technology. The rate of these changes will probably only accelerate over the coming years.

IS FASTER ALWAYS BETTER?

Rapid growth in an occupational area does not necessarily mean a large number of jobs will be available in that area. This is because (1) The public's perception of a high demand may cause them to over-prepare for an occupation and thereby decrease the number of opportunities; and (2) if only a small number of jobs are represented in an occupational area, rapid growth in that occupation won't cause a significant increase. For example, even though high-tech job opportunities will grow more than 25 percent between 1982 and 1995, the percentage of total employment in this fast-growing sector will be only about 4 percent in the United States, according to a representative of the Department of Labor. And even though computer-related careers dominate the foregoing list of fast-growing occupations, only 1.5 percent of the total employment will be in computer occupations in 1995.

Surprisingly, slow-growth occupations that employ large numbers of workers can create more jobs than fast-growth occupations that employ relatively few. For example, from 1982 to 1995, the number of custodians in the United States is predicted to increase by 779,000 (a slow-growth occupation employing many workers), while the number of paralegals may double, creating approximately 50,000 jobs.

Despite the Bureau of Labor Statistics prediction for above average job growth in professional and technical areas, the greatest growth will be outside of highly skilled areas. A recent study conducted by Stanford University reveals that of the 10 occupations predicted to have high growth rates through 1995, only two will require postsecondary education — teaching in the lower elementary grades and nursing. And, contrary to popular opinion, many jobs in high-tech industries are for unskilled production workers rather than for college graduates skilled in math, science, and computing.

High-growth service jobs, which will account for 25 percent of all new jobs generated in the 1980s, include secretaries, sales and general office clerks, cashiers, and fast food service workers. With Americans spending increasing percentages of their incomes on recreation, personal services, travel, and restaurant meals, even more service jobs will become available for hair stylists, waitresses, cooks, child care workers, weight-reduction instructors, and hotel and motel personnel.

EXOTIC JOBS OF THE FUTURE

Besides the frequently named high-tech jobs, *The Futurist* magazine (February 1984) published a list of exotic occupational titles of the future, including plant therapist, treasure hunter, ocean hotel manager, and shyness consultant. Jobs from the human resource development profession were well represented in this list; for example, relocation counselor, career consultant, job developer, color consultant, image consultant, retirement counselor, benefits analyst, community psychologist, wellness consultant, and certified alcoholism counselor.

Consider job market and outlook information as you plan for your career, but don't rule out your area of interest if it is not represented in the high-growth occupations. Finding satisfying employment is often a matter of identifying what you want to do and then persistently getting out there in the marketplace to look for it.

8

How to Set and Reach an Employment Goal

The next step after exploring your work options and your new job market is to specify an employment goal by evaluating how well your preferred options match your priorities and qualifications. While this deciding aspect of work and life planning is often the most difficult, it will enable you to maintain control over your life.

Many relocating spouses, particularly those who relocate on a regular basis, come to believe it is useless to make employment plans. Aimless, they accept whatever work (if any) comes their way, and their lives become a series of postponements as they wait for their next moves. Beyond the external barriers and prejudices, relocating spouses often raise their own barriers — they have no goals, or, if they have them, they do not stick to them.

Granted, the relocation factor complicates planning for the future, but you can set long-term goals if you step back and examine your life as a whole. As a spouse who relocates regularly and cannot always find paid employment in your field, your goal may be to continue in your field by volunteering, taking courses, and involving yourself in other self-development activities. On the other hand, your goal may be to keep working, which may mean accepting whatever is available. If the work you have been doing or want to do is not compatible with the locations you are or will be in, perhaps you will decide to revise your employment goals and acquire new skills so you can find satisfying work over the long run. Regardless of your situation, goals will help you get to where you want to go.

HOW TO SET AND REACH AN EMPLOYMENT GOAL

CASE IN POINT

Alice Reems had just returned to the United States after six years in the Spanish-speaking world and was faced with a dilemma — one that made her friends envious. Before actively seeking reemployment, Alice had been asked to apply for jobs in two organizations, and now, with job offers from each, she needed to decide between being an administrative assistant in a professional association of economists or being an office manager in a family education center.

Confronted with making a choice between two jobs that appealed to her, Alice was confused. Initially, she had every intention of working. Since two of her three children were in college, she had looked forward to accumulating some money through the higher American salaries before returning to Latin America.

Realizing it may be shortsighted to take either of the two jobs, Alice took steps to evaluate what it was she really wanted to do. She says, "I concluded that my long-term goals were (1) to be hired from the States to work abroad as a consultant in bilingual education on issues related to language policy and planning or English as a Foreign Language (EFL), and (2) when in the States to work with Hispanic refugees. Even though I had worked steadily in Latin America and had gained a lot of experience, I recognized that I needed more academic training in the States to fulfill my long-term goals and to command more money."

Alice turned down both jobs in favor of getting a master's degree in linguistics, which will provide portable skills for her future relocations. She says, "It was a big decision to spend money on my education and turn down a salary that would contribute to my children's education." When Alice received a full fellowship, it was a welcome surprise.

The greatest advantage derived from setting well-thought-out goals is the enormous sense of control it gives you over your life.

DEFINING YOUR GOAL

To identify an employment goal, follow these steps.

1. Ask yourself, "Where am I now?" and, depending on the time frame you are comfortable with, "Where do I want to be in one, three, or five years?" Let yourself dream.

2. Write down all the options you have considered. Besides paid work, consider volunteer work, academic studies, and other alterna-

tives. Generate possibilities by looking to your past, your dreams for the future, and the options covered in Part II of this book. Now, brainstorm. Examples of options include acquiring CPA certification, finishing a degree, becoming a real estate agent, and working with learning-disabled children. As you come up with ideas, consider what you learned about the job market and employment trends in the previous chapter. Transfer your most appealing options to a page you have drawn like the accompanying exercise.

EXERCISE TO NARROW YOUR OPTIONS

OPTIONS	CRITERIA						
A.							
B.							
C.							
D.							

3. Determine your criteria for selecting a preference from among your options. Criteria, in this case, are those things that you hold important and feel you must have in terms of, for example, your values, preferred lifestyle, skills, and ideal job specifications. If you completed the exercises in Part I, you will have the criteria for choosing among your options. (If you skipped this important section, turn there now before continuing.) Examples of criteria:

- provides international employment opportunities
- is a field with a progressive career ladder
- offers part-time programs
- projected to be a high-demand field throughout the United States
- allows a steady income within six months
- requires only a short commute
- presents writing opportunities

Transfer your most important criteria to the Exercise to Narrow Your Options.

4. Compare each of your options with each of your criteria in the exercise and write + or - in the adjacent boxes to indicate whether or not the options fulfill your criteria. For example, if one of your options is *a position in advertising* and you have no advertising experience, this option probably would not meet your criterion to *make more than $20,000 a year within six months*.

Narrow your choice of a goal even further by writing the advantages and disadvantages of your preferred options on a page you have drawn like the following Exercise on Pros and Cons of Preferred Options. From the previous exercise, select two options you believe meet many of your criteria. After writing down all the possible advantages and disadvantages of each, you may find that the disadvantages outweigh the advantages. When this is the case, select two more options and repeat the process until you target a goal.

EXERCISE ON PROS AND CONS OF PREFERRED OPTIONS

| OPTION C || OPTION F ||
advantages	disadvantages	advantages	disadvantages

At this point, you probably have some idea about what your goal might be.

ACHIEVING YOUR GOAL

Often our employment goals are vague and overwhelming because of how we express them; for example, "I hope to find a challenging job," or "I want a professional job working with people." Since you cannot *do* a goal of this nature, you must design an *employment action plan* that will help you reach your goal.

Employment Action Plans

Besides specifying a realistic goal, your action plan will name specific *objectives* and *tasks* that are attainable, measurable, and time limited. Whereas objectives are mileposts that enable you to see progress toward your goal, tasks are short-term, action-oriented details for carrying out your objectives.

The time span of your plan depends on what you hope to accomplish. If you plan to continue with the same work you are doing now, a one-year plan may suit your needs. If you opt for a drastic change in your field of work, a four-year plan may be more realistic because of possible reeducation or the necessity of working in several lower-level positions before reaching your targeted employment. Regardless of the time frame you choose, set deadlines, write them down, and make sure you meet them.

Do not make the mistake of thinking your next job has to be *the* job when you are making a total career change. It is acceptable to have three jobs in five years if they will enhance your qualifications and help you work toward your employment goal.

CASE IN POINT

Mary Parker had been a typist when she decided to enter the world of accounting. To make this career transition, she took two accounting courses by correspondence while living abroad.

While Mary envisioned herself as the supervisor of an accounting department in a medium-size company, she did not apply for jobs on that level. Describing her approach, Mary says, "I knew I had a lot to learn before I could get to where I wanted to be. I realized nobody was going to put me in charge of a department. Yet if I could begin in an entry-level accounting job, I would be able to go on to another job and then another with increasing responsibility. Therefore, as I read the employment ads, I looked under *accounting assistant* and *accounting clerk*."

Moving up the ladder in her field, Mary became a supervisor as she had hoped and then set higher employment goals. In preparation for taking the CPA exam, she is now completing an accounting degree through evening classes at a local community college.

The following is an example of an action plan with its combination of a goal, objectives, tasks, and accompanying time limits:

GOAL: To become skilled at word processing.

Objective 1: Take word processing courses at local community college starting next spring.

Action-oriented tasks:
- I will finance my tuition with savings from my previous job.
- I will register for Word Processing I on January 5.
- For transportation I will use local bus #L-7.

Objective 2: Starting mid-winter, develop contacts to facilitate job-finding in companies that have a variety of word processors.

Action-oriented tasks:
- By January 23 I will inform my 21 targeted contacts about my new job direction.
- To begin networking, I will join a community group and Women in Information Processing by February 19.

To gain more control over your life, use the following guide to develop your own plan.

EMPLOYMENT ACTION PLAN

Employment Goal _____

Objective 1: _____

Tasks for carrying out Objective 1:   Time Limit
_____   _____
_____   _____
_____   _____

Objective 2: _____

Tasks for carrying out Objective 2:
_____   _____
_____   _____
_____   _____

Objective 3: _____

Tasks for carrying out Objective 3:
_____   _____
_____   _____
_____   _____

If your plan involves an academic or work commitment that must be fulfilled in your current location, try to get your spouse to agree to your action plan. While relocations are not optional matters in many work environments, they are in some.

CASE IN POINT

At the age of 36, Marion Cooke enrolled in a two-year community college program to become a travel agent. She had tried going to school in years past, but because of relocation, she had always dropped out before completing her studies. Marion knew that would not happen this time. She says, "I decided it was important to devote some attention to my career, and my husband agreed. We sat down and mutually decided not to accept a transfer from his employer until I finished school."

Marion finished school and worked as a travel agent before relocating. Looking back, she says, "Since my husband's organization allows only a few days to decide about a transfer, we might have made the wrong decision if we hadn't worked it out together ahead of time."

Since you will change with time, regularly examine and revise your employment action plan. To keep up your momentum, sit down with your calendar once a week and evaluate your progress toward your goal. For example: Are you staying within the time limits you set? Do you need to add more elements to your action plan?

Managing Your Time

Consider whether or not you are using your time most effectively to accomplish your goal. If you view the elements in your action plan as things you will do *if* you have the time, you will not get to them. Each of us has 168 hours a week — this is true for you, and it is true for the high-level executive. But time, like money, can get away from us. Most people have no idea how much time they spend on their daily tasks.

In his book, *How To Get Control of Your Time and Your Life*, Alan Lakein speaks of working smarter, not harder. He advises labeling those tasks that lead to your most important goal — perhaps the ones in your action plan — A's. Label the most important task A^1, the next most important one A^2, and the next most important one A^3. Those tasks that are important to you because of your other lifetime goals should be labeled B's, and those that are not important to either your employment goals or your lifetime goals can be labeled C's. Using a time management log like the one at the end of this chapter, keep an honest tabulation of the time you spend on various activities. You may be shocked by what you see.

Do not be discouraged if you have trouble managing your time at first. Like bicycle riding, time management is a learned skill and will improve with practice. Here are some basic steps to get you started.

1. Figure out what your procrastinating behavior is. It is human nature to do the easiest activities first; yet these may tire us and prevent us from getting to the tasks that contribute to our long-term goals. Work on your A tasks, as designated on the accompanying log, before allowing yourself to work on other things that do not contribute to your employment goal.

2. Just as you block out periods of time to attend meetings or classes, block out time to work on the tasks in your action plan.

3. Reward yourself when you complete a task in your action plan. Save something you really enjoy doing until you cross the task off your list.

4. To get organized, detail which aspects of your life you are going to change. Could you delegate more to other family members? Could you eliminate some tasks?

5. Set up a desk and work space for yourself where you live. Do not let your personal life spill into this area. Set up card files and manila folders to house the materials related to your action plan.

6. Let nothing interfere or interrupt you! Consider every potential interruption a *decision point*. You do not have to answer the telephone or the door. You are not obligated to go somewhere just because you were invited. Be clear and consistent with those around you about your available time and interests. If, after all this, you still find your home environment distracting, work on your tasks at a library or another quiet place.

TIME MANAGEMENT LOG

List below your daily activities, from the time your alarm sounds until you turn in at night. In the Priority column, use these letters: A=important and contributes to my employment goals; B=important to my other lifetime goals but does not contribute to my employment goals; C=not important to either my employment or my other lifetime goals. You can refine your categorization by breaking each A, B, or C task into A1, A2, A3, B1, B2, etc. depending on their value to your goals (the "1's" would be top, the "3's" lowest). In the Result column, indicate whether the activity could have been consolidated with other activities, eliminated, delegated, delayed to another time or day, etc. Record each activity as you complete it rather than waiting until the end of the day to work on this sheet.

Start	Stop	Total Time	Activity	Priority	Result

9

Career Planning Assistance

Many people find it difficult to make career decisions independent of the support of others. If that happens to you, ease your career transition by choosing from three different forms of career assistance — workshops and courses, one-to-one counseling, and career resources. Your spouse's employer may offer you some assistance, but it may be to help you locate a job rather than to help you plan your career. However, refer to Chapter 11 to learn about the programs directed at you, especially if you are a corporate, military, or foreign service spouse. To locate high-quality assistance available to the general public, get recommendations from your contacts and supplement them with the listings of services and counselors as described here.

Employment-related services may be available at your new location from college career counseling centers, YWCA's, women's centers, and the chamber of commerce. In addition, check a variety of headings in the *Yellow Pages* of the telephone book: career consultants, career and vocational counseling, employment counselors, guidance counseling, job counselors, vocational consultants, and women's organizations and services. Whenever you call one group in a geographic area, ask for the names of others.

Appendix C of *What Color Is Your Parachute?* has four excellent lists of individual and group career counseling services throughout the United States: (1) Places Which Counsel Anyone, (2) Help for Women (many of these also serve men), (3) Group Support for Those Who Are Unemployed, and (4) Directories of Career Counseling

Services in Various Cities/States. Author Richard Bolles stresses that his lists include only a sampling, and he does not go so far as to recommend them.

Catalyst, a not-for-profit organization dedicated to addressing issues related to the career advancement of women, offers a listing of more than 180 career resource centers located throughout the United States (and a few abroad). These centers provide a range of career guidance services including counseling, employment referral, test administration, internships, and career information via libraries. An increasing number of these firms are experienced in working with relocating spouses. For a free copy of the listing, "National Network of Career Resource Centers," write to Catalyst at their address in the Publisher/Distributor Contact Information section near the end of Appendix C.

WORKSHOPS AND COURSES

Group experiences are alternatives for individuals who may benefit from an organized program and the support of others. Whereas career resource centers and counseling services typically specialize in short workshops and one-to-one counseling assistance, colleges and other academic institutions are the most likely sources of longer credit and noncredit career development courses. Since credit courses often take a different approach and require more from students than noncredit courses, you may get more out of a credit course even if you do not need college credit.

CASE IN POINT

When 37-year-old Malcolm Weintraub learned that his wife was to be transferred to a nearby state, he enrolled in a one-credit career development course at a community college. Having been dissatisfied with construction management for some time, Malcolm looked to the relocation as the impetus to enter something more gratifying. He hoped the course would help him decide on a new field. On the first night of the 14-session course, Malcolm was pleased to see that many of the students were about his age and not enrolled in degree programs at the college.

Malcolm reports that the course work was demanding: "I had not counted on devoting time outside of class to homework. There were interest inventories and personality preference tests. The self-assessment exercises — especially skills identification — took many hours. The in-

> structor had us interview three people, each of whom was employed in a field related to our interests. Then we had to use four different resources to write about the career fields. Toward the end of the 14 weeks, we were told to develop resumes using two different styles. While I sometimes resented giving up my free time, I learned an incredible amount about myself and about the world of work."
>
> Malcolm credits the course with his reemployment in a new field after only two months. He says, "If I hadn't taken that $60 course, I would still be out there looking instead of contentedly working as a manager in state government."

ONE-TO-ONE COUNSELING

You may need more individual attention than a course or even a small workshop can provide. If so, you'll want to track down a career counselor with whom to work on a one-to-one basis.

Increasingly, the field of career counseling is requiring formal credentials, and you can get a listing of nationally certified career counselors in your area by contacting the National Board for Certified Counselors (NBCC) through the American Association of Counseling and Development, 5999 Stevenson Ave., Alexandria, VA 22304, 703-823-9800. Also request their free brochure, "How to Select A Counselor."

Although it is preferable to work with a trained and experienced counselor, these qualifications do not ensure you will develop rapport with the counselor or that he or she will communicate career information clearly and effectively. Many able and experienced counselors without certification or counseling degrees provide excellent services. Others can refer you to a counselor or career service, but it must be up to you to make the final selection.

While no fail-safe method has been devised to screen out poor counselors and screen in effective ones, there are ways to minimize your risk. Interview several counselors asking open-ended questions such as the following:

"Would you please describe your program to me?" (Beware of any service or counselor who offers or guarantees to find you a job – that is your responsibility, and not the role of a legitimate career service or counselor. Likewise, beware of numbers-game zealots who advocate flooding hundreds of employers with resumes in the hope that a few will "catch.")

The purpose of a career counseling service is to guide you in a decision-making process and to provide you with techniques and resources for launching or advancing your work and life goals. A worthwhile program should approximate the four stages covered in this book: self-assessment, exploration, choosing, and taking action.

"What do you perceive each of our roles in this program to be?" (Beware if it sounds as though everything will be decided for you, including what you do and where you will do it.)

An effective counselor serves as facilitator while training clients to do the hard work — making effective career decisions and taking action in the form of contacting employers, writing resumes, and interviewing.

"Do you guarantee that your methods will work?" (Beware if you are quoted an astounding success rate or are practically guaranteed a job.)

An effective and ethical counselor using the recommended self-directed method of finding employment will tell you honestly that a client's lack of motivation or follow-through sometimes contributes to lack of success with the methods. The self-assured counselor may say something to this effect: "Since it is important to me that my clients succeed, I put a lot into my counseling relationships and, in return, expect a high level of commitment and work from those with whom I decide to work." Just as counselors should not claim unreasonable high success rates, they need not take responsibility for clients' failures.

"Are you the counselor I would be working with, from beginning to end, if I decided to enroll in this service?" (Beware of committing yourself to a service and then discovering that the first party you met with was only a salesperson.)

Meet whomever you will be working with and ask about the counselor's experience or training if that is important to you. Trust your intuitions, and don't enter a counseling relationship with anyone you don't feel comfortable with. Although the counselor may hold impressive credentials and be dynamite with others, he or she will not be effective with you if the chemistry is not right.

"How much time will the program take, and what will it cost?" (Beware of shelling out big bucks beyond what you can afford.)

Whereas some services require that fees be paid up front, others charge by the hour or for increments of several hours at a time.

Avoid expensive up-front career services — say, more than $400 or $500 — because there is little that they could deliver worth that much. However, many counselors rightfully request up-front payment for several hours' worth of counseling at a time to increase their clients' motivation and commitment to the counseling process.

CAREER RESOURCES YOU CAN USE AT HOME

Career development workshops and one-to-one counseling may not be accessible if you are in a remote U.S. or overseas location. In any case, you will find a wealth of information in books, manuals, pamphlets, and audio and video cassettes. Appendix C offers a listing and order information for resources on subjects ranging from career planning to dressing for work.

IV

TAKING ACTION

There are risks and costs to a program of action. But they are far less than the long-range risks and costs of comfortable inaction.

John F. Kennedy

10

Broadening Your Opportunities With New Skills

Once you have determined your employment goal, you are ready to enter the job search stage of the career planning process. However, job search skills alone will not enable you to locate satisfying employment. To qualify for the work you've chosen and to keep abreast of the rapid changes in the job market, you may need to acquire new work-content skills, as described in Chapter 2. For example, language skills besides English are necessary for many overseas jobs, and even if you don't want a high-tech career, computer literacy will enable you to deal with the computer hardware and software that may be peripheral to your job. New opportunities arise for those who acquire up-to-date and relevant skills.

Skills can be acquired in a number of ways, including:

- course work
- audio/video cassettes
- entry-level jobs
- part-time work
- temporary work
- avocations
- volunteering
- internships and apprenticeships
- self-development
- self-employment

> **CASE IN POINT**
>
> A nurse off and on for 15 years, Joanna Liponski always found it easy to find a job. The fact that two relocations and three children had interrupted her employment history did not seem to concern prospective employers. However, as the years passed, she noticed that the nurses sought after for the plum jobs had high-tech skills. Joanna says, "I knew that if I wanted to work at the best hospitals in top-rate positions, I had to keep learning — which, in my field, meant, among other things, knowing how to use a computer at the bedside. That realization led me to learn all kinds of things I had not been receptive to before." Proud, confident, and in demand, Joanna now perceives herself as a high-tech nurse.

'RETURNING TO SCHOOL': VARIATIONS ON A THEME

When you think about developing new skills, you probably first imagine returning to school. Yet there are many different ways to "return to school":

- traditional degree programs, taken on a part-time or full-time basis, at high schools, colleges, and universities
- individual credit courses at academic institutions
- noncredit courses through adult education divisions of community colleges, county agencies, and departments of recreation
- company-sponsored training programs during employment
- university-sponsored conferences or workshops
- professional development programs through professional associations or independent groups: for example, "How to Start Your Own Private Practice" through the American Association of Counseling and Development, and "How to Develop a Promotional Brochure" through the American Society for Training and Development
- correspondence courses
- external degree programs
- courses open to military spouses at military installations, and courses open to foreign service spouses at the Foreign Service Institute in Washington, DC

The following sections take a closer look at these last three options.

Correspondence Courses

An option particularly compatible with the needs of a relocating spouse, home study provides convenience, speed, and economy. Some courses take only a few weeks to complete, while others take up to four years; you usually can set your own pace within guidelines determined by an individual school. You can choose from more than 12,000 courses on subjects ranging from accounting to beekeeping in two broad categories of schools:

Proprietary: Includes privately owned, profit-making schools that provide technical or vocational courses, from the basics of writing and mathematics to unconventional subjects such as yacht designing.

Postsecondary: Generally includes public and private colleges and universities that offer home study courses, some of which can lead to a degree. If you are interested primarily in getting a college degree, you may be able to use correspondence courses from postsecondary institutions to earn an external degree.

To avoid disreputable businesses when selecting a home study course, find out whether the school has accreditation from the National Home Study Council. While accreditation implies the school has met strict standards, lack of it does not automatically mean the school is incompetent or unethical. If you find that what you want to study is offered only at a school that has no accreditation, check it out through the Better Business Bureau or the department of education in the school's state.

External Degree Programs

In response to the demand from adult learners who are unable to complete traditional, on-campus courses of study, many institutions have developed alternative programs for earning degrees. External degree programs fall into three basic types:

Packaged Programs: In this type of program all course work required for a degree is available through the degree-granting institution via correspondence, videotapes, and/or audio cassettes. The professors assigned to each course are accessible by telephone for guidance and questions. When selecting this option, evaluate the level of counseling support and, as appropriate, the value placed on the degree by graduate schools.

Nontraditional Options for Earning Academic Credits: This approach is particularly suitable for spouses just beginning a course of study and for those who have already completed much of their college-level work. While academic guidance and counseling are critical with this method, the possibilities for earning credits include independent study, work study, individualized projects, contract learning, review of work and life experiences, customized tests, and standard course work through class attendance and/or correspondence. In various subjects, students may study with a privately contracted mentor-professor.

Review and Accrediting Programs: While offering no academic courses, this option is an excellent vehicle for pulling everything together for an academic degree. It is a good choice if, through the years, you have earned many college credits, worked as an employee, actively volunteered, independently studied various subjects, and/or developed a specialized hobby. Counselors and advisers help evaluate your skills and accomplishments and translate them into academic credits. If tests are administered to fill requirements in specific subjects, the numerical scores determine the amount of credit awarded. If additional course work is required, it may be earned through correspondence courses or independent study. This is not a suitable program for those who do poorly on tests or who have never attended college.

Consider the College Level Examination Program (CLEP) if you want to receive undergraduate credit for your knowledge in various areas. By passing a 90-minute test on any one of this program's exams in five general areas and 30 different subjects, you can receive either three or six credits, depending on the type of test. At a cost of $35 these tests are given throughout the United States by colleges and universities, and overseas by more than 300 educational advising centers. Approximately 2,000 U.S. universities accept CLEP credits. For more information about this program, order the *Guide to the CLEP Examinations* (Publication #002938), available for $8.95 from College Board Publications, Department B10, Box 886, New York, NY 10101.

Special Opportunities for Military and Foreign Service Spouses

While the policies as well as the type and number of courses differ among the branches of the uniformed services and even among installations of the same branch, military spouses may be able to take advantage of noncredit and credit courses on their bases. As described in the following chapter, the larger installations have a huge variety of outstanding programs ranging from personal effectiveness to financial planning and word processing. Courses may be sponsored by universities, family advocacy programs, hospitals, and chaplains' offices. At this writing, the uniformed services have succeeded in gaining, from 38 of the 50 states, in-state tuition rates for military family members. Without venturing far from home, military spouses can add to their educational background in order to qualify for the categories of employment described in Chapter 5.

Family members of foreign service and State Department employees may be eligible for functional training, in anticipation of prospective employment abroad. Under this arrangement, spouses may enroll in the same courses taken by junior, and in some cases mid-level, foreign service officers and be eligible for professional or nonprofessional work in the administrative, personnel, budget and fiscal, or consular areas in embassies. Grading and testing are done on the same basis as for regular employees.

To take advantage of the functional training, check with the Family Liaison Office (FLO) at the State Department in Washington, DC, to learn about positions that may be open in the missions to which you have been assigned. If you have interest but no training in the available areas, submit to the FLO Office an SF171, the application for federal employment. Then, if you qualify and if the regional bureau to which your spouse is assigned approves the training, you may take courses on a space-available basis at the Foreign Service Institute.

Since federal employment enables spouses to earn credits toward direct appointment eligibility in the civil service as described in Chapter 5, they have an advantage over other job seekers because, when this is coupled with their current or recently expired security clearances, they can be hired more quickly. An increasing number of foreign service spouses are taking advantage of the functional training because it helps them to find work more consistently over the long run.

Other types of training available to foreign service spouses, depending on the relocating employee's agency and assignment, include language training and intercultural training. It is important for anyone working abroad to understand how a culture functions — for example, the work values, office hierarchy, relationships among supervisors and colleagues, acceptable hours of work, and the general customs of the society.

How to Pursue Graduate Studies Abroad

Useful resources for those interested in graduate studies while overseas include the *Guide to External Degree Programs in the United States* and *The Independent Study Catalog*. The following strategies have been recommended by the Family Liaison Office at the Department of State:

1. After selecting schools in the United States with attractive programs in your field of interest, write to admissions offices and department heads for information about degree requirements, including the required number of residence units.
2. Investigate the availability of courses in your overseas location that might fulfill some of the course requirements.
3. Request approval from the U.S. institutions' department heads to take overseas courses that meet the degree requirements.
4. Through a Bi-National Center of the United States Information Agency, apply for and take the Graduate Record Exam (GRE) abroad. For information on taking the GRE, contact the Educational Testing Service, Graduate Record Examinations, Princeton, NJ 08541; 609-771-7670.
5. Get transcripts of your undergraduate work.
6. Collect recommendations, including at least one academic reference.
7. Submit applications with, possibly, a resume of your work experience and writing samples.
8. Arrange for the overseas credits to be accepted by the U.S. institution you have chosen.

An alternative to these steps is to get your graduate acceptance while overseas, but postpone enrollment until your return to the United States.

AUDIO AND VIDEO CASSETTES

An increasing number of educational and instructional programs are becoming available on audio and video cassettes. While both allow you to set your own pace, audio cassettes enable you to learn while driving or running. Some tapes can be purchased in bookstores, but educational cassettes are primarily available through mail-order firms, which often offer free catalogs and generous trial periods.

Language studies once dominated the learning-by-audio-tape method, and now, more choices are available than ever before. Audio study courses are available for more than 50 languages on tapes produced by Berlitz Language Center, Linguaphone, and the Foreign Service Institute.

Moving beyond languages, the audio industry has produced a potpourri of courses for high school, college, and continuing-education students. These include accounting, business law, word processing, history, health, psychology, and child care, among other topics. For professionals such as lawyers and engineers, audio tapes provide a way of keeping abreast of new developments in their fields.

A smaller percentage of the available video tapes fall into the educational and how-to categories, but many can be rented or purchased from mail-order houses.

For a list of firms offering audio and video tapes, refer to Appendix C.

LEARNING BY DOING

Entry-Level Jobs

Entry-level jobs can offer a form of on-the-job training for higher-level jobs by providing opportunities to acquire the appropriate skills. As an insider, you will also learn about attractive opportunities before they are publicized. Since employers like to hire people they know, taking an entry-level job may give you a better chance of getting your preferred work.

CASE IN POINT

Betsey Hughes had followed her husband as the Navy took him from place to place. A teacher, she was able to find work — if only as a substitute — after most relocations. But when she moved from Connecticut to the San Francisco area, where there was a surplus of teachers wanting jobs, she decided it was time to make a transition into something new. "I realized I did not have much to offer," she says, "but I knew I was relatively intelligent, and I knew I was a hard worker. I had the feeling that if I got myself in the right environment, I could probably grow if somebody would just let me in. That is what I conveyed to Prudential when I went to them."

> Starting in an entry-level job at a salary less than what she made as a substitute teacher, Betsey says, "I had many different responsibilities, and found it invigorating. Within one year, I became assistant supervisor of an office of about 40 people. I monitored our computer system. I did presentations for new clients. I did quality control. I did a lot of training. I interviewed and I terminated people. I went about as far as I could, though I suppose I could have been supervisor."
>
> By the time Betsey relocated again, she had picked up many skills. She says, "Your potential success is not so much where you start as it is getting in a spot where there are obvious opportunities. Then you will grow."

To ensure that an entry-level job works to your advantage, choose it carefully. It is very difficult to move up once you enter some positions; for example, secretaries rarely are considered for management openings.

Part-Time Work

Besides providing a means of easing into the job market, part-time work is a way to acquire skills and experience to enhance your qualifications. To acquire a variety of skills and diversified experience, work several part-time jobs simultaneously. For more information about part-time work, refer to Chapters 3 and 11.

Temporary Work

Besides its other benefits, temporary work provides opportunities for updating old skills and developing new ones relevant to your job target. It is also a way of acquiring the recent work experience and references you may need before applying for permanent positions. For more information about temporary work, refer to Chapters 3 and 11.

Avocations

Hobbies are a much-overlooked source of skills. You could develop new skills by becoming involved with home video, microcomputers, gourmet cooking, gardening, or researching your ancestors, to name but a few areas.

Volunteering

Adults on all career levels choose volunteering as the method to fill in their skill gaps. If you move repeatedly and occasionally find yourself in places where you are unable to find paid employment in your field, do volunteer work to keep your skills up-to-date and to develop new skills. As you evaluate volunteer jobs, keep in mind the skills you hope to develop. Look for assignments offering a variety of experiences, training, adequate guidance and direction, satisfactory work space, opportunities for recognition and promotion, and assurance that you will be treated as a co-worker by paid employees.

CASE IN POINT

After following her husband from Boston to Washington, DC, Thelma Cox decided to take some time off before seeking paid employment. Besides needing an interval to recover from an intense two year master's degree program in career counseling, she wanted to get her young children settled in their new community, redo her home, and thoroughly evaluate the marketplace.

Although Thelma was determined not to work for one year, she did volunteer one day a week in her field to get experience working with adults on a group basis, maintain a steady employment record, and learn about the opportunities Washington, DC, had to offer. Years later, she has this to say about her year with Wider Opportunities for Women (WOW): "Even though I had prior experience in the human resource development field, that seven-hour-a-week volunteer job enhanced my qualifications considerably and made me more attractive to employers. I realized I needed to beef up my skills before I could get to where I wanted to be. My work with groups at WOW gave me the confidence to offer the large career planning workshops I give today throughout the Washington area."

Since then, Thelma has had been employed in several counseling and training jobs in university and federal government settings, but she continues to list the volunteer job on her resume:

<u>Career Adviser</u>, Wider Opportunities for Women, Washington, DC. 1979 to 1980.
> Regularly conducted five different career development workshops, including resume writing and interviewing skills. Counseled individuals and groups of women of all ages on a variety of career concerns. Assisted members in the use of career library.

For more information about volunteering, refer to Chapters 3 and 11, and for relevant resources, to Appendix C.

Internships and Apprenticeships

The relationship between volunteer work and internships or apprenticeships is very close. In addition to offering excellent methods for developing skills, all three can be integrated with paid work on resumes and application forms.

In contrast to a volunteer job, an internship is of limited duration. While they sometimes are required aspects of academic programs, internships also can be arranged independently by individuals who need up-to-date skills and work experience. In hard-to-crack fields, an internship can provide the all-important break, as shown by the following examples:

- Madeleine Cohen, assistant curator in a midwestern museum, got her start in museum work as an unpaid intern in a large Canadian art gallery.
- Andrew Flask, a legislative aide on Capitol Hill, was a political science major who spent a semester as an intern working for a California congressman. He says, "I have this job today because I accepted a low-paying internship instead of an offer for a more financially rewarding job."
- Rather than seek paid employment, Laurie Chu interned as an editorial assistant on a large city newspaper and became first in line for several attractive opportunities.

Besides the excellent opportunity an internship provides for acquiring new skills, it also enables you to be sheltered in an *informational job* whereby you can learn from others. In contrast to the one-time meeting for information described in Chapter 6, this arrangement allows you to meet an unlimited number of times with people throughout the organization. For example; you can go with your co-workers and supervisor to lunch and their professional meetings.

The term *apprenticeship* often refers to a formal arrangement in the blue-collar trades, but it can also apply to an unpaid work situation that is arranged independently for the purpose of acquiring on-the-job learning. For example, if you plan to open a retail store, the best preparation is to work side by side with the owner of a similar business to learn about all the aspects of business ownership, including inventory, payroll, budgeting, taxes, and supervising.

SELF-DEVELOPMENT

As a relocating spouse, you may find yourself in a geographic area that does not offer paid employment in your field of work. Try to look upon this as a new opportunity. Granted, your work options may be bleak for the short-term, but you can use the time to develop interests and new portable skills for the long-term.

You can, for instance, set up a self-directed reading program for yourself, by subscribing to all the trade or professional journals in your field or by immersing yourself in a subject area in which you have always wanted to be knowledgeable. Of course, self-development requires motivation, effective time management, and a willingness to set other things aside. But you can do it, if you decide to do it.

CASE IN POINT

Two days before Laurie Filbert had an interview for an editing job, she realized she might be given a test requiring a knowledge of proofreaders' symbols. Anxious to get the position, Laurie spent half a day in a public library memorizing all the symbols, which she found in the dictionary under 'Proofreaders Marks.' "Even though I had never done formal proofreading, I entered the interview prepared to apply my new skills," she says. When my interviewer asked if I was proficient at proofreading, I confidently said that I was. I got the job." With her mobile lifestyle, Laurie has found proofreading to be a portable skill that is always in demand.

SELF-EMPLOYMENT

Although it is wise to have some background in an area related to your business venture prior to launching it, you can start a small-scale mini-business and learn as you go. The Small Business Administration offers many resources, including books and personnel, that describe the ins and outs of operating a small business. To pick up relevant skills, new or potential entrepreneurs may want to apprentice themselves, even on a part-time basis, to experienced business owners in the same field. For more information about starting and running a business, refer back to Chapter 4 and to the extensive list of resources on this subject in Appendix C.

Skill development is an investment in your future — like money in the bank. A decision to learn even one new skill a year will be a step toward keeping prepared for the upcoming shifts in the job market.

11

Tracking Down the Job Openings

Even in times of high unemployment, relocating spouses find many satisfying work opportunities by using imaginative job-search techniques. These techniques vary greatly in terms of how actively the job seeker participates in the process. At one extreme you take charge of the entire process, while at the other extreme you relinquish control by letting others decide what work you should do and where you should do it. As this chapter reveals, the effectiveness and rewards of these extremes vary substantially.

The easiest way to get a job is to transfer within your present organization — a possibility if your employer has a division where your spouse is relocating. This arrangement is a rare but fortunate opportunity; even if you make a lateral transfer or drop in status, it may be better than seeking immediate outside employment, losing your benefits, and facing the other ramifications of termination.

Another relatively easy way to get a job, especially for the spouse of a corporate employee, is to secure employment with your mate's firm. In two national surveys, more than 80 percent of the companies surveyed had no policy preventing employees' spouses from working for the same company, as reported by Catalyst in *Corporations and Two-Career Families*. While the majority of these companies would not allow a spouse to work in the same department or assume the same function, large companies were less restrictive in this regard than small ones. Since employers often realize the relocation may not come about if the accompanying spouse is not satisfied, it may be worth your while to urge your spouse's organization to consider hiring you.

CASE IN POINT

A high school guidance counselor for nine years, Louis Mallen had recently taken a position within his northern Virginia school system when his wife, Bette, received a high-level appointment from the governor of a large western state. Bette was thrilled about the idea of a substantial salary and being in charge of the state's parks and recreation.

Louis, however, was satisfied with life as it was and uninterested in moving 600 miles away. He had passed an intensive round of interviews to get a coveted position in one of the region's top high schools and was just beginning to feel comfortable in his new job. Eventually, Louis and Bette decided the quality of their lives was more important than the dollars they brought home.

Sensing that Louis might be the point of resistance, the state offered him three all-expenses-paid job hunting trips to interview for state government jobs. He was unimpressed, but went on the interviews anyway.

Now he has this to say about his experience: "It was clear that the state wanted Bette badly, and they went to great lengths to make the move palatable to us both. After many interviews, I accepted a job as supervisor of training programs. Although it's not the perfect job, I decided to give it a try." Louis realized this was a chance to try something new, and he could return to his school system if he and Bette moved back to the northern Virginia area. The couple learned that when an organization really wants you, you can ask for whatever it is you feel you need to be satisfied with a relocation.

WHAT CAN YOUR SPOUSE'S EMPLOYER DO FOR YOU?

Often employees are more likely to accept relocation if their spouses are offered employment assistance at the new location. Awareness of this, coupled with an increased sensitivity to the plight of the relocating family, has prompted the development of specific spouse employment assistance programs in the corporate, military, and foreign service sectors. Varying in sophistication and quality, these programs are continuing to evolve.

Corporations

Many firms have, or at least are contemplating, spouse employment assistance programs. In a survey conducted by Catalyst, only about a fifth of the companies had specific relocation policies for spouses with careers, but at least half of those surveyed were considering such policies and the numbers are expected to escalate. It makes sense economically to create policies to ensure that transfers are successful because, between 1968 and 1983, the cost of relocation increased five times, according to Runzheimer and Co. — a Wisconsin consulting firm.

The companies with such policies have devised creative incentives to persuade spouses to move. Some large corporations provide informal contacts with other employers, typically by sharing job openings and spouses' resumes with personnel representatives from area firms. Others offer career counseling on a one-to-one or group basis, focusing primarily on resume preparation and job-search strategies. Relocation policies in some companies provide payment for spouses' job-hunting trips. One large corporation, aware that transfers often create career setbacks for their employees' working spouses, offers an allowance of one-and-one-half months' former pay to reimburse spouses for lost income. And a few progressive companies attempt to find in-house employment for spouses accompanying relocating employees.

Corporations without in-house assistance programs sometimes refer spouses to outside services such as employment agencies or relocation firms. Consequently, spouse employment assistance programs are springing up in real estate relocation management firms, outplacement companies, and counseling and consulting groups. Some of these groups are creating programs simply to keep up with their competition.

Before entering a spouse employment assistance program, evaluate its quality and approach in terms of your needs. Depending on your work experience and personality, you may benefit from one-to-one help or you may need the support of a group. Similarly, under one set of circumstances you may need 10 sessions, while under another set you may be satisfied with two. If you have assessed your needs, you will be in a better position to make an informed choice about a program.

When only one program is available and it does not meet your requirements, request what you would like to have. Since most spouse employment assistance programs are in the start-up phase, your suggestions may be incorporated.

Well before you relocate, find out what, if any, assistance program is offered by your spouse's company. This may take some initiative on your spouse's part. While some organizations clearly announce the availability of spouse employment assistance, in others it is a well-kept secret. When spouse assistance is not publicized, it may mean that the programs are informal and negotiable on a case-by-case basis.

The Military

While the corporate world continues to contemplate the issue of spouse employment assistance, the uniformed services have been giving it their direct attention and have been targeting resources in the form of money and personnel. The Family Policy Office under a deputy assistant secretary of defense evaluates existing programs and recommends new ones to enhance federal employment opportunities for military spouses; for example, they are now awarded preference points when applying for domestic and overseas jobs with the Department of Defense.

At their installations throughout the United States and abroad, the Army, Navy, Air Force, and Marines offer spouses and family members comprehensive employment assistance workshops that cover some of the same options and strategies presented in this book.

Personnel offices at military installations offer spouses information about application procedures for a variety of positions on installations in the United States and overseas in the following categories of employment: civil service, contract, exchange system, nonappropriated fund, bank and credit union, and Department of Dependents School (DODDS) employment. Family or community service centers at some installations provide spouses with direct placement assistance for local and base-centered jobs.

As an example of what is being done in the uniformed services, the Army suggests that all installations offer spouses three employment-related services: information and referral; training and counseling; and a job bank. In addition, it recommends that each base offer individualized workshops according to the needs of the spouses there. Among the workshops regularly presented at a large base in the Washington, DC, area are Stress Management for the Mobile Spouse, Dynamics of a Mobile Lifestyle, Understanding the Local Job Market, and Educational and Employment Resources in the Area.

Since each of the Marines' employment resource centers has compatible computer software and hardware, they are able to offer spouses access to job listings in other parts of the country before they move.

If you are a military spouse, investigate the availability of employment-related services at your installation.

The Foreign Service

The Foreign Service has been the leader in offering employment assistance to spouses accompanying relocating employees. The growing tendency for foreign service employees to request Washington, DC, in preference to overseas assignments, in part because spouses are unable to find sufficient suitable employment abroad, has prompted a number of progressive actions. Moreover, there are initiatives afoot to make substantive improvement to the spouse employment picture as it is today.

As demonstrated in the Foreign Service Act of 1980, the top echelon of the State Department is clearly committed to the spouse employment issue. To quote that act,

"1. The Secretary may facilitate the employment of spouses of members of the service by
    a. providing regular career counseling for such spouses;
    b. maintaining a centralized system for cataloging their skills and the various government and nongovernmental employment opportunities available to them; and
    c. otherwise assisting them in obtaining employment.

2. The Secretary shall establish a family liaison office to carry out this subsection and such other functions as the Secretary may determine."

In actuality, the Department of State's Family Liaison Office (FLO) was established in 1978. Besides its other family-related services, the office offers short-term career counseling for spouses returning from or departing for overseas posts. It also maintains a file of current jobs offered by employers who want to hire foreign service spouses. Among the employers are the Department of State, the Agency for International Development, the United States Information Agency, and the Peace Corps, as well as employers in the Washington, DC, area. FLO also sends a weekly list of job offerings, known as the Network Mailing, to foreign service spouses in the Washington area who sign up for it. For those going abroad, FLO provides detailed information about employment opportunities and, wherever possible, international companies located at various posts. During 1987 FLO implemented an automated, centralized data base of spouse skills. Though the data base is designed to be used by foreign affairs agencies in the United States and abroad, it is also available to private employers who want to take advantage of the skills.

Other assistance is available to spouses of foreign affairs personnel through the Overseas Briefing Center (OBC) at the Foreign Service Institute (FSI) — the training arm of the State Department. For each of the foreign service posts, OBC maintains files that sometimes include job market information. OBC also has contact information on foreign service families who have recently returned from posts around the world. Since the late 1970s, FSI has offered four-day, semi-annual, career planning workshops for spouses of U.S. foreign affairs personnel. These workshops, which have recently increased in number and length, cover how to find jobs in the United States and abroad. By taking advantage of these resources, relocating spouses can begin their employment planning prior to their moves.

Additional employment assistance, in varying degrees, is available to spouses through community liaison offices at posts throughout the world.

A resource not to be overlooked is the Association of American Foreign Service Women (AAFSW), which works hard to advance the rights of foreign service spouses. This private, nonprofit group, which is not restricted to women, lobbies on behalf of spouses on issues including employment and publishes a monthly newsletter.

To facilitate the employment of family members of diplomatic and consular employees assigned abroad, bilateral work agreements have been negotiated between the United States and the foreign governments of some countries. In these countries, spouses from the United States are able to work on the local economy, and spouses from those countries may work on our economy. While more formal bilateral agreements are being negotiated, many other countries have informal work arrangements that allow spouses of diplomatic and consular employees to work on local economies. Even with these strides, many feel that progress in this area is slow.

Other Employers

Employment assistance programs may not be firmly established for relocating spouses of academics, the clergy, state government employees, and others. However, many organizations offer informal assistance on a case-by-case basis. If your husband or wife is valued by the recruiting or transferring organization and you resist relocation because of your employment, your spouse's organization is likely to help you, in some manner, to find employment. If not, decide what you need to make the move palatable and ask for it.

CASE IN POINT

Helen Stanton was taking child development courses in preparation for paid employment when her husband was selected to be the minister of a large urban church in Indianapolis, IN. Helen and her children were reluctant to leave Austin, TX, because they had lived in their community for 11 years and had many friends. For herself, Helen felt the move would be a setback professionally. Besides her current courses, she had a degree and experience in religious education that she knew would equip her for employment in the Austin job market. Furthermore, she had many contacts through her church, community, and academic work. "I knew I could get a good job as soon as I finished my course work," she says. "Although I hated being so obstinate when my husband was presented with such an attractive offer, I thought, 'It's my turn now!'"

Aware of Helen's resistance, the recruiting church's search committee took steps to woo her. A few inquiries convinced them that Indianapolis in fact had more employment opportunities in Helen's field than Austin had. Church members, committing themselves to supporting her in a job search, circulated her resume and arranged for her to fly to their city to meet with the directors of five day-care centers and preschools. Helen says, "That trip *did it* for me! After talking with those directors, I soon realized my qualifications would be in demand in Indianapolis. The fact that I was from out of town prompted day-care staff members to reveal upcoming job openings they may not otherwise have thought of mentioning."

Several months after getting established in her new home and community, Helen took a part-time job in a suburban day-care center. Two years later, she became the director of the center's after-school program. She attributes much of her success to the initial support she received from church members who were anxious for her husband to accept his job offer.

LONG-DISTANCE STRATEGIES

Finding employment is difficult enough in your home town, where at least you know your way around. When you add in a new location with unknown employers, the task may seem insurmountable. Nevertheless, there are some things you can do before you relocate to simplify your job search:

- Contact the chamber of commerce and the regional economic development commission for lists of businesses and information about them.

- Get in touch with your professional society in your new locale, and try to get the membership directory to identify contacts. As soon as you move, join other groups such as a church, political club or health club, and throw a party for all your neighbors.
- Contact your college placement office, regardless of how long ago you graduated, to see what assistance they can provide.
- Write your college and/or high school for alumni lists of your graduating classes. Get in touch with past classmates who live where you will be moving.
- Get names of organizations by consulting out-of-town telephone directories at large public or academic libraries. If you can't find telephone directories in your present location, borrow them from contacts in your new location.
- As outlined in Chapter 6, refer to the appropriate directories for the work settings at which you will be directing your efforts. For example, if you want to work for a corporation, use *Standard and Poor's Register of Corporations*.
- Ask your contacts in the community to which you will be moving to monitor vacancy announcements; for example, by checking bulletin boards in the organizations where they work.
- Use the placement services offered by organizations you learned about while exploring your options in Part II. For example, The American Society of Association Executives publishes a weekly trade paper, *Association Trends*, that lists employment opportunities.
- Attend job fairs to help you identify employers in your new location. These often are scheduled in large metropolitan areas by groups of firms in technical fields.
- Subscribe to the newspapers from your new location and read the business pages and employment ads to discover business trends and who is hiring.
- Write to get annual reports from those firms that appeal to you.
- Especially if you are in a high-demand field, contact one or two recommended employment agencies in your new location, or executive-search firms. Have them generate interest with companies on your behalf. Even if this strategy doesn't produce a job, it will help you learn about major employers and their needs. For help in identifying firms, refer to *Consultants News' Directory of Executive Recruiters*.
- Take several trips to your new location. During your first trip, concentrate on gathering information and developing contacts. On later trips, after you are well prepared, approach the organ-

izations on which you have focused. The relocation policies of some corporations now include provisions for financing one trip for the spouse of a relocating employee.

CASE IN POINT

Marshall Fox says it was his membership in the American Association of Counseling and Development (AACD) that enabled him to get so quickly reemployed after relocating with his wife to New Orleans. While he was a rehabilitation counselor in Ann Arbor, MI, Fox had had little to do with the professional society even though he had been a member for eight years. When he learned that AACD's annual convention would be held in New Orleans two months before he moved, he renewed his membership and flew down.

The atmosphere, typical of most conventions, was festive and the participants talked easily and openly with each other. Marshall says, "It was incredible what happened on that trip! I met dozens of people, many of whom worked in the New Orleans area. Besides the employers who interviewed me at the AACD convention placement service, I made contacts in both public and private institutions. When I moved, I had a number of interviews lined up and soon thereafter had several job offers."

The offer Marshall finally accepted was several levels removed from a contact he had met the first day of the convention.

If you want to schedule interviews before relocating, write to employers telling them you will be visiting the area during a specific time period. Say that you will be telephoning to arrange a convenient time to visit, and if possible, include the number of a friend or relative in your new location who can take local phone messages. This long-distance approach may yield more interviews than if you wait until moving, because the psychological effect of making an effort by traveling a distance may prompt more employers to see you.

Tips for Seeking Overseas Employment

While many of the same job-search strategies apply internationally, there are additional steps you can take to identify organizations and job opportunities abroad.

- Use the networking techniques described in Chapter 6 to locate people who know about the country where you will be moving.

TRACKING DOWN THE JOB OPENINGS 139

- Identify and meet with faculty members and students from that country.
- Before moving abroad, contact the country's embassy or consulate for information. Besides requesting information on specific organizations, say, for example, "My spouse and I are going to your country. How best can I contribute my time while I am there, either for pay or no pay?"
- Refer to the *Directory of American Firms Operating in Foreign Countries, Moody's Principal International Businesses*, and the other directories listed in Chapter 6 and Appendix C.
- Contact the U.S. Chamber of Commerce, which is located in countries where there's a big American presence.
- For a list of approximately 30 resources and agencies reporting opportunities for employment or voluntary service abroad, write for the International Resource and Agency List from the American Friends Service Committee (1501 Cherry St., Philadelphia, PA 19102, 215-241-7105).
- To identify firms receiving federal contracts, regularly review the "Contract Awards" section of the *Commerce Business Daily* as well as the *Federal Register*.
- For information and advice on employment with nonprofit international organizations, contact InterAction: American Council for Voluntary International Action (a coalition of more than 100 U.S. organizations), 200 Park Ave. South, New York, NY 10003, 212-777-8210; or 1815 H St., N.W., Suite 916, Washington, DC 20003, 202-822-8429.
- For information on more than 1,400 recruiting firms that may be able to give you information on organizations hiring abroad, refer to the *Directory of Executive Recruiters – International*.
- If you are a foreign service spouse, visit the Family Liaison Office at the U.S. Department of State in Washington for information about international companies and other employment opportunities at various posts.
- After identifying companies having overseas branches at your new location, contact the offices in the United States to learn the names and titles of personnel who have the authority to hire.
- To have your skills incorporated into a computerized inventory for full-time, part-time, and contract jobs in South, Central, and North America, send your resume to Director, Department of Human Resources, Organization of American States, Room 660, Washington, DC 20006, 202-458-3285. Positions are in the following areas, among others: economic and social affairs,

education, cultural affairs, and sciences. Examples of specific positions include public information specialists for radio and television programs, trainers in computer sciences, and archives curators.
- Contact the International Monetary Fund's office — after arriving in Latin America, Paris, Geneva, or other places where they are located — for positions in areas such as the following: economics, finance, international trade, computer science, secretarial work.
- To pursue a position with the World Bank, which has offices throughout the world, send your resume to the Staffing Office, 1818 H St., N.W., Washington, DC 20006, 202-477-1234. Specify where you want to work, and then plan on waiting six to eight weeks for a response. You can also contact the World Bank office in the country where you want to work.
- For a position with the Inter-American Development Bank, contact them for an application form and submit it to: Deputy Manager, Human Resources Administration, Administrative Department, 1300 New York Ave., N.W., Washington, DC 20577, 202-623-1000. An alternative is to directly contact their field offices, which are located in Latin America, the Caribbean, Paris, and London. While employment opportunities in the field are limited by an office's specialty, positions exist in the following areas, among others: energy, construction, agriculture, economics, transportation, engineering, feasibility studies, budget preparation, management, accounting, and finance. As you might expect, field offices hire their own office staff directly.
- If you are interested in a short- or long-term public- or private sector assignment in the Middle East or North Africa, join MATCH, a free computer-based personnel search service operated by AMIDEAST, the largest nonprofit U.S. educational organization serving in that region. With nine offices in the Middle East and North Africa, MATCH has placed candidates in a wide range of positions that include the following job titles: administrative assistant, financial analyst, secretary, personnel manager, engineer, computer scientist, and post-secondary teacher for English as a Foreign Language (EFL). For more information or to subscribe, contact MATCH, AMIDEAST/Washington, 1100 17th St., N.W., Washington, DC 20036, 202-785-0022. Information is also available through AMIDEAST regional offices.
- Subscribe to the *International Employment Hotline*, a monthly

TRACKING DOWN THE JOB OPENINGS 141

publication that monitors international employment opportunities. Order a subscription from International Employment Hotline, PO Box 6170, McLean, VA 22106 ($28.00 for one year if you live in the United States or Canada; $40.00 those living elsewhere). While Hotline's staff are concerned about spouses' lack of freedom to relocate to the available jobs, decide that for yourself after becoming a subscriber.
- Subscribe to the "Job Opportunities Bulletin," a bimonthly job-listing service, for positions in international development with private voluntary organizations, consulting firms, and other worldwide development groups. This publication has a "Job Seekers" section in which you can announce your availability. For an annual subscription costing $15, contact The New TransCentury Foundation, 1724 Kalorama Rd., N.W., Washington, DC 20009, 202-328-4400. TransCentury has additional job listings and a talent bank at its offices, and, for a small admission charge, holds monthly job fairs.
- Purchase Drs. Ronald and Caryl Krannich's book, *The Complete Guide to Public Employment* to learn about other organizations providing job listings and placement services for international nonprofits. Among these are CODEL, PACT, Employment Abroad, International Employment Opportunity Digest, Friends of the World, Overseas Jobworld, and Foreign and Domestic Teachers' Bureau. CODEL (Coordination in Development) is a consortium for more than 40 Christian development agencies whose members work abroad; write to 475 Riverside Dr., Suite 1842, New York, NY 10115, 212-870-3000. PACT (Private Agencies Collaborating Together) is a consortium of 26 nonprofit agencies working abroad; write to 777 U.N. Plaza, New York, NY 10017, 212-697-6222.
- To improve your chances of having your skills incorporated into a contract for overseas work, make your contacts with U.S.-based organizations before moving abroad, and keep in touch with them. This approach may also enable you to be paid in American currency rather than foreign currency, which is sometimes preferable. If you have already moved, visit the contracting officer at the World Bank, AID, or other field offices overseas to learn the names of the consulting firms and host country firms doing business in your area of interest. For more about contract work abroad, see Chapters 3 and 5.

For an extensive list of written resources on working abroad, refer to Appendix C.

HOW TO FIND ALTERNATIVE WORK ARRANGEMENTS

Many of the same strategies and resources apply regardless of whether you are seeking full-time, part-time, or another kind of work, but if you want other than full-time work, consider the following ways to find jobs.

Contract Work

While some contract jobs are advertised — for example, in the *Commerce Business Daily* — most are located through networking and by contacting organizations directly. Refer to the *Consultants and Consulting Organizations Directory*, the central library at the Agency for International Development (Rosslyn, VA), the other sources of information in Chapter 6, and the services and resources in the previous section.

Part-Time Work

Ways to locate part-time jobs include word-of-mouth, classified ads, and identifying or creating them on your own. Part-time professional jobs are scarce and are most often obtained by switching from full-time to part-time status within an organization.

The Association of Part-Time Professionals, primarily an advocacy group, provides publications related to part-time, professional work. It also offers memberships, local job listings, and workshops, including "How To Get a Part-Time Job." For more information, write to 7655 Old Spring House Rd., McLean, VA 22102 or telephone 703-734-7975.

Temporary Work

Although it is possible to secure temporary work on your own, you will find it easier through employment agencies specializing in hiring temporary employees for organizations. Temporary agencies serve as middlemen between workers and employers. They interview and test applicants' skills, make appropriate matches, check references, and issue paychecks. While some agencies offer a spectrum of employment opportunities, others specialize in specific fields of work; for example, hospital and medical care, hospitality services, and word processing.

TRACKING DOWN THE JOB OPENINGS

Consider the following points as you choose temporary agencies and later work with them.

- Consult the *Yellow Pages* for listings of "Employment Contractors, Temporary Help." Register with several services in your area after asking other temporary workers about the reputation of agencies you are considering: Do they pay promptly? Do they offer good assignments? Do they call well ahead of assignments? What are their wages and benefits? Do they offer training?
- State your assignment preferences in terms of location, hours, number of days per week, size of office, long-term versus short-term employment, and type of duties.
- Inquire about the agency's clients, types of tests, reference checks, and how much advance notice they will offer you.
- Keep in mind that there's no obligation to accept or continue assignments you dislike.
- Check the agency's policies on accepting permanent employment as a result of a temporary assignment.
- If you have any questions about working for temporary agencies, write or call National Association of Temporary Services, Inc., 119 South St. Asaph Street, Alexandria, VA 22314, 703-549-6287.

Job Sharing

According to New Ways to Work in San Francisco, CA, worker proficiency and work quality generally are higher than average when workers share a position. Many employers, however, resist this way of working. Job sharing is more readily accepted when two (or more) applicants present themselves to employers as one unit after having worked out all the details, such as who will work when. To convince employers of the merits of job sharing, convey that the members in your unit offer specialized and complementary skills that, when used together in one job, offer even more than one very qualified employee.

Volunteering

While you can identify volunteer jobs on your own, you can also find them through nonprofit volunteer bureaus, often in county governments, that serve as clearinghouses. Similarly, military installations and foreign service posts sometimes have personnel who disseminate information about volunteer activities.

For volunteer jobs overseas, clearinghouses operate to match the interests of potential volunteers with the needs of member organizations. For example, those interested in health and medical services to the poor of the developing world should get in touch with International Liaison, a Roman Catholic organization with broad contacts and concerns beyond the Catholic Church. *International Health News*, a publication of the National Council for International Health (Appendix B), frequently lists organizations seeking volunteers for international health placement. A recent listing included Goodwill Industries International, Lutheran World Ministries Volunteers, Peace Corps/ACTION, and Project HOPE.

TRADITIONAL JOB-HUNTING METHODS (THERE'S GOT TO BE A BETTER WAY)

Before reading the remainder of the chapter, take a few minutes to jot down all the ways you can think of to locate employment — be creative! After generating at least 10 ideas, compare your list with the possibilities described here.

If you are like most job seekers, you probably thought first about these traditional ways of finding jobs:

- answering classified advertisements in newspapers — local, metropolitan, regional, and national
- answering advertisements in newsletters or journals issued by trade and professional associations
- going to federal, state, or private employment agencies
- contacting college placement offices that deal with alumni or the general public
- using registers, clearinghouses, or other forms of job exchanges
- contacting personnel offices in organizations

> Expenses related to your job search are tax deductible on federal tax returns. This includes the cost of stationery, postage, resume reproduction, travel, books to help you with your job hunt, career counseling, and the like. If you believe the expenditure is deductible, keep very detailed records.

Job seekers who have the most success using traditional job-finding methods are generally clerical, semi-skilled, and unskilled workers or individuals in high-demand fields.

Traditional approaches to the job search require a low output of effort and are relatively passive. Unless combined with more active methods, traditional approaches usually are not very effective for relocators, career changers, or individuals seeking employment in fields with a low demand. When relying on traditional methods, most job seekers simply submit application forms or resumes in response to publicized job openings. However, these pieces of paper are endowed with far less power than the unsuspecting job hunter would like to believe.

CASE IN POINT

After five years in fund raising, Clifford Moore decided to accompany his wife when she transferred with her organization from Milwaukee to Baltimore. At the same time, he decided to change careers.

Describing his approach to the job search, he says, "I bought many Sunday newspapers — the *Washington Post*, the *Baltimore Sun*, the *News American* — and went through the ads and chose all the jobs I thought I could somehow fit into. If something looked good, I'd write a letter and send a resume. Most of those communications went unanswered, and I got frustrated with the process. I decided there was no magic I could create in writing that would cause me to stand out among the crowd. I could put together a professional message to an employer, but many other people could probably do the same thing."

It wasn't until he clarified his own goals and undertook an intensive, self-directed approach that Clifford got results. He is now happily employed in computer sales.

When sending out resumes in response to publicized job openings, you put yourself in a position of being evaluated along with perhaps hundreds of other job seekers. What are your chances of surviving such scrutiny? While some career advisers advocate mailing out hundreds of resumes with the hope that at least a few seeds will sow," most participants in this numbers game have found it ineffective.

Consider the other disadvantages that characterize the traditional job search methods:

- In some cities — as an example, Washington, DC — as many as 80 to 90 percent of the professional job openings are never advertised. Although a higher percentage of nonprofessional jobs may be advertised, many still are not.
- Employment agencies often handle no more than five percent of the available jobs, and their loyalty rests with employers rather than with job seekers.
- Although there are exceptions, most employment agencies will not devote much time to placing clients unless they are qualified in high-demand fields such as secretarial work, nursing, data processing, or engineering.
- Employment agency personnel sometimes try to persuade clients to take jobs below their capabilities because the agencies earn quick money by making easy placements.
- Personnel administrators often are not aware of all the job openings within their organizations, especially on the professional level, and therefore may inadvertently reject applicants who could qualify for such jobs.
- The competition is stiffest when you use traditional methods because most job seekers go this route.

SELF-DIRECTED JOB-HUNTING METHODS (THE BETTER WAY)

The self-directed methods require the job hunter to take a great deal of initiative in seeking out and applying for positions in the *hidden job market* — the job market of unadvertised jobs found through research and the contacts developed through networking.

CASE IN POINT

After 142 rejection letters and 29 dead-end interviews, Anna Skelton — a spouse relocating to the Midwest from California — finally found a job. In the process, she discovered that networking works in mysterious ways.

"I answered a newspaper ad — the world's worst way to get a job — for a technical writer," she recalls. "Later, after I'd been on the job awhile, I talked to the guy in personnel. He told me why my resume stood out in the pile of 432 that came in from the ad: He'd gone to the same college I had. It was the old school tie that caught his eye. Of course, it helped that I was qualified for the job."

But Anna's networking story doesn't end there. Unhappy with the

TRACKING DOWN THE JOB OPENINGS 147

> technical writing job, she used a self-directed approach to find her next position. "During the 18 months I was a technical writer, I also joined and took on leadership positions in two professional organizations: the International Association of Business Communicators and a local group for professional women."
>
> "Through the grapevine," Anna says, "I heard that a woman I'd met through both organizations was leaving her job to get her Ph.D. I casually questioned her. 'Are they looking for somebody to take your job?' She said, 'Yes.' As we talked about her job, I kept saying, 'I can do that. I really want to do that. I'm sending you my resume.' She suggested I send my resume to the personnel department. Instead, I sent it directly to her. She took it to her boss and told him she'd been impressed with my abilities in the professional organizations. He interviewed me and offered me the job. That job had not been advertised in the newspaper." Hired as manager, Anna now is director of corporate communications for a large telecommunications company.

The higher the employment level, the more important it is to use self-directed means, including:

- writing a proposal for a job after researching an organization
- taking advantage of all of your contacts — family, friends, neighbors, fellow students, current and former co-workers and supervisors, your spouse's colleagues, and more
- contacting organizations you identify through directories organized by local industry or other categories; for example, the *Washington Information Directory*, the *Dun and Bradstreet Million Dollar Directory*, and others from Chapter 6 and Appendix C.
- contacting decision-makers with the authority to hire, rather than contacting personnel departments (switchboard operators and receptionists in companies are good sources of the names and titles of the people you want to reach)
- contacting individuals you identify through membership directories from organizations with which you are affiliated
- contacting individuals and organizations mentioned in business sections and other sections of newspapers
- contacting employees in organizations to which you are referred by your spouse or by your spouse's co-workers
- taking temporary or volunteer jobs to develop contacts and, therefore, to become aware of job openings for permanent positions before they are advertised to the general public

> "... You put yourself in a situation where opportunities are likely to happen... It's not that you have charisma, and it's not necessarily that you are smart. Although those things help, what really helps is knowing someone on the inside."
> — a successful relocating spouse

There are many additional ways to find jobs, and it is important to take time to investigate the job-search strategies that are appropriate for the work settings at which you are aiming, and then create your own methods.

While the self-directed methods require more work and initiative on your part, they are more productive than the traditional methods. This doesn't mean, however, that you must abandon those less effective methods. Use them in combination with the self-directed approaches to maximize your chances of locating satisfying employment.

A note on timing: Many experienced relocators advise getting your personal life, including the home front, in order before accepting employment or entering an intensive job-search process. Although the time it will take you to adjust to a relocation will depend on the nature of your move and personality, you may need a few weeks or months to learn about your new community and where to purchase goods and services, arrange for child care, help children to reestablish themselves socially and academically, and attend to the physical setup of your home.

12

The Relocation Resume

If your career has been interrupted one or more times, as is the case with many military spouses, it is especially important to communicate well with employers about yourself. Unlike application forms, resumes offer you the opportunity to list, in the order of your choosing, what you want to share with employers. This chapter tells how to create resumes that will work to your advantage.

A resume's primary purpose is to generate employers' interest so they will want to interview you. For this to happen, your resume must communicate your experience, marketable skills, and education in terms of an employer's requirements. Instead of trying to list all the experience you've ever had, focus on your employment goals and eliminate information that does not support them.

DO YOU NEED A RESUME?

In some fields of work, resumes are unnecessary. For example, application forms may be sufficient for blue collar, restaurant, clerical, and retail sales jobs.

In other fields where resumes are normally acceptable, you may discover that, because of your particular background, a resume works against you; for example, your education and experience are in areas other than the one in which you are applying, but you believe you are qualified. When this is the case, you may choose to send a letter — instead of a resume — outlining good reasons why the employer should hire you. For this purpose, use the cover letters in the following chapter as a guide.

If you decide you need a resume, it is not unreasonable to spend 10, 20, or even more hours developing this important employment communication.

WHY SO MANY RESUMES FAIL

Anxious to get on with the job hunt, job seekers often make the mistake of writing and distributing *past-oriented* resumes. Since they have not yet decided what they want to do, they fail to convey how they could help solve employers' problems. For expedience, they skip the three steps necessary to develop *future-oriented* resumes that generate interest and produce interviews. As implied in the Introduction, these steps are: (1) assessing your skills, interests, values, and other priorities, (2) exploring work options, and (3) making choices about work. When job seekers do their homework in these areas, they are able to communicate effectively with employers during the job search.

CASE IN POINT

Eva Otteson had been a research assistant for five years before changing careers to social work. After relocating from Des Moines, IA, to Nashville, TN, she decided to return to research because of the job market and a desire for more income. Proud of the resume she had developed the previous year, Eva distributed it to a number of St. Louis employers in response to their ads.

Her efforts produced only a stack of rejection letters, and she decided to find out why. Describing her experience, Eva says, "I was new to the city and wanted to learn what I was doing wrong, so I telephoned the employers who had rejected me or had not responded to my mailings. Although many employers were hesitant to answer my questions, I heard enough to realize that my resume stressed social work rather than research."

Eva revised her resume and is now doing challenging research work in a small management consulting firm.

A second problem with resumes is that companies often receive hundreds of them for a single job opening. In the face of such competition, you may have difficulty excelling on paper. Richard Bolles, the career development guru, speaks of resumes as being most effective when accompanied by something else — preferably you. In line with this, he advises leaving your resume behind after visiting a prospective employer, when possible, rather than sending it ahead. You can leave your resume behind as you explore your options by talking with people, as described in Chapter 6. When you cannot leave it behind, accompany it with a cover letter as described in the following chapter.

CATEGORIES TO CONSIDER

As you decide what to include and what to omit from your resumes, keep in mind the word *relevant*. And, since employers often do not read all the information listed on resumes, put the most important information first and to the left. Although some of these categories are best omitted from some resumes, the following will be covered in this chapter:

- contact information
- work experience
- education
- honors and awards
- credentials, licenses, special skills
- publications
- memberships
- languages
- interests
- personal data
- references
- job objective

Contact Information

If you believe that the first thing on your resume should be information on how you can be reached, you are correct. Please don't put this information at the bottom of the page, or on a second page as some job hunters do. Located on the left, center, or right of a page, depending on your personal preference, contact information includes name, address, and telephone number(s). Since employers are more likely to call you during the day than the evening, you may want to list an office telephone number as well as your number at home if you are working. Resumes must be as concise as possible, so omit the words *name, address, telephone number* as well as *resume* at the top of a page.

Work Experience

Most employers say work experience is the most important section on a resume, so take special care in presenting it. As a relocating spouse, you will want to emphasize your strengths and downplay the interruptions to your career.

Before writing this section, thoroughly document each of your past paid and unpaid work experiences. If you have completed your job description records from Chapter 1, you will have most of the necessary material for the work experience section of your resume. If you skipped this step, do it now before proceeding with this chapter.

The preferred resume styles for presenting work experience are (1) the chronological and (2) the combination functional/chronological. One will probably be more suitable for you than the other.

Chronological style: A chronological resume presents your work experience within the time frames you spent on each job, in a reverse time sequence. This is the most traditional and the best choice for individuals with steady and increasingly responsible work experience and for job hunters whose recent employment is relevant to the job for which they are applying now. Refer to the chronological resume samples at the end of the chapter.

The following steps will help you create the work experience section of a chronological resume:

1. Reproduce copies of your job description records from Chapter 1.
2. Cut the sentences into strips.
3. From each of your job description records, transfer the following information to 3" by 5" cards: job title, organization, city, state, inclusive years. For example:
Instructor, Beatte & Smith, Inc., Richmond, Virginia, 1975 to 1979.
If you wish to avoid calling attention to your dates of employment, do not put them on the left side of the page.
4. Arrange your sentence strips under the cards in order of relevance to your job target.

THE RELOCATION RESUME

5. Eliminate those sentences that won't really enhance your qualifications in the eyes of an employer.

6. As necessary, revise your sentences according to the section entitled "Using the Language of your Future Work" later in this chapter.

Combination functional/chronological style: The combination style resume provides a skills section, enabling you to cluster similar skills and accomplishments from throughout your work life into functional areas such as promotion, training, sales, writing, and others as listed on page 154.

Although many employers prefer the traditional, chronological-style resume, it can work against job seekers whose career paths have been somewhat erratic. Since a combination-style resume focuses on what you have done rather than where you have been, it works well for individuals reentering the job market or changing careers, and for those whose recent work does not support their new career interests. Since job titles, names of organizations, and dates are not listed in the skills section of this resume, volunteer jobs and gaps in employment cannot be identified as easily as with the chronological format. For these reasons, the combination style may be the right choice for many relocating spouses.

CASE IN POINT

Pamela Mann chose the combination style resume because her mobile lifestyle between Latin America and Washington, DC, created an erratic work record. While Pamela worked almost consistently, she had often accepted whatever was available, especially while abroad. Now back in the States, she decided to pursue work as a manager of volunteers.

"I realized I had the right background for what I wanted to do, but it certainly didn't come across well on a chronological resume," she says. In fact, my most recent volunteer job wasn't relevant by any stretch of the imagination — I had prepared a study on Chilean education for a multinational diplomatic group. Using the combination resume format, I grouped my wide-ranging experience into three categories — Management/Community Organization, Training, and Public Relations — all of which were appropriate for my job target."

Besides effectively camouflaging her relocations, Pamela's approach made it impossible to discern which of her jobs were volunteer and which were paid.

A work history section, similar to that on a chronological resume, generally follows the skills section on a combination resume. Although it includes job titles, organizations, cities, states, and dates, this style omits a description of experience because that is integrated into the skills section. Again, it's probably wisest to avoid listing employment dates on the left side of your resume. For a variety of samples, refer to the combination functional/chronological resumes at the end of the chapter.

The following steps will help you create the skills section of a combination functional/chronological-style resume:

1. Reproduce copies of your job description records from Chapter 1.
2. Cut the sentences into strips.
3. Refer to the accompanying list of functional headings.

FUNCTIONAL HEADINGS/SKILL AREAS

Program Coordination	Social Work	Evaluation
Clerical Work	Food Service	Employment
Graphic Design	Supervision	Interviewing
Materials Handling	Organization	Public Speaking
Volunteer Management	Purchasing	Fund Raising
Market Research	Acquisition	Teaching
Instruction	Planning	Testing
Construction	Scheduling	Advertising
Data Processing	Administration	Secretarial Work
Presentations	Programming	Public Relations
Community Affairs	Publicity	Accounting
Investigation	Legal Services	Budgeting
Program Development	Human Services	Nursing
Staffing and Directing	Promotion	Retailing
Career Development	Consulting	Sales
Product Development	Production	Research
Writing and Editing	Communication	Finance
Personnel Management	Training	Counseling
Systems and Procedures	Advising	Recruitment

Community and Professional Relations

---

4. Using the list as a guide, analyze your strips of sentences to identify the major skill areas. Unless you plan to acquire some new

skills, identify major areas in your experience that match the field in which you plan to apply.

5. As appropriate, add your own categories to the functional headings list.

6. Now check off the functions in the list that best describe your abilities and are in line with your job target.

7. Narrow your choices to two to five functional headings that best describe your experience and your preferred field of work.

8. Write those headings on 3" by 5" cards.

9. Arrange your sentence strips under the cards in order of relevance to your job target.

10. Eliminate sentences that add little or do not fit into your categories.

Using the Language of Your Future Work: The difference between an effective resume and a poor resume rests in how well paid and unpaid work experience is described and related to an employer's needs. While you may need to develop a general, unfocused resume to use as you talk with people about work options, as described in Chapter 6, it is important to create a focused, future-oriented resume after clarifying what you want to do. Unless you want to continue being a volunteer, avoid sounding like a volunteer. The same holds true for those who are changing fields of work, be they teachers, librarians, or military personnel. Consider the following examples of how to change the implication of words by making them more generic:

> *church* could become *nonprofit organization*
> *Boy Scouts* could become *youth* or *members*
> *children* could become *participants* or *individuals*
> *bulletin board* could become *visual aid*
> *school* could become *facility* or *institution*

CASE IN POINT

While Ginny Taylor was overseas and her children were young, she could always find jobs as a teacher, and the work schedule was compatible with her family demands. Ready to try something new when she returned to the States, Ginny enrolled in a teacher transition course. She says, "The course taught me how to rephrase things accomplished in teaching; for example, 'decorated a bulletin board' would change to 'developed three-dimensional learning materials' and 'wrote a new math curriculum' might

> be, 'developed a new mode of learning.' I remember it was hammered in, 'Don't use the language of teaching as you write your resume to go into the business world! Present yourself not as a teacher but in terms of the skills you want to use'; for example, 'I am a public relations person,' 'I am a trainer,' 'I am a program planner.' "
>
> Ginny's approach helped her get a management-level job in a government agency and later in a national association.

Here are some additional guidelines for writing and revising your sentences:

- Avoid *I* and other personal pronouns. While *real* sentences always have subjects, resume sentences do not.
- Begin all sentences with action words of the correct tense. When describing something you are currently doing, say, for example, "*Conduct* daily tours of museums for groups of 15 adults." When describing something you did in the past, using the same example, say, "*Conducted* daily tours of museums. . ." For a list of action words, refer to Chapter 1.
- Instead of using unnecessary phrases such as "was responsible for," substitute an action word.
- Put abbreviations in parentheses the first time you use them, preceded by the terms for which they stand.
- To ensure that your relevant qualifications are obvious, prioritize your sentences and list the most important ones first. Eliminate extraneous information.
- Use natural and understandable language. For example, instead of saying, "Imparted knowledge about abstract concepts to advanced learners," say, "Instructed adults how to design brochures."
- Be concise, to the point, and clear.
- Refrain from self-evaluation or the use of subjective words, such as *efficient* and *energetic*, to describe yourself. Save these for the interview, when there has been an opportunity to develop rapport with the employer.
- Do not label work as *volunteer* or *part-time*. Integrate such jobs into your work experience section rather than placing them in a separate section.
- Stress accomplishments rather than merely describing job duties. The experience section should not read like a company-issued job description.

Education

The location and order of your academic work on a resume depend on your employment goals and what you want to communicate to an employer. Although it is more usual to list education after work experience, you may list your education first if, of the two, it is the more relevant or you are a recent graduate.

CASE IN POINT

When Gomer Macomb's wife, Sheila, took a job as a hospital administrator in Houston, he moved from Philadelphia with her. Six years before, he had received a master's degree in urban planning from the University of Pennsylvania, but he had never worked in that field because the supply of urban planners in Philadelphia exceeded the demand. Excited about the opportunity to apply his training in a growing city like Houston, Gomer created a traditional resume that listed his education after his work experience.

"It wasn't until I was face-to-face with an employer who hadn't previously seen my resume that I realized the error I had committed," he says. "By listing my education near the bottom of my resume, I screened myself out of some of Houston's best firms. My experience in other fields was relatively insignificant compared to my urban planning degree from a top-rate university."

When Gomer reversed the blocks, he was able to get interviews and convince employers of his worth.

List degrees in reverse chronological order with the highest degree first. Each entry should include the degree, the major field of study, the institution, city, state, and year of graduation or, if you did not graduate, inclusive years of study. For example: "B.A., Psychology, Wells College, Oakland, California. 1966." Special situations include the following:

- If you do not have a degree but expect one soon — within a year or less — list the information as though you have a degree, but instead of dates, specify, for example, "Degree expected 1985."
- If you have course work but are not aiming toward the degree, you could list, for example, "Course Work Toward B.A. Degree."

- Individual workshops, seminars, or courses — credit and non-credit — may be presented in a running list of subjects as on the Smith resume at the end of this chapter. Your completed educational records from Chapter 1 may remind you of training experiences to list on your resume.
- If you are a recent graduate, it is acceptable to make a brief listing of courses that are relevant to your employment goal but not obvious from your major.
- When you have college-level course work, do not list your high school education on your resume.
- Academic-related internships may be listed with either education or work exprience. Many job seekers prefer to list internships, whether paid or unpaid, in the experience section and describe them as jobs. (They *are* jobs.)
- Academic honors may be listed with education or in a special section entitled "Honors and Awards."

Honors and Awards

Honors and awards may spring from many activities, such as paid and volunteer work, professional and civic memberships, and academic work. Keep in mind, however, that this is an optional category on your resume. Unless you are a recent graduate, list only those honors and awards that are related to your employment goals. Exceptions to this rule are widely recognized academic honors such as Phi Beta Kappa.

If you have academic honors or awards, consider listing them with your degrees rather than in this separate section located near the end of your resume.

Credentials, Licenses, and Special Skills

In certain fields of work, such as nursing, counseling, social work, and law, applicants are required to have specific credentials and/or licenses. If you are in such a field, be sure you have them, and be sure you list them.

Depending on your situation, your resume might have one category entitled "Credentials, Licenses, and Special Skills," or you might break this down into three separate categories. Another possibility is to integrate this information into the "Education" or "Experience" categories. Keep in mind that cardinal criterion, relevance to the job.

Publications

While this category usually refers to your published works, you may include unpublished materials as well if they are relevant to your job target. Since writing experience is applicable to many jobs, review your background for handbooks, guides, pamphlets, or special lengthy reports.

If you have written only a few publications, list them on your resume, either after your education or after your experience. If you have many publications, list them on a separate page, and either send them with your resume or take them with you to interviews.

CASE IN POINT

Soon after moving to the Phoenix area, Sarah Faulkner was offered a paid job to write for a small community newspaper. Recalling her feelings about being selected, Sarah reports, "Of course, I was thrilled, but I knew immediately that it wasn't just good luck. I got that offer because I had worked hard in three volunteer jobs to create *products* I could list on my resume. I had written a guide to my community, which was adopted by the regional tourist bureau in my section of Tennessee. I had researched and written a 20-page handbook for parents about the guidance services in my son's junior high school. And finally, I had written a number of articles for my college alumni magazine."

Memberships

At or near the end of your resume, this optional category should include only current affiliations that have some relevancy to the field in which you are seeking a job. (An exception: Recent high school or college graduates who lack information for their resumes may list past memberships and extracurricular activities from school, even if these involvements are irrelevant to their job objectives.) Avoid emphasizing potentially controversial affiliations such as political party or religion. If you are an officer in an organization, say so, because it shows leadership ability — a plus in most employers' eyes.

If you aren't a member of any group, check to see if there are associations in your field that you *should* join. Memberships provide relocating spouses with a variety of important benefits, including opportunities to learn about or keep current in their fields through publications, workshops, and seminars. Furthermore, memberships may offer listings of job openings and, through meetings and membership directories, contacts. Specific memberships may enhance your qualifications in some professions, including nursing, law, training, and counseling. Besides providing many benefits, memberships are impressive on your resume.

Languages

In certain regions, proficiency in a particular language may be a real asset regardless of the job for which you are applying. For example, in Washington, DC, and in San Antonio, TX, where the population includes many Spanish-speaking residents from other cultures, Spanish is a valued second language.

"Languages" is an optional category that should be listed only if you believe you could effectively use the language in a job. Omit the category if you are so rusty you would be hard pressed to communicate in a foreign language. If you are fluent in a language, specify that. You might even add, "fluent in reading, writing, and speaking," if that is the case.

The language category should be near the end of your resume.

Interests

This optional category belongs near the end of a resume and generally refers to interests outside your work life, such as hobbies. Include interests if they are relevant to your field of work. While canoeing may appear frivolous to an employer of health-care professionals, it may not be to one in the environmental field. Again, recent high school or college graduates may include interests that are unrelated to employment goals, since employers might otherwise have too little information on which to base hiring decisions.

---- CASE IN POINT ----

The proud recipient of a B.A. degree in marine biology from Duke University, Susan Barlow moved to Annapolis, MD, after her graduation and marriage. She wrote her resume and applied to environmentally oriented firms she identified through the *Yellow Pages*. Before long, she had a job offer.

"I credit my *outside interests* with helping me land that job," Susan says. "I had listed scuba diving and photography on my resume, and my interviewer immediately latched on to that. He brought it up repeatedly throughout the interview, and now that I am employed, I frequently fly with him over the Chesapeake Bay and take photographs from the plane."

Personal Data

Personal data usually refers to statistics such as age, marital status, number of children, height, weight, and health.

Unless you believe employers truly need this information because it is relevant to your job objective, eliminate it. It could work against you. For example, *married* brings forth the issue, for women, of pregnancy and length of employment; *children* may raise questions about child care.

If you feel you must include personal data about yourself, put it at or near the end of your resume.

References

To avoid wasting space and having your references contacted unnecessarily, do not list the names, addresses, and telephone numbers of your references on your resume. Instead, take that information with you to your interviews, and offer it to the interviewer after mutual interest develops. If your references cannot be readily reached, bring copies of their letters of recommendation.

At the end of your resume you may state, "References Available Upon Request," or, since this is often assumed, the phrase may be omitted.

As a matter of courtesy and to ensure that employers receive favorable reports about your past work, always contact your references in advance for permission to list them. Describe to them the work you hope to secure, and tactfully remind them of your accomplishments.

Job Objective

Job objectives on resumes can raise more questions than they answer, so think twice before listing one.

Job hunters often set themselves up for rejection by specifying job objectives that organizations cannot possibly fulfill. For example, if you state that you want to be a management trainee when the firm to which you apply has no such job, you are likely to be screened out.

It may be advantageous to include a job objective when writing your resume for only one type of job; otherwise, integrate your objective into an individually typed cover letter that will accompany your resume. If you do decide to include a job objective, place it near the top of the resume and state it in terms of an employer's needs rather than in terms of your needs.

Examples of job objectives that are vague and expressed in terms of the applicant's needs rather than employers' needs:

- To work in a challenging administrative job where I can use my leadership skills and grow professionally.
- To work in a high-growth investment firm where I can contribute my capabilities to a dynamic team.

Examples of acceptable job objectives, presuming the applicant intends to apply only to the specified positions:

- Private secretary to a senior executive who requires shorthand, word processing, and meeting planning skills.
- To work in a state conservation agency as an energy consultant.

An alternative to the job objective is to write a brief "Summary of Experience" that would be located near the top of a resume after the contact information.

THE VISUAL FACTOR

Rightly or not, employers often form opinions of resumes based on their appearance alone. The following tips will help you to get screened in rather than screened out:

- Capitalize and underline headings and indent as appropriate to ensure that your resume will be easy to read and visually pleasing (see samples at end of chapter).
- Allow 1" to 1 1/2" margins at the top and sides of your resume and plenty of white space throughout to increase readability.
- Make your resume no longer than one to one-and-one half pages (one page is preferable).

THE RELOCATION RESUME

- Neatly type your resume, and enlist the help of others in proofreading for grammar and spelling errors, including incorrectly hyphenated words. Typesetting is unnecessary and, if you target your resumes to particular jobs, impractical. However, if you use a word processor to type your resume, you can make periodic changes with little effort. Some copying and duplication businesses will provide this service for you.
- For the body of your resume, stick to the standard type fonts rather than italics or other unusual fonts.
- Use white, off-white, or pale grey paper and avoid photographs of yourself on your resume.
- When your resume has been typed and proofed, take it to a printing shop to have it reproduced.
- Accept only excellent copies on high-quality, medium- or heavy-weight bond paper.

CRITIQUE YOUR RESUME

When you have completed your resume, ask yourself the following questions:

- Have I selected the most appropriate resume style for my particular background?
- Have I deemphasized the interruptions in my career?
- Have I highlighted benefits for a potential employer, and are my relevant qualifications obvious?
- Have I put the most important information near the top and left side of my resume?
- Have I stressed accomplishments rather than only job duties?
- Have I used natural and understandable language?
- Have I left off irrelevant personal information?
- Is my resume brief, to the point, and clear?
- Have I been consistent in my use of underlining, capitals, spacing, and margins?
- Is my original copy clean, clear, and of good contrast?
- Have I chosen high-quality bond paper on which to reproduce my resume?

As mentioned earlier in this chapter, your resume will generate the best results when *you* accompany it. Barring this opportuntiy, send it with a well-written cover letter as described in the next chapter.

Chronological Resume

```
            Martha Smith
           500 Main Street
        Fairfax, Virginia 22030
            (703) 323-5467
```

PROFESSIONAL EXPERIENCE

Administrative Assistant, Personnel Department, George Mason University, Fairfax, Virginia. 1982 to present.

Analyze institution's staff for percentage of female and minority group member distribution, develop institutional affirmative action goals, write required reports, and comply with and enforce federal Equal Employment Opportunity laws. Researched, designed, and wrote six 20- to 40-page administrative and procedural handbooks for student and faculty use. Supervise two work/study students, coordinate their work schedules, and monitor their work loads. Appraise their strengths and weaknesses in order to recommend appropriate promotions. Test and interview clerical job applicants, and then assess their suitability for employment with the university.

Secretary to Equal Employment Opportunity Officer, Personnel Department, Data Beta Manufacturing Company, Falls Church, Virginia. 1978 to 1980.

Assisted supervisor in developing and organizing summer program for disadvantaged minority youth. Researched sources for securing potential female and minority group member applicants, and then advertised all company job openings therein. Oriented new clerical and hourly employees to company's policies, procedures, and benefits. Expedited employment inquiries for supervisory review and, as appropriate, wrote rejection letters or arranged for interview appointments.

EDUCATION

B.S. Psychology, Pennsylvania State University, State College, Pennsylvania, 1976. Phi Beta Kappa

Workshops in counseling, equal employment opportunity, communication effectiveness, speed reading, testing and assessment, and industrial relations.

PROFESSIONAL MEMBERSHIPS

American Association for Counseling and Development
Council of Affirmative Action Professionals

THE RELOCATION RESUME   165

Chronological Resume for a Recent High School Graduate

```
                    Francis Sloanacker
                    36710 Wayford Court
                  Seattle, Washington  98199
                       (206) 763-2188
```

EDUCATION

    High School Graduate, Fairbanks High School, Fairbanks, Alaska. 1984.

SPECIAL SKILLS: Typing -- 50 words per minute
                      Bookkeeping
                      Competent at using calculators,
                          office reproduction equipment,
                          and cash registers.

WORK HISTORY

    <u>Clerical Assistant</u>, Northfield Hospital, Urbana, Illinois. 1982 to 1983.

        Maintained medical records on all outpatients in large urban hospital. Secured medical data from appropriate departments and calculated laboratory, surgical, and physicians' fees. Communicated with proper personnel regarding errors. Billed clients and recorded incoming receipts.

    <u>Food Service Worker</u>, Wendy's Restaurant, Toledo, Ohio. 1982.

        Calculated bills and collected money. Used cash register and totaled end-of-evening receipts. Took orders from patrons and served them food. Periodically closed restaurant in manager's absence.

    <u>Other Employment:</u> Lifeguard, child care worker

AWARDS

    Received Employee of the Month Award from the Allegash Regional Restaurant Association

INTERESTS

    Reading, hiking, fishing, furniture refinishing, and bridge

REFERENCES
    Available upon request

Chronological Resume
(All Jobs Listed Are Volunteer)

```
Sarah Lee Hoya
321 Appleby Boulevard
Hanover, Pennsylvania 17331
(717) 699-9754
```

WORK HISTORY

<u>Mental Health Worker</u>, Apt Community Outreach Program, York, Pennsylvania. 1980 to present.

Counsel approximately 12 youth per week to help them solve their drug dependency and alcohol problems. Create innovative approaches appropriate to the specific needs of the individuals participating in the program. Maintain accurate client records by detailing weekly counseling sessions. Facilitate group meetings for clients with long-term addictions.

<u>Coordinator</u>, York Boys' Club, York, Pennsylvania. 1977 to 1980.

Implemented plans for the creation of this 125-member organization that was formed to provide supervised recreational activities for youth. Independently wrote a 20-page proposal, and then gave a one-hour presentation to the town council to explain the merits of the proposed organization. Recruited and supervised 12 volunteer staff members to oversee building and grounds maintenance. Designed and produced all publicity and member-recruitment handouts. Ordered office and athletic supplies and equipment for facility's first year of operation.

<u>Facility Resource Consultant</u>, Fort Riley, Fort Riley, Kansas. 1974 to 1977.

Coordinated written relocation information developed for incoming personnel to large facility. Consulted with medical, educational, and food distribution services to obtain literature pertinent to the needs of relocating individuals. Initiated and planned functions for new residents. Assessed and revised existing procedures for helping individuals of all ages adapt to the facility.

EDUCATION

Undergraduate work in Psychology, English, and Business Administration, Iowa State University , Ames, Iowa. 1968 to 1970.

<u>Other Workshops and Training</u>: Communication, Word Processing.

LANGUAGES
Spanish (fluent), Portuguese (fair)

MEMBERSHIPS
Hanover Citizens Association
Youth Assistance Council of Greater York

Combination Functional/Chronological Resume

Malcolm Radnor
21 North Darby Drive
Princeton, Massachusetts 01541
(617) 292-7027

AREAS OF COMPETENCY

Editing and Writing
Edited and rewrote news articles for a 16-page weekly newspaper with a county-wide circulation of 100,000. Wrote brochures for fund-raising campaigns of $50,000 to $250,000 for academic and medical institutions, nonprofit social agencies, and private interest groups.

Research
Designed survey for psychological research study and collected data from 700 students in large state university. Compiled results, analyzed data, and wrote final report at conclusion of yearlong study. Investigated information for news articles for large county newspaper. Researched information for high school textbooks on ancient history.

Management
Hired, organized, and monitored a three-person staff during $250,000 fund raising campaign for a large urban hospital. Supervised the work of these individuals, assessed their performance, and then discussed evaluations with them. Budgeted for administrative overhead, including supplies, rent, and campaign expenses. Directed the publication of five brochures and supervised their distribution.

PROFESSIONAL EXPERIENCE

<u>Copy Editor</u>, Middlesex County Journal, Acton, Massachusetts. 1978 to present.

<u>Research Aide</u>, Newbury Press, Newbury, Massachusetts. 1964 to 1969.

<u>Proofreader</u>, Ginn and Company, Boston, Massachusetts. 1960 to 1964.

EDUCATION

B.A. English, Duke University, Durham, North Carolina, 1963.

MEMBERSHIPS

American Society of Journalists and Authors
International Women's Writing Guild

Combination Functional/Chronological Resume for a Teacher Redirecting Her Experience Toward a Career in Training/Human Resource Development

Barbara Bowman
601 Ariel Avenue
Omaha, Nebraska 68101
(402) 981-2154

AREAS of COMPETENCE

TRAINING — Review literature and prepare training proposals. Design, deliver, and evaluate education and training for diverse participants. Plan and conduct in-service workshops and seminars. Develop program materials and select audio-visual aids. Use a variety of training techniques, including role plays, group discussions, and lectures. Identify and resolve conflicts and facilitate group interaction among students to promote optimum learning. Coordinate and manage programs. Evaluate and assess participants' skills.

PUBLIC RELATIONS — Organize and deliver public presentations to large and small groups. Advertise and effectively market programs. Write and edit newsletter for professional organization. Translate technical material into language understandable to audience. Establish liaison with community and social services.

ADMINISTRATION — Organize people, time, and materials. Monitor production and work of diverse individuals, and delegate authority as appropriate. Supervise training of interns and paraprofessionals. Oversee personnel appraisal system. Implement and interpret institutional policies. Manage annual budget, and order materials and supplies according to funding.

WORK EXPERIENCE

<u>Instructor</u>, Hoover School, Omaha, Nebraska. 1982 to present.

<u>Staff Assistant</u>, Farway Center, Omaha, Nebraska. 1980 to 1984.

<u>Coordinator</u>, City Youth Center, Eugene, Oregon. 1975 to 1979.

EDUCATION

M.Ed., University of Oregon, Eugene, Oregon. 1979.
B.A., Carleton College, Northfield, Minnesota. 1975.

MEMBERSHIPS

American Society for Training and Development
National Society for Performance and Instruction

Combination Functional/Chronological Resume for a Woman Redirecting Her Volunteer and Part-time Experience Toward a Full-time, Salaried Career

Marcie Jones
113 Acton Street
Lewiston, Maine 04240
(207) 872-9361

SKILL AREAS

SALES and FUNDRAISING

- Sold cosmetics and household products to 400 private clients, grossing more than $10,000 in sales in one year.
- Raised more than $250,000 for national nonprofit medical association through annual fund-raising event.
- Increased Saturday sales in clothing store by 30 percent in nine months.

MANAGEMENT

- Managed medium-sized clothing store during manager's absences.
- Planned and coordinated major fund-raising activity for national firm.
- Oversaw promotional activities, recruited and interviewed staff, and administered agency budget.
- Planned and administered educational events and trips for adolescents.

SUPERVISION

- Supervised a staff of five volunteers for nonprofit medical association.
- Supervised the recreation activities of 10 youth over a two-year period.
- Managed group of 75 youth and seven adults on weekend area-wide camping trip.

WORK HISTORY

<u>Salesperson</u>, Joe's Clothing Store, Lewiston, Maine. 1978 to 1983.

<u>Sales Representative</u>, Avon, Inc., Louisville, Kentucky. 1972 to 1978.

<u>Manager</u> of Walk-a-Thon, Cancer Society, Louisville, Kentucky. 1975 to 1976.

<u>Youth Coordinator</u>, Boy Scouts of America, Louisville, Kentucky. 1969 to 1971.

EDUCATION

Courses in Business Management and Finance, Sullivan Junior College of Business, Louisville, Kentucky. 1976 to 1978.

13
The Customized Cover Letter

The purpose of a cover letter is to encourage an employer to read your accompanying resume or, perhaps, an application for federal employment. Although you may send the same resume to many different employers, you should write each cover letter individually and relate your qualifications to an employer's specific needs. Nothing turns an employer off more than a reproduced cover letter.

With organizations receiving thousands of resumes annually, it is difficult to make a favorable impression in the face of such competition. However, a resume accompanied with a well-written cover letter will help you move beyond the competition.

CASE IN POINT

Anxious to get a part-time job after relocating, Velma Martin went into town late each Saturday night for the Sunday newspaper, and then read the employment ads before going to bed. Early each Sunday morning, Velma carefully composed cover letters specifying how her qualifications met the employers' requirements, and later the same day, she dropped the letters in the mailbox. This is how she got her job as coordinator of cooperative education at a Boston-area college.

Describing what happened, Velma says, "The job was advertised just before Christmas, and the student services department hoped to hire someone immediately because the present coordinator was leaving right after the holidays. My papers were among the first to be reviewed because

THE CUSTOMIZED COVER LETTER

> of the routine I had established. I was interviewed and hired while resumes were still arriving."
>
> Velma was told she got the job because of her cover letter and the speed with which her papers arrived. "Since I had thoroughly analyzed every phrase in that ad, I was able to write a letter that matched my qualifications to the department's needs," she says. The department eventually received over 100 resumes, but few were accompanied with high-quality cover letters.

APPEARANCE

- Type your letters on high-quality 8 1/2" x 11" paper, preferably white or off-white bond. Avoid colored paper.
- While personal letterhead stationery is attractive, it probably will not make much of an impression on employers.
- Likewise, an effort to coordinate your envelopes and stationery probably would not be noticed by employers.
- Select a standard typeface, and be sure that the ribbon is sufficiently dark.
- Write the letters in clear, concise language.
- Keep the letters brief — not more than one-half to two-thirds of a page long.
- Proofread several times for spelling and grammar errors.

ADDRESS

If possible, address your cover letters to specific individuals and use their titles. If you do not have this information, telephone the organization and ask whomever answers for the name and title of the individual in charge of the department in which you want to work. In any case, take care to spell all names correctly.

Of course, when responding to a "blind" ad, in which the employer is unspecified, you will be unable to use a person's name. You will have little choice except to write, "Dear Madam/Sir:" or "To Whom It May Concern:" Don't expect a high return on the time you invest responding to blind ads.

When an ad requests that you send a resume to the personnel department, it is acceptable to send a cover letter and resume to a departmental supervisor as well as to personnel if you let both parties know you are doing this.

OPENING PARAGRAPH

The opening paragraph of a cover letter may be as short as one sentence or as long as several sentences. Mention how you found out about the organization or the position, and, when possible, use the name of a mutual contact. The purpose here is to catch the readers' attention and make them want to read further. Some examples:

- "After reading about Knox and Witte in the *Chicago Tribune*, I spoke with Gertrude Baskin, who mentioned your need for an additional staff person in your fund-raising activity."
- "As a specialist in working with problem learners, I was interested to learn from an Apt, Inc. employee, Malcolm McKee, that your organization is launching a new program to tutor learning-disabled children and adults."
- "I see from the *Washington Post* that your organization has recently added an extended health-care facility. This is why I am writing to you today."
- "As a high-speed typist with excellent word processing skills, I believe I can make a significant contribution to your publications business."
- "I recently read that your organization's food service operation has been modernized. You may be interested in my background as a certified Food Service Institute graduate."
- "I understand that you have recently received a large grant from the National Academy of Sciences to study environmental causes of rheumatoid arthritis."

BODY OF THE LETTER

Devote the center of the letter to brief facts about your background that will benefit the organization. You want to imply, "Since I have done it in the past, I can do it for you in the future." Do not repeat your resume, but draw attention to it.

When responding to an ad, assume the employer has advertised because he or she has a problem that needs solving. To figure out what that problem is and show how you can be of service, dissect the ad and carefully describe how your particular experience or education qualifies you to handle the organization's work. If an ad gives so little information you are unable to do this, call the employer for more data. Since employers do not want to be bothered by unnecessary calls, make sure you have a legitimate need for information. To avoid being obtrusive, briefly and politely ask two or three questions you have written out ahead of time.

When writing to organizations you have identified without ads, you may need to independently research their requirements using the methods described in Chapter 6. In any case, read company publications and trade journals in the field for which you are applying.

There are three ways to present your qualifications in the body of a cover letter:

- in paragraph form (refer to the Martin letter near the end of this chapter)
- with bullets — a bullet is a small "o" on the typewriter, filled in with felt-tip pen (refer to the Adler letter)
- a graphic approach (refer to the Wright letter).

The tone in the body of your letter should be very positive without being aggressive. Do not risk overselling yourself by using adjectives, such as *organized* and *successful*, to describe yourself. Save that for when you are face-to-face with an employer in an interview and there has been a chance for personal chemistry to develop. In either case, always focus on employers' needs rather than on your needs.

THE CLINCHER PARAGRAPH

In this part of the cover letter, make a bid for a meeting with the employer in a manner that clearly shows you expect the meeting to occur. Since the word *interview* can put off employers, use *meeting* instead. If you wait for an employer to contact you, the connection may never occur. Consider specifying a day when you plan to telephone, and then call on that day to arrange a time to meet. (While you have more control with this strategy and can relax about the possibility of missing employers' calls, do not telephone repeatedly.)

When responding to an advertised position, you may feel more comfortable by not naming a day when you will call. In that case, word the message in a way that leaves an opening for you to contact an employer without discouraging him or her from making the contact. A typical closing might be, "I look forward to a meeting to discuss my qualifications and to learn further about your requirements." You could include the times you can be reached and leave alternative phone numbers. You might say, "Please don't hesitate to call me at my office."

To alleviate your concern about missing employers' calls, rent an answering machine during your job search. The rental charges are tax deductible along with your other job hunting expenses.

Initially, you will find that writing cover letters requires concentrated effort. Yet with time and practice, not only will you become more proficient, but you will also accumulate a supply of cover letters from which to adapt paragraphs.

Refer to Chapters 6 and 15 for information about other employment-related letters, and to Appendix C for resources on cover letters.

Cover Letter in Paragraph Form

91 Sharon Court, S.E.
San Diego, California 92104
July 10, 198_

Ms. Maria Martin
Training Director
TRW Systems, Inc.
123 Albemarle St., S.W.
San Diego, California 92101

Dear Ms. Martin:

    As a specialist in human resource development, I was delighted to read about TRW's innovative approach to supervisory training. You and your staff must be proud of the very descriptive article written by Ms. McCoombs in <u>Training News</u>.

    Aspects of my background are particularly relevant to your activities. For example, having recently completed a 75-hour professional development program, I am now a certified training specialist. As an instructor with eight years of experience, I am competent at designing effective learning environments. Repeatedly, I have been commended on my approaches to needs assessment, curriculum development, and training evaluation. You can see from my enclosed resume that my other related experience in personnel and training has been in both profit and nonprofit institutions -- a balance that has enhanced my professional development.

    Although I presume you are not in a position to add staff members to your department at this time, I believe a brief meeting would be of potential benefit to both of us. I will telephone you on Thursday, July 17, to make arrangements to get together.

                                    Sincerely,

                                    Elizabeth A. Boyd

Enclosure: Resume

Cover Letter Using Bullets

5342 Clifton Avenue
Wilmington, Delaware 19810
December 10, 198_

Ms. Bernadette Adler
Government Contracts Advisor
Tuck & Tuttle International Corporation
321 Third Avenue
Wilmington, Delaware 19804

Dear Ms. Adler:

I recently read about Tuck & Tuttle's new ventures and understand from Brian Williams that you may have a need for an additional staff person for your government contract work.

I am interested in this position and believe you will find the following aspects of my background particularly relevant:

- As project manager for a community-wide fund-raising campaign, I recruited and supervised personnel, administered the budget, and oversaw the development of promotional materials.

- As a manager of volunteers for an organization of 300 people, I handled diverse management functions including planning work schedules, evaluating personnel, organizing supplies and equipment, and controlling cash receipts and other assets.

- Recently, I have acquired word processing skills and am knowledgeable about a several software packages.

Since I am difficult to reach, I will telephone you on Thursday, July 27, to arrange for a meeting. I look forward to learning more about your needs and describing my background as it relates to the work at Tuck & Tuttle.

Sincerely,

Suzanne A. Carrier

Enclosure: Resume

Cover Letter Using Graphic Approach

```
                                        Box 20301
                                        Indianapolis, Indiana  46222
                                        January 2, 198_
```

Mr. Malcolm Wright
Food Service Manager
Air Rights Corporation
65 Twelfth Street, N.W., Suite 310
Indianapolis, Indiana 46227

Dear Mr. Wright:

I was interested to read in the <u>Indianapolis Tribune</u> that, as a part of Air Rights' expansion program, you hope to hire a maitre d' for your executive dining room. I believe that my food service experience is especially applicable to your needs:

<u>Your Requirements</u>	<u>My Qualifications</u>
Food Service Institute certification	Food Service Institute certification
3 years maitre d' experience	5 years maitre d' experience
1 year corporate experience	3 years corporate experience
Knowledge of French or Spanish	Knowledge of French <u>and</u> Spanish
Willingness to assume other food service roles	Able and willing to serve as waiter, cook, and cashier

Additional qualifications are covered in my enclosed resume.

I am interested in this position and look forward to meeting with you so we may learn more about each other. I can be reached weekdays at 542-7601 between 10 a.m. and 7 p.m. or at 987-9726 other times. Thank you for your consideration.

```
                             Sincerely,


                             Francesca Garcia
```

Enclosure: Resume

14

The Application Form

In some jobs — including federal employment — your application form will be an interviewer's first impression of you. In others, after you have presented a resume, you may be asked to complete an application to provide information not normally covered on resumes, such as salary history, the names of previous supervisors, and reasons for leaving jobs. In either case, your goal is a carefully completed form that is high-quality in both content and appearance.

NONGOVERNMENT FORMS

Well in advance of a job interview, ask your prospective employer to send you two application forms, or stop by and pick them up yourself. Use one as a working copy and the other as a final copy. If you are unable to get a second form, reproduce a working copy from the original. If you cannot get even one application before your interview, bring along your work portfolio (see Chapter 1) for reference in filling out the form.

If at all possible, type your application forms. Otherwise print, preferably with black pen. (If your printing is hard to read, write neatly in script.)

Filling in the Blanks

Avoid leaving any empty blanks, even when a question on the application form calls for information you have already provided on your resume. When a question does not apply to you, write *N/A*, meaning not applicable. A word of caution: Never put any false information on an application form, because employers frequently check on data submitted. Besides, according to many employers, falsifying an application form may be grounds for dismissal if you have already been hired.

Past Supervisors: If you are unable to locate a past supervisor, list a co-worker or someone else who can verify your employment.

Salary History: When requested to provide salary history, you may want to add in bonuses or other fringe benefits that could be considered part of salary. This may enable you to command a higher rate of pay. However, provide an explanation for the increased figure.

Reasons for Leaving: Examples of what you might list if you are asked your reasons for leaving your previous employment include fulfillment of job requirements, reduction in force, career or financial advancement, desire for more challenging job duties, relocation, and to work in a new field. Never indicate that you had a personality problem with a supervisor.

Work Experience: Your completed job description records from Chapter 1 will provide the information requested in the work experience sections of application forms. If you have not yet documented your experience on these records, do so now before proceeding with this chapter.

To help you compensate for employment gaps, job-hopping, and underemployment in your work history, Fred Hechlinger and Bernadette Curtin offer creative solutions in their book, *Training for Life*. If you are asked to specify periods of unemployment, avoid the negative word *unemployed* and instead list what you were doing at the time — career research, consulting, traveling, improving your home, raising your children, developing your qualifications. If there was a period when you had many jobs of only a few weeks' duration, lump them together under one general description or eliminate some. If one of your past job titles did not reflect the skills and accomplishments you utilized in a job, change the title to emphasize your expertise; however, *never* exaggerate to the point where what you say is an untruth.

References: List individuals who have been associated with you in a paid or unpaid work capacity or in a school capacity and can attest to your value in a work situation. References may be from past or present supervisors, teachers, and co-workers. As mentioned in Chapter 12, contact your references for permission to list them as a matter of courtesy and to increase your chances of receiving good recommendations. Tell them about the work you hope to secure, and remind them of your positive attributes. If you have written recommendations from references instead of contact information for them, mention that on your application forms.

When you have completed your form, proofread it at least three times — preferably with the help of another person — for spelling and grammar errors.

SF171: THE APPLICATION FOR FEDERAL EMPLOYMENT

If you have decided to pursue work with the Federal Government, apply by submitting an SF171, which you can get from a federal job information/testing center, listed in Appendix A, or a federal civilian personnel office. This four-page form is used for three basic purposes:

- to obtain the highest possible rating from the Office of Personnel Management (OPM)
- to apply for specific job announcements at federal agencies
- to secure promotions and advance your federal career.

The information you provide about your experience, education, training and development, awards, and outside activities is used to determine whether you are eligible to be considered for the jobs you choose, and, if eligible, how you are rated for them. As you complete your SF171, consider it a test, because your rating determines how you are ranked against other applicants. Depending on your background, it is not unreasonable to spend up to 50 hours completing an SF171. Besides the content, pay close attention to the format and appearance of your SF171.

Your SF171 will be read by many decision makers, including personnel specialists who will determine whether you have the qualifications for vacancies, review panel members who will evaluate your experience and rank you against your competitors, and program managers or selecting officials who will interview you during the selection process.

To develop a superior SF171, consider the following tips:

THE APPLICATION FORM

- Do not submit the original of your SF171 to OPM or to agencies. Keep it and make copies and revisions as necessary. If you are outside the government, write a comprehensive SF171 that covers much of your background and submit a copy to OPM. When you apply for a specific agency position, revise your form to reflect the requirements specified on the vacancy announcement.

- Read and reread the SF171 instructions and give all the requested information. Fill in every space on the form, except those you are instructed on the following pages to leave blank. When a question does not apply to you, type *N/A* (not applicable).

- Remember all your qualifications and describe them in a detailed yet concise manner. Many applicants are screened out because they fail to list information for which they could receive credit.

- When adding additional pages to the SF171 form, as described in this chapter, renumber your pages in sequential order.

- Omit uncalled-for attachments; for example, resumes, recommendations, certificates, and awards. Instead, list relevant information in the appropriate spaces on the SF171. For example, if you received an award for work described in an experience block, consider listing it at the end of that block under a heading entitled *accomplishments* as shown in the sample experience block later in this chapter. Since it is acceptable to list your qualifications in more than one place on the SF171, list your award a second time under the *honors, awards, and fellowships* section.

- Type your SF171, if possible; otherwise, print with black pen.

- Type your name and social security number on the top of each page in case the pages are separated.

- Use adequate and consistent margins and indentations.

- Get assistance in proofreading your SF171 many times for spelling, grammar, and clarity.

- Reproduce one side only, not back to back, and accept only high-quality copies with good contrast.

- Send your SF171 to the hiring official *before* the closing date for the announcement.

- Do not fold your SF171 or use a government envelope to mail it.

**Page 1: General Information; Availability;
Military Service and Veterans Preference**

Page 1 is the most straightforward and easiest to complete of the four SF171 pages. The following will cover only those questions that need some explanation.

Kind of job: Leave the original blank. On the OPM copy, list the position category or name and announcement number from OPM. When you are ready to submit a copy of your SF171 to an agency, list the exact job title and announcement number, if you know it; for example, personnel specialist, No. 81-112.

If the announcement lists several job titles: Leave the original and OPM copies blank. On the copies you submit to agencies, name the additional jobs for which you are applying, if applicable.

Name and address: If your address changes after you apply for a rating or vacancy, notify OPM and agencies to which you have applied.

Other names ever used: If you have education or experience under a previous last name, this is an especially important item. Later put your previous name(s) in parentheses at the end of each work experience block to which it applies.

Previous federal employment: Give information on the highest grade you previously attained, including grade level, classification series, and job title.

Applications on file with OPM: Leave your original copy blank until you receive your notice of eligibility from OPM (four to eight weeks), then fill in the requested information. On your copy to OPM, check *no* or write *N/A* if this is your first time filling out an SF171 or your previous eligibility or rating has expired. After you receive notice of eligibility from OPM, include the appropriate information on your SF171, including the regional office where your form is on file. If you start job hunting before receiving your notice, state that your application has been submitted to OPM. While some agencies will accept this, others will not. If applicable to you, type "Noncompetitive Eligibility under EO 12585" (see Chapter 5).

THE APPLICATION FORM

When you can start work: Leave your original SF171 blank. On the copy you send to OPM, specify the earliest date you expect to be available. On copies you send to agencies, specify the month that is about two weeks after the announcement's closing date or type, "two weeks notice."

Lowest pay you will accept: Leave your original SF171 blank. On the copy you send to OPM, specify grade rather than salary, because the Federal Government thinks more in terms of grades. If you are willing to accept the entire range, put the lowest grade you would accept. While you will not be considered for grades lower than you specify, you will be considered for higher. If the lowest grade you specify is higher than the level at which you qualify, OPM will not provide you with a rating. If you are unsure of the grade you are qualified for, refer to *Handbook X-118 — Qualification Standards for White Collar Positions Under the General Schedule* (see Appendix C). As you apply for agency positions, fill in the grade.

Page 2: Work Experience

The work experience section is the most important part of the SF171. The information you provide will be used in determining whether or not you qualify for a rating or a position, and will have a significant impact on whether you are evaluated as a highly qualified candidate in competition with other applicants. Since 50 to 60 percent of your score is based on the quality of your experience, you must show that you have the knowledge, skills, and abilities for the work you want to do. *Knowledge* can be defined as an organized body of information, usually of a factual or procedural nature; for example, knowledge of accounting or Spanish. A *skill* is an ability or physical competence that you demonstrate in the course of your responsibilities, performing your duties, or making your contributions; for example, typing skill. An *ability* is the potential to use a knowledge or skill when needed; for example, the ability to edit technical documents.

Divide your work experiences into blocks and list them in reverse chronological order, with your most recent or present job first. Start a new block each time you changed employers or got a promotion. (A promotion involves a new job title and/or new job responsibilities and, sometimes, a pay increase.)

Regarding the top portions of the blocks, be brief in listing reasons for leaving jobs; for example, relocation, reduction in force, professional advancement, promotion, and financial advancement. If the duration of your qualifying experience is close to the required 18 months for noncompetitive eligibility as described in Chapter 5, specify the exact days as well as months and years of your employment to avoid being deemed ineligible.

You may summarize work beyond 10 years in a paragraph or list one-line entries with dates, job titles, organizations, and locations. However, if the work is relevant to your current job objective, describe it fully in the standard blocks.

As requested on the form, integrate and describe relevant volunteer work with your paid work experience. If the work or a part of the work resembles the job you are applying for, you may receive credit for your experience with religious, community, service, cultural, and other organizations.

Whereas other application forms and resumes are brief, an SF171 should be detailed. Expand the experience blocks and add additional blocks according to what you need to describe your work. To expand the blocks and improve the appearance of your SF171, use scissors to eliminate the lines and use paper cement, a ruler, and black pen to reconstruct the blocks. Make certain to paste on the "for agency use" block. If you would prefer to use ready-made forms, order "The New Expanded 171 Forms Kit" (see Appendix C and example, page 185). Letter the small boxes – C, D, E, etc. – up to the number of jobs you describe. Unless the description is longer than a full page, do not split a job between two pages.

To develop comprehensive write-ups, such as the sample experience block on page 185, adapt sentences from your completed job description records (Chapter 1). To develop additional sentences, refer to the "Model for Documenting Your Experience," also in Chapter 1.

As requested on the SF171, describe your experience in terms of your duties, responsibilities, and accomplishments, which are defined by the Federal Government as follows:

Duty: A specific activity that is expected of you in the day-to-day performance of your responsibilities; for example, "Audit bank records."

Responsibility: An area of work where you have authority, make decisions, and exercise independent judgment; for example, "Determine which banks are audited."

THE APPLICATION FORM   185

Expanded Experience Block, Page 2 of the SF171

1. Name (Last, First, Middle)	2. Social Security Number
Watson, Rebecca Anne	313-83-4074
3. Job Title of Announcement Number You Are Applying For	4. Date Completed
Management Analyst	August 1986

ADDITIONAL WORK EXPERIENCE BLOCKS

C

Name and address of employer's organization (include ZIP Code if known)	Dates employed (give month and year)	Average number of hours per week
Jarvis Moulton, Inc. 20 Acorn Lane Reston, VA 21194	From 4/80 To 6/82	40
	Salary or earnings Starting $12,100 per year Ending $14,800 per year	Place of employment City Reston State VA

Exact title of your job	Your immediate supervisor		Number and job titles of any employees you supervised
Secretary	Name Mary Fortune	Area Code Telephone Number 703 868-0442	one typist

Kind of business or organization (manufacturing, accounting, social service, etc.)	If Federal employment (civilian or military), list series, grade or rank, and the date of your last promotion	Your reason for leaving
manufacturing	N/A	financial advancement

Description of work. Describe your specific duties, responsibilities and accomplishments in this job. If you describe more than one type of work (for example, carpentry and painting, or personnel and budget), write the approximate percentage of time you spent doing each.

Served as senior secretary to the purchasing agent and five buyers for a 350-member firm that manufactured extreme low-temperature refrigeration systems for military and industrial purposes.

DUTIES AND RESPONSIBILITIES
- Directed the work of a part-time, temporary typist, and delegated typing to other clerical employees during peak work periods.

- Prepared semi-annual performance appraisals on part-time typist, and made recommendations for career development.

- Interacted directly with senior officers of the company and officials from other companies.

- Planned monthly and annual procurement meetings and conferences for 30 to 80 senior staff members from regional companies.

- Welcomed approximately 35 visitors weekly and 12 delegations of visitors from abroad annually.

- Reviewed all incoming mail and routed it to staff members according to their areas of speciality. Wrote responses to routine inquiries directed to the purchasing agent.

- Typed a variety of materials from drafts or dictation, including letters, memoranda, reports, statistical charts, and budgets.

- Maintained time cards and coordinated annual leave schedules for staff members of the Purchasing Department.

ACCOMPLISHMENTS
- Designed and implemented a new time-card retrieval system for the Purchasing Department using the MultiMate Word Processing software package. Trained five employees on how to use and maintain similar systems.

- Consistently received excellent performance evaluations and above average merit salary increases.

Accomplishment: A contribution of substantial value, made independently or as part of a team, that is not normally expected of you and contributes something out of the ordinary to the goals of your organization or office; for example, "Devised a new auditing technique that was adopted by my organization." If you have no accomplishments, you need not worry — many applicants don't.

Vacancy announcements often list *selective placement factors* that you must meet to be an eligible candidate, and they sometimes specify *quality ranking factors* that you are not required to meet but through which you can earn extra rating points from an evaluation panel. Agencies sometimes ask applicants to address these factors on a separate sheet of paper, but if the agency does not, attach your own supplemental sheet, as shown in the example on page 187. In either case, also make these factors obvious throughout your SF171.

Consider the following as you write the work experience section of your SF171:

- Relate your experience to a position's requirements. Useful resources for learning about job requirements are vacancy announcements, the *Handbook X-118,* and the *Position Classification Standards* (see Appendix C).
- Describe your actual work experience in your own words rather than copying or attaching position descriptions.
- Avoid describing your employer or organization unless it bears directly on your experience.
- Show career growth and progression. Reflect your breadth of experience in your write-ups.
- Use separate blocks for military service experience, and describe your duties in terms a civilian can understand.
- When using acronyms, spell out the term on first reference, followed by the acronym in parentheses.
- Use action words and avoid the phrase "responsible for."
- Write in first person and use the correct tense (as an example, for a current job: "Instruct potential retirees. . ." and, for a past job: "Instructed potential retirees. . ."). It is unnecessary to use "I" on SF171s and resumes.
- Use clear, simple, direct sentences. Describe fully without being wordy.
- Use adverbs to show passage of time and job growth (*initially, subsequently, later, then*).
- Don't exaggerate but don't be humble either.

Supplementary Statement to SF171*

(Applicant's Name)

Narrative Statement Relating Background to Selective Placement Factors for the Position of Personnel Specialist, Nuclear Regulatory Commission.

1. Knowledge of personnel policies and procedures with an emphasis on recruitment of professional personnel.

I have acquired more than eight years of experience in personnel administration while working at Allen Hamilton & Associates and the Department of Energy (DOE). Through this experience I have become familiar with personnel policies and procedures as they pertain to the private sector and the Federal Government. My knowledge from these work experiences covers wage and salary administration, benefits administration, training, occupational safety and health, affirmative action, and recruitment. In terms of recruitment, I am well versed on federal, state, and local labor and equal opportunity laws as they affect child labor and hiring with regard to age, sex, religion, or national origin.

During my eight years in personnel, I recruited more than 400 professional employees. For each new hire, I consistently worked from the beginning to the end of the recruitment process. For example, I traveled to colleges and universities throughout the eastern United States and interviewed undergraduate and graduate students. I also developed advertisements for use in professional journals and newspapers and then screened the resulting applications before circulating them among appropriate supervisory staff. I coordinated all on-site visits of potential employees to the organizations I was associated with and issued offers of employment. In addition, I developed and supervised the orientation programs that were offered to new hires.

2. Knowledge of position classification methods.

As a personnel specialist with DOE I spent more than three years working closely with the position classification specialists to reevaluate the grade designations held by the agency's technical personnel. In this regard I regularly assisted classification specialists throughout the reevaluation process. While participating in over 180 reviews, I developed competency in assessing and establishing proper grade levels of technicians, engineers, physicists, chemists, and geologists. In the absence of the position classification specialist, I independently conducted evaluations. As a part of this, I met with an interagency board composed of other technical reviewers to share cases and mutual concerns.

---

* The information on this page is intended to be only a partial sample.

All editions of the SF171 request information about periods of unemployment longer than three months, but the 1984 edition is a better choice for the job seeker with gaps in employment. Whereas the 1984 edition directs you to list periods of unemployment on the last page of the SF171 and only as far back as 10 years ago, the previous editions require that you list unemployment with your work experience, as it occurred, and specifies no time limit. In either case, it is preferable to describe some relevant volunteer work rather than say *unemployed*. If you cannot think of anything, record the dates, your address during your period of unemployment, and the word *unemployed* in the spaces provided on page four of the 1984 edition or, in previous editions, on the last line of the job that followed the unemployed period.

Page 3: Education; Special Skills, Accomplishments and Awards; References

This page is closely scrutinized by examiners at OPM and federal agencies. Too often, job seekers offer only brief information to questions that could make the difference between their being hired or rejected. Do not hesitate to repeat appropriate information here from your work experience blocks.

Whenever you need more space, borrow from elsewhere on the page by cutting and pasting or continue on page 4 of the form. If you need more space than either of these alternatives allows, attach an extra page before or after page 3. Type your name and social security number at the top, followed by the category you are continuing (see the example in the case in point on page 190).

Education: Since course work can be substituted for experience in determining qualifications, this section may be very influential. If you cannot remember the exact number of your semester or quarter hours, estimate them.

One education section, often overlooked but very important, asks for other courses and training related to the kind of jobs for which you are applying; for example, trade, vocational, military, or business. To jog your memory, review your completed education records from Chapter 1, and list pertinent information for seminars, workshops, conferences, leadership orientations, military training, correspondence courses, private study, and the like.

Special Qualifications, Skills, or Accomplishments: Many applicants neglect this box, yet other factors being equal, the information included or omitted here could be the deciding factor between applicants. You may include relevant skills with machines (including office machines), important publications, public speaking and writing experience, patents or inventions, and memberships. This is also the place to highlight other skills; for example, you could describe your excellent research skills. You may even include hobbies — for example, computer programming, video, and cataloging of slides — if they are applicable to the job you are seeking.

You don't have to be a polished speaker to include public speaking. List experiences where you had to teach, brief, or persuade audiences; for example, presentations or reports to clubs. If you have extensive public speaking experience, be concise by summarizing your speeches into categories; for example, "As guest speaker at libraries and community groups, gave 20 presentations on dressing for success.

Make a complete list of your writing experience, including dates of reports, guides, handbooks, instructions, and pamphlets. There is no need to submit actual copies of these.

While the SF171 asks for memberships in professional and scientific societies, you can stretch this to include civic and community affiliations and others, both past and present, that are remotely relevant, with dates. Specify if you were an officer or committee member, and if your involvement was extensive, describe it in a block in the work experience section.

Languages: It's best to omit languages in which your skills are so rusty you would be hard-pressed to perform on the job.

Honors, Awards, and Fellowships: List letters of commendation, recognitions, certificates, and exceptional salary increases based on performance, with the years they were received. For ideas, look to your employment, community, church, school, and professional or civic affiliations, and don't be modest!

References: List references who can attest to your work-related abilities rather than your character. While you are not allowed to list the same supervisors named in your work experience blocks, you may list co-workers from paid and unpaid jobs, teachers, and, in a pinch, classmates.

CASE IN POINT

Since John Garvis realized his wife would be regularly relocating with the Federal Government, he decided to simplify his life by joining her as a federal employee. Recalling the application process, he says, "Getting a government job was a matter of the utmost importance to me. I spent hours on the application form, and my efforts really paid off. After being hired as a management analyst, I learned that the way I presented my special qualifications impressed the reviewers." After page 3 of his SF171, John had attached a page that included the following information:

```
John Garvis                             213-34-4068


Special Qualifications, Skills, and Accomplishments

Computer Skills
     • Word processing skills using MultiMate and
       Wordstar on IBM-PC.
     • Experienced at using personal accounting
       packages and financial spreadsheets.

Public Speaking
     • Participated on three panels for Little Rock
       Chamber of Commerce.
     • Led four workshops for Abacon Associates on the
       techniques of supervising entry-level employees.
     • Run monthly meetings of condominium members.
     • Taught groups of 10 to 15 nine-year-olds for two
       years at weekly church school.

Writing Experience
     • Wrote 20-page affirmative action program for
       Haas, Inc.
     • Developed eight pages of handouts for partici-
       pants in Abacon workshops.
     • Wrote promotional literature for academic
       enrichment program.
     • As a member of a team, contributed to four
       proposals for government contract work.

Memberships
     American Management Association
     National Association of Credit Management
```

Page 4: Background Information: Additional Space for Answers; Signature, Certification, and Release of Information

Read this last page carefully and answer *yes* or *no* to the questions. Use the spaces provided to explain your *yeses*, or, if explanations are lengthy, use a separate piece of paper. Because each copy must be individually signed and dated, do not sign your original.

If an agency requests that you submit a performance appraisal with your SF171 and you do not have one, you can get a letter of evaluation from a previous employer, or get a blank appraisal from an agency and send it to a previous employer to complete.

After You Complete the SF171

After your SF171 is evaluated, you will receive a notice informing you whether or not your experience is acceptable for the level for which you applied and how long your name will remain on the agency referral list. If you have questions about the evaluation of your SF171 or if your name, address, or preferred work location has changed, contact the office that reviewed your form.

Several months before your eligibility is scheduled to expire, you can request that the office extend it. In any contact you make with OPM offices, give your full name, date of birth, social security number, and the level for which you applied.

15

Interviewing With Confidence

Job interviewing — probably the most important aspect of all the job-search activities — is dreaded by many job seekers. As a relocating spouse with several strikes against you already, you may feel particularly vulnerable when sitting face-to-face with an employer. Yet, by thinking through your particular situation, you can prepare for the difficult questions in your interviewing encounters. And take heart: effective interviewing is a skill that improves with time and practice, and employers, too, have fears about the interviewing process.

YOUR GOAL IN AN INTERVIEW

During an interview, your goal is to find out as much as you can about a job while presenting yourself as positively as possible. It is your responsibility to steer your interviews in the direction you want them to go. You will be most successful when you have a firm understanding of your qualifications and employment goals and can effectively relate them to employers' requirements.

According to Richard Bolles, employers want answers to four basic questions in interviews:

1. "Why are you here?" (Translation: "What *in particular* attracted you to this organization?")
2. "What can you *do* for me?" (Translation: "Do you know

about yourself?") You will be able to respond to this question if you have completed the self-assessment exercises in Chapters 1 and 2. Be prepared to describe how your skills could be used to solve employers' problems.

3. "What kind of person are you?" (Translation: "Will you fit in and get along with others in the organization?") Be prepared to communicate some of your important personal traits as revealed in Chapter 2.

4. "How much would it cost me to hire you?" Prepare for this question by finding the general salary range for the job you are applying for and determining the minimum amount you will accept.

Employers may ask their questions directly or indirectly in an interview. The information in this chapter will help you respond.

CASE IN POINT

Soon after relocating to Chicago, Joanne Baskerville learned that a major trade association had a nine-month contract job for a conference coordinator. She sent off her resume, and soon the association contacted her for an interview. Before her appointment, Joanne did two things: (1) she refreshed her memory on her relevant skills by reviewing her self-assessment data and past resumes, and (2) she got in touch with a very good friend who had held a similar position in the past. After spending an hour and a half on the telephone with her friend, Joanne had reviewed the skills required for conference coordination and was prepared to tackle the interview with a list of appropriate questions.

Joanna reports that her foresight paid off: "I was able to discuss the job knowledgeably. I got the job and was paid at my salary level. I recruited staff; I set up the office; I arranged everything. I did my homework on that one, and, in a sense, enhanced an available opportunity."

HOMEWORK THAT PUTS YOU A STEP AHEAD

Most of your work for a job interview takes place before you are actually face-to-face with the employer. By following these steps, you will put yourself well ahead of your competition:

Call ahead to learn the name, title, and level of responsibility of the person or persons with whom you will be talking. This will prepare you in the event a panel interview is scheduled. Although panel interviews may seem frightening initially, they have some advantages over interviews conducted by one person: you may be able to get more information about the organization, and, because there is less chance for subjectivity, your odds are better for creating a favorable impression with at least some of those interviewing you.

Familiarize yourself with important points about the organization, including length of time in business, products or services, growth and trends, and training programs. As described in Chapter 6, you can do this by reading annual reports, company brochures, trade journals, business periodicals, and directories. Your familiarity with the organization will impress your interviewers and allow more time to discuss your qualifications and job details.

CASE IN POINT

Concurrent with her move from Kansas to Maryland, Sheila Simpson decided to leave day-care teaching for something more lucrative in the profit-making world. She found an appealing employment ad for a sales representative with a cosmetics firm, and, as the ad directed, she telephoned to arrange for an interview. After a brief screening over the phone, Sheila was scheduled to meet with the sales director the following week.

Remembering the advice she had heard in a career development course, Sheila spent a few hours in the public library learning about the firm before going on the interview. She says, "I discovered how many divisions the company has and where they are located, when it was founded, the name of the chief executive officer, and all about the product lines. When I got to the interview, the first question the sales director asked me was 'What do you know about our organization?' In answering the question, I gave details even he did not know."

Sheila was the only applicant invited back for a second round of interviews. She got the job and received a promotion sooner than she had expected.

Write out and memorize important and specific points about what you can do for an employer. For help with this process, refer to the "Model for Documenting Experience" or to your completed job description records, both of which are in Chapter 1. At a minimum, include an adverb, verb, and object; for example, "Effectively analyze statistical data," or "Quickly and accurately type

INTERVIEWING WITH CONFIDENCE 195

documents using word processors." As these sentences reveal, self-evaluating words that were verboten on resumes are acceptable in interviews.

You may want to take something to the interview that underscores your enthusiasm for the position and shows your uniqueness.

CASE IN POINT

Before meeting with a new West Coast publisher, Mary Abrams, a managing editor, composed a list of 10 ways she could make their magazine a success. The following is a partial list of what she presented to her prospective employer as the interview came to a close:

- Establish smooth copy-flow systems and schedules for each phase, from story planning to printing.
- Serve as a link between editors and art department.
- Develop a style book that reflects the nature of the magazine and its readership as well as the editors' consensus.
- Conduct an editorial readership survey to assess charter subscribers' response to early issues and to define readers' needs.
- Infect others with enthusiasm, exuberance, energy, and dedication at a time when stress typically runs high.

Know exactly what you want to say and don't want to say during an interview. Anticipate questions about problem areas in your record and be prepared to respond to them. Review your resume, and write out and memorize answers to difficult questions. Rehearse your answers as you are driving your car or standing in front of a mirror, and role-play interviewing situations with your spouse or a friend. With practice, you will become more relaxed and confident about answering questions that initially seemed difficult. For examples of questions employers may ask relocating spouses, refer to the list here, and for optional ways to respond, turn to the end of the chapter.

1. Tell me about yourself.
2. Why do you want to work for us?
3. What kind of work are you looking for?
4. Why did you leave your last job?
5. What does your husband (or wife) do?
6. What are the most important factors you require in a job?

7. How is your experience relevant to the job you are applying for here at our organization?
8. What do you consider to be your outstanding achievements?
9. Describe a time when you felt particularly effective.
10. What do you consider to be your greatest strengths? Weaknesses?
11. Most people have some long-range goals and objectives. Where do you want to be in the next 5 to 10 years?
12. What are your salary expectations for this position?
13. Based on the number of places you have lived, I prsesume your husband (or wife) is _____ (with ABC Corporation, in the military, in the Foreign Service, etc.). How long are you going to be here?
14. I don't normally hire _____ (corporate, military, foreign service, etc.) spouses. Why should I hire you?

According to the Equal Employment Opportunity Commission, there are no illegal interviewing questions per se, but employers cannot use the responses to non-job-related questions to discriminate against broad categories of applicants. If an organization has a written policy showing that a particular factor is necessary for job performance, the policy must be applied equally to all categories of applicants; for example, males and females, blacks and whites. With respect to individuals 40 to 70 years old, employers cannot deny employment on the basis of age, according to the Age Discrimination in Employment Act of 1967, as amended.

The following list includes subject areas that could discriminate against applicants.

- Age ("How old are you?")
- Religion ("What is your religious background?")
- Your sex; unless sex is a bona fide occupational qualification, the interviewer should not make comments that imply your sex may be used to eliminate you from consideration.
- Marital status ("Are you married?", "Are you divorced?", "Are you single?")
- Children ("Do you have children at home?" "How old are your children?" "Who cares for them?" "Do you plan to have more children?")
- Physical data ("How tall are you?" "How much do you weigh?" "Do you have any physical or mental handicaps?")
- Housing ("Do you own your home?" "Do you rent?" "Do you live in an apartment or a house?")

When you are interviewed by individuals working outside of personnel departments, they may be unaware these subjects should be avoided. Therefore, they may unknowingly ask you questions on sensitive areas as they engage you in casual conversation in an effort to get to know you. You can respond in one of several ways:

1. Answer the question, possibly in a general and light manner. Demonstrate through your answer that the factor in question would not detract from your ability to do the job. The following are examples: "I am in my mid-forties, and accomplish twice what I did in my twenties," "My children are six and eight and have a marvelous sitter."
2. After repeating the question, answer it with humor and then lightly ask your interviewer the same questions. Consider the two examples that follow:

- "How old am I? I'll be 39 forever. And how about you?"
- "Do I have children at home? I have three and a wonderful sitter who lives next door. Do you have children?"

3. Instead of answering the question, say, "I think that is not relevant to the requirements of the position."
4. Show annoyance, refuse to respond, and contact the nearest Equal Employment Opportunity Commission office.

If an interviewer's questions become too personal, consider whether or not you want to work for someone who is so concerned about that aspect of your life. If you do want the job, however, you may want to respond in the first or second way. The third response may put off an employer and indicate you have something to hide. Whatever your answer, you can follow it up with a question on another subject to divert your interviewer.

If you sense that an employer would like the answer to a question but realizes it should be avoided, consider voluntarily providing the information.

CASE IN POINT

After moving to California, Connie Talbot interviewed for a part-time waitressing job in an elegant, 150-seat Mexican restaurant. The hours of work were 6 p.m. to 10:30 p.m., three evenings a week.

Connie sensed that her interviewer was concerned about his employees' frequent absences. It was obvious to the interviewer that Connie was new to the San Diego area, lived 15 miles from the job, was married, and might have young children at home. Instead of ignoring the employer's concern, Connie confronted it by saying, "You needn't worry about my being late or absent from work. I have a very helpful husband who is home from work by 5 p.m., and I have excellent back-up assistance in the event he can't get home before I must leave." When Connie said this, she detected a sigh of relief from her interviewer, and soon thereafter he told her the job was hers.

Develop a list of well-thought-out questions for your interviewer. Part of the purpose for an interview is to find out about the organization and the position. Develop a list of your own questions to help you determine the following: Will the job use the skills you most enjoy? Will it provide you with opportunities for advancement? Is the environment the kind in which you want to work? Is the turnover at a reasonable level? For examples of questions to ask interviewers, refer to the accompanying list.

- Why do you want to hire someone for this position? Is it a newly created job, or did the previous employee leave? Why?
- How many people have had this position in the last six years? Where have they gone within the organization? Outside the organization?
- Is there a job description for this position? If so, may I see it?
- Would you please describe the duties and responsibilities of the job as you see them?
- What are the qualities you want in the person who fills this job?
- What is the potential for growth in this job?
- Would you mind sharing the things you like most and least about working in this organization?
- Are you interviewing many people for this position?
- When can I expect to hear from you?

Add at least 5 to 10 more questions that pertain to your specific situation.

Your questions will help you to focus your own thoughts and to steer the interview in the direction you want it to go. Used effectively, they may divert an interviewer from the negative line of questioning you may encounter as a relocating spouse. It is acceptable to keep your list of questions at hand and refer to it occasionally during an interview.

Calculate the rock-bottom salary you can afford, and decide how much the job and experience are worth to you in the long run. Be aware that almost every salary is negotiable, and that absurdly low aspirations may even disqualify you. While you can always back down after naming a high figure, you will find it all but impossible to come up from a low rate. To get the best results, estimate the employer's range before you negotiate by referring to a variety of sources, such as the following:

- your local contacts
- personnel departments — salary ranges for a field of work may be offered upon request
- *American Almanac for Jobs and Salaries*
- employment ads
- employment agencies and recruiters
- *Occupational Outlook Handbook*
- trade journals and other publications in your field

For resources on salary negotiation refer to Appendix C.

Know well ahead of the interview what you are going to wear, and make sure your total appearance is appropriate to the job and organization to which you are applying. "Appropriate" will have different meanings in different regions and in different seasons. Moreover, dress codes vary depending on whether an organization is a large or small corporation, a college or university, or in the public or private sector. Be aware that, for the same level of job and with the same outfit, you could be perceived as projecting too much power in one environment and too little in another. One way to discover what is appropriate for a particular organization is to stop by a few days before your interview to see how the employees dress. A well-thought-out investment in an interviewing outfit is money well spent because you will be more effective in interviews when you are confident about how you look. Since you probably will not know your interviewer, a good rule is to be conservative.

Assemble relevant employment information to take to your interviews. In preparation for completing application forms, you will need the exact dates of your past employment, salaries, employers' names, and your social security number. Take a list of references or letters of recommendation — copies, not originals — and copies of your resume. Check your work portfolio for any other documents you might need to bring along.

> **CASE IN POINT**
>
> When Walter Best interviewed for his job as program director at a community college in the East, he took along brochures that he had developed while doing volunteer work for a religious organization and while working on a federal government grant. The brochures included course descriptions similar to those in the tabloids published by the department with which he was interviewing, so he brought a copy of the department's publication as well.
>
> Walter says, "My brochures were striking and were visual evidence that I had been doing something relevant. The other program directors were impressed that I was so familiar with their course publication and had brought it with me. This was a simple and obvious thing, but they told me afterward that other people had not bothered with it. They hadn't known the courses or programs offered, and they didn't have ideas about new ones. It is difficult for me to imagine how someone could go to an interview without that kind of background information."

Know exactly how to get to your interviews, and be prepared to arrive early and stay late. Take some time before your interviews to learn the best route, how long it will take, and where to park. By arriving early, you will be more relaxed and can spend time evaluating the work environment, taking your time with application forms, rereading your resume, and talking with the receptionist. Do not schedule appointments too close together. If you are nervous about missing other engagements, you may have difficulty being effective in your interview.

FACE-TO-FACE WITH THE INTERVIEWER

If you enter an interview thoroughly prepared, having completed the items specified in the previous section, the actual interview is more likely to be successful, especially if you very carefully follow these steps.

1. Be nice to *everyone*, because interviews begin from the time you are in sight of the facility you are visiting. Comments from even the lowest-level employees in organizations can influence hiring decisions.

INTERVIEWING WITH CONFIDENCE　　　　　　　　　　　　　　　　　　201

CASE IN POINT

After her second round of interviews for a personnel job with a prestigious trade association, Lucy Heims received some very disturbing feedback. "Ten days had gone by, and I hadn't heard from the personnel director so I phoned repeatedly," says Lucy. "When I finally reached her, she reluctantly told me the receptionist had been put out by my behavior the day of my second interview. The receptionist had said I showed irritation when told my interviewers weren't readily available to see me."

Lucy was shocked by what she heard and realized she had lost her chance at a very attractive job. She recalled how she had rushed to the interview on a 90° August afternoon after finally finding a parking place in downtown Chicago: "I was exhausted and, therefore, delighted to have a few minutes to cool off, gather my thoughts, and make some final notes before coming face to face with a department head. Perhaps my preoccupation offended the receptionist."

Now a successful real estate agent in St. Louis, Lucy says, "While I still have trouble accepting that a receptionist's subjective impressions had so much influence, it's a possibility I won't ignore in the future."

---

2. To establish rapport, try to shake hands (firmly) and smile while looking your interviewer in the eye.

3. Get comfortable before your interview begins, so you will be more effective during the interview. For example, if the sun is in your eyes, ask if you may move your chair.

4. Think of your interview as a two-way conversation rather than just a time to sit back and respond to an employer's questions. Take some responsibility for leading your interviews where you want them to go. Since you are unlikely to get the job if your interviewer learns too little about you, make an effort to talk for more than 50 percent of the time.

5. Listen very carefully as employers reveal new factors for you to address, and then relate your past experience in a manner that shows you have potential for solving employers' problems. But never assume an attitude of having all the answers.

6. Do not volunteer negative information about yourself, and never deal in personalities; for example, do not criticize a past supervisor.

7. Because it conveys important information to interviewers, be aware of your nonverbal communication such as eye contact and posture. Avoid fidgeting, smoking, and gum chewing. Maintain a reasonable amount of eye contact without staring an interviewer

down. Use an attentive posture, and put energy into your interviews. Smile and be sincere.

8. Be alert to clues to areas that may be important to you, including work environment, staff turnover, and personality traits of supervisors and colleagues.

9. Try to delay money talk until you sense the employer's mind is made up about hiring you. To determine the employer's state of mind, say, "Before we discuss salary, tell me about your objectives and how I might fit in." Then, after communicating how you can meet the organization's requirements, you will be worth more in the interviewer's eyes when salary is discussed. Do not be the first one to raise the issue of salary, especially in the first interview. When the employer brings it up, the following approach will work to your advantage:

- If the employer names a salary range, build a rationale for the higher end.
- If the employer avoids naming a salary and asks you to name one, you might say, "It depends on the fringe benefits," or "What do you pay others in this category?"
- If you are pushed to name a salary, specify a range rather than one figure.
- Never answer in terms of how much you need; instead, talk about how much you are worth — your accomplishments, productivity, efficiency, and what you can do to make life easier for the employer.

10. If mutual interest develops between you and the employer, offer your list of references or written recommendations.

11. Do not accept or reject a job offer on the spot, whether the offer is made during an interview or later. It is good practice to sleep on a decision of such importance, and discuss it with someone close to you. Say for example, "I need time to think this over and will get back to you in two (or three) days."

Before giving a final answer to an employer, consider all your priorities. If you need answers to more questions, do not hestitate to recontact the company. Ask yourself:

- Do I understand exactly what I would be doing if I took the job?
- Have I met the person I would be working for?
- Do I know where I would be sitting?

INTERVIEWING WITH CONFIDENCE

- Do I know what the benefits are and how often my salary will be reviewed?

12. Before leaving an interview, to avoid being left hanging, ask when you can expect to hear from the interviewer about a decision.

FOLLOWING UP

If you are inexperienced at interviewing or out of practice, think of your initial interviews as learning experiences. Evaluate your mistakes by jotting down anything you think you did incorrectly and failed to convey. If you correct these the next time you go on an interview, your interviewing skills will improve.

Send a brief follow-up letter to thank your interviewer. While guarding against going overboard, stress points in your background that qualify you for the position, and review any strengths you forgot to mention during your interview. You might want to send a copy of materials, such as a report, that exemplify your competencies. When you have interviewed with employees from several departments — for example, personnel and purchasing — send a thank-you letter to the interviewers from each of the departments. As a guide, use the Reems letter near the end of the chapter.

If you believe a superior recommendation would improve your chances of getting a job for which you have interviewed, you could ask one of your references to call or write the prospective employer about your excellent qualifications.

If you are not contacted within a week of the time the employer said you would be notified, telephone to restate your interest and to find out when a decision is expected.

If, after all you've done, you are rejected, there are still a few things left to do — things your competition may not bother with:

- Telephone to thank your interviewer for his or her time and efforts on your behalf and try to find out why you were not hired. While many job seekers call out of sheer curiosity, others seek information to help them improve their interviewing skills. You may or may not learn the real reasons for your rejection, but it is worth a try.
- To keep your name coming across the employer's desk, write a letter that expresses your continued interest and hope for future contacts. As a guide, use the Bacon letter later in this chapter. If the employer's first choice fails to work out, you may have a chance to be hired.

If, after all your hard work, you have the good fortune of being selected for a position, be sure the specifics are in writing. Richard Irish, in *Go Hire Yourself An Employer*, advises applicants not to accept a job until salary and meaningful fringe benefits have been agreed upon and clearly written out in an *employment agreement* describing details of employment (including time of your salary review). If such a letter isn't forthcoming from the employer, write one of your own that formally accepts the position and restates all verbal agreements. This letter will go into your personnel file and prevent misunderstandings in the event the individual who hired you forgets his or her promises or leaves the company. Keep a copy of the letter for your own files. Use the Rosenberg letter near the end of this chapter as a guide.

Thank-You Letter Following an Interview

3954 El Camino Real
Palo Alto, California 94301
October 21, 198_

Ms. Jeanette Reems
Director of Purchasing
Centron International, Inc.
19 Santa Cruz Avenue
Menlo Park, California 94025

Dear Ms. Reems:

    I want to thank you for the time you spent with me on Monday describing the activities of the Purchasing Department and your requirements for additional staff.

    I am enthusiastic about the prospects of working for Centron and believe that my experience is very relevant to your needs -- especially my most recent work as a buyer at Cebulex. I have enclosed a copy of an annual inventory report I developed for the company's president. From this, you will be able to see the various aspects of purchasing I coordinated during my employment there.

    Please contact me if you want more information about my education or experience. In the meantime, please thank Mr. Rosen and the other members of your staff for the tour of your facilities. I will be out of town between November 1 and 5, but otherwise you can reach me at the numbers I gave you at our meeting. I look forward to being in touch.

Sincerely,

Francis B. Bartlett

Enclosure

Letter Sent to an Interviewer After Being Rejected

12 Alameda Boulevard
Oklahoma City, Oklahoma 73127
June 17, 198_

Mr. Milton Bacon
Chief of Support Services
Elkins & Elkins, Inc.
41 Appian Way
Oklahoma City, Oklahoma 73130

Dear Mr. Bacon:

    I understand you were faced with a difficult decision in choosing between me and the applicant you finally selected for the new position in your department. While this has not turned out to be the right time for my employment with you, I continue to be enthusiastic about Elkins & Elkins and its production coordination activities.

    Since we last met two weeks ago, I have been investigating a variety of ways to approach the quality control problems you portrayed. Although I am sure you are aware of the new Strathmore techniques, have you considered the Bitcom strategies as described in Boynton Balasar's new book, <u>Quality Control Systems for A New Age</u>? At your convenience, I would welcome an opportunity to discuss this book and my other research findings with you.

    I want to thank you again for your time and consideration throughout our past meetings. I will look forward to being in touch soon.

                                          Sincerely,

                                          Barbara A. Jaffrey

Letter Sent After Receiving an Offer of Employment

3124 Euclid Place
Portland, Maine 04104
February 22, 198_

Ms. Amanda Rosenberg
Personnel Administrator
Floral Design Center
21 Academy Lane
Portsmouth, New Hampshire 03801

Dear Ms. Rosenberg:

I am enthusiastic about the prospect of working for James McCartin in your organization's insurance division. Before I formally accept the position, I want to confirm some of the points covered in our discussion last Thursday.

- I will begin employment with the Floral Design Center at an annual salary of $17,500. After six months of employment, Mr. McCartin will evaluate my performance and I will have an opportunity for a merit salary increase of up to 6 percent depending on the quality of my work. Six months after that, or one year from the date of my employment, Mr. McCartin will reevaluate my work, and I will have another opportunity for an salary increase of up to 6 percent. Thereafter, my salary will be reviewed on an annual basis.

- In addition to merit increases, the Floral Design Center also offers annual cost-of-living increases that have averaged from 5 to 10 percent over the past four years.

- Although FDC normally offers its employees three weeks paid vacation, I will receive 11 days during my first year of employment. Thereafter, I will be eligible for three weeks. Other paid time away from FDC includes 10 paid holidays and <u>personal time</u> for medical appointments and family emergencies.

- Additional fringe benefits include 50/50 sharing in the Blue Cross/Blue Shield Health Plan and full company financing of both life and disability insurance.

If I have understood you correctly on the above points, you can assume I have accepted the position with Mr. McCartin. Please sign the copies of this letter, and ask Mr. McCartin to do the same. Please keep copies for yourselves and mail one to me.

I look forward to working for Mr. McCartin beginning March 10. In the meantime, please telephone me if you would like to discuss any of the points raised in this letter.

Sincerely,

Lane A. Wilcox

_____   _____
Amanda Rosenberg   James McCartin

Enclosures

OPTIONAL WAYS TO RESPOND TO QUESTIONS FROM INTERVIEWERS

The numbers that follow correspond to those on pages 195 and 196.

1. Time is limited, so don't try to cover your entire life. Instead, talk about your work life, and emphasize aspects of your background that are relevant to the job at hand.

2. By thinking this through before an interview, you will put yourself ahead of your competition. This answer must be sincere and personal to you and might be related to the knowledge you gained from reading about the organization (this is where you can show off how well-prepared you are).

3. If you don't know the answer to this question, you are not ready to go on job interviews; instead, you should be talking with people about your options. Don't expect employers to look over your resumes or application forms and tell you where you would fit into their organizations — that's your responsibility.

4. You can name any number of things, including:

- to move ahead in my field
- the project I was working on came to completion
- reduction in force, relocation, financial advancement
- to pursue work-related training
- to devote some time to self-development
- to take some time away from the work world to reevaluate my career in preparation for pursuing a new line of work.

5. This kind of question is not relevant to the job, and you could say just that. However, to avoid offending the employer, you may want to answer the question directly. Then immediately come forth with one of the well-thought-out questions you developed just for this purpose. (Be sure to have a long list of questions, so you don't run out.) An alternative to naming your spouse's position is to specify the organization he or she works for; for example, "My wife works for the Federal Government." If you do name an occupation, give a generic answer; for example, when the spouse is an officer in the military, say, "My husband is an administrator of a scientific laboratory," "My wife manages a staff of 50 employees," or "My husband is a technical specialist."

6. Think about the factors ahead of time and clearly state them, keeping in mind that you don't want to be demanding. They should be in line with what the job can offer; otherwise, don't pursue it. Your research before the interview may have given you some tips about this.

7. Again, by thinking this through ahead of time and by learning about the company, you will be able to answer this question easily. But to build on your prior research, try to get the interviewer to tell you about the organization and the job before you answer this question. Then describe *specific*, pertinent responsibilities in sufficient detail so the interviewer can understand what you did.

INTERVIEWING WITH CONFIDENCE

8. Be prepared to name and describe some specific work-related accomplishments that have some relevance to the job for which you are applying. Ideally, they will be some things you enjoyed and would like doing again.

9. Name something job related that will make an employer think you could do the same thing for him or her. Think this out ahead of time, write it down on paper, memorize it, and rehearse it in front of a mirror. Since most other applicants won't bother to prepare so carefully, this attention to detail may very well get you a job.

10. Think of those job-related qualities that may enhance your image in the eyes of an employer. This is not a time to be humble. Remember that no one will know about your positive attributes if you don't tell them. Since everyone has some weaknesses, be prepared to name something. It is particularly effective when you can turn a weakness into a strength. Consider these examples:

- "I get very frustrated when I can't see the end of a project. I am not satisfied until I can see it to completion."
- "I put a lot of pressure on myself to do perfect work, and I tend to have the same high standards for others I work with. That tendency sometimes comes out as impatience."

11. Don't let this question overwhelm you; many professionals employed for years don't have long-range goals. Sometimes interviewers are just trying to get you to talk or see how you would handle such a question. Consider variations to these responses:

- "It has always been very important to me to do the best possible job and to continue growing and achieving. With this attitude, in 5 to 10 years I assume I will be moving steadily ahead."
- "Since each new position brings fresh opportunities and I am the type of person who does not let favorable opportunities pass me by, I cannot name my exact work goals at this time. However, because of my drive and initiative, I am confident I will be competent in my field of work."

Of course, if you know exactly what your long-range goals are, name them.

12. If you have done your homework, this question should not throw you. However, it is preferable to get the interviewer to name a figure first. You could respond, "What is the range that you pay your employees doing this type of work?" Then, if the interviewer names a range, you can state why you feel you should be near the top (if you think you deserve that, based on your abilities and experience). Many employers will try to get you to name a figure first. When that happens, name a range when possible. You could say that you are primarily interested in the nature of the job and are confident that salary can be worked out when mutual interest develops (if salary is raised early in an interview). Always be realistic about salary expectations in terms of your qualifications.

Sometimes, if the salary offered is lower than your expectations, you can work out an arrangement for an early review. In any case, find out when salary reviews take place; get this and any other special arrangements in writing.

13. As a relocating spouse, you probably dread this question, yet the average length of time that even nonrelocated employees stay with jobs is relatively short these days. Familiarity with statistics on local employee turnover may enable you to make a better case for your possibly abbreviated stay. These statistics may be available from local groups such as an economic development commission or a chamber of commerce.

If you are empathetic, you may be more successful at winning over employers; for example, "You are concerned that I won't be able to fulfill the requirements of the job. I can understand that." Follow this up with a response such as these:

- "Here's why I expect to be able to fulfill the requirements of the job..."
- "This job sounds very attractive to me, and I look forward to staying as long as possible."
- "I have no plans to move again."

After giving a brief response, get the interviewer off the subject with one of your own questions. In addition, be prepared to convince the employer that you would be a valuable employee (see number 14).

14. You might show empathy with the employer about not wanting a short-term employee, and then add that you are not the average relocating spouse. Be prepared to offer convincing reasons about how and why your skills and attributes would be very valuable to the organization. (Also draw on the responses provided in number 13).

Epilogue

With the guidance of this book, you have successfully progressed through four of the crucial levels of work and life decision-making: self-assessment, exploration, choosing, and taking action.

What next?

Level V of this process is *adjusting to transition* — after you make a change of any kind, you need to get accustomed to it and grow with it. Since relocation is likely to set one's career back somewhat, you may be especially eager to move ahead quickly after reestablishing yourself in your new position. The following guidelines will help you make the most of your growth potential:

- Based on your self-assessed priorities, devise and follow a plan for developing within your position.
- Communicate well orally and in writing with your work associates, both inside and outside your organization, who may directly or indirectly have the power to influence your career. Do not miss opportunities for effectively presenting your work.
- Develop sharp analytical skills and the ability to present concise and convincing solutions to problems. Avoid presenting problems without suggestions for solving them.
- Be productive and increase your visibility and influence by offering your assistance to others outside your immediate area.
- Be willing to consider and embrace new ideas and methods.
- Develop technological literacy.
- Keep yourself up-to-date: Be well-read in your field. Enroll

in challenging courses or workshops. Be active in work-related organizations and other groups. Network to develop contacts outside of your place of employment.
- After identifying what you need in terms of guidance and support, invite mentoring from a variety of people, both inside and outside your organization, who can contribute to your career development.
- Learn about all aspects of your organization and demonstrate your understanding of and interest in it: Circulate and meet everyone you can within your department, division, or the entire organization. Develop mutually supportive relationships with employees on all levels.
- Apply good interpersonal skills with everyone you meet, including co-workers, supervisors, subordinates, and outside contacts.
- Demonstrate a caring, respectful attitude toward people of all backgrounds and on all levels. When living and working abroad, appreciate and adapt to the culture and customs.

Eventually, you, your job, or your status will change, and you will feel the need for *reevaluation*. It may be when you are approaching another relocation or have outgrown your job. When you reach this point – level VI of the decision-making process – it's time to repeat the cycle, beginning with the self-assessment exercises at level I. So, in one sense, this book is ending where it began.

> *. . . do you not see how everything that happens keeps on being a beginning*
>
> Rainer Maria Rilke

Appendix A

Federal Job Information/Testing Centers

The offices listed below provide general information on federal employment, explain how to apply for specific jobs, supply application materials, and conduct written examinations when required. This information is available by mail, by telephone, or by visiting an Office of Personnel Management (OPM) field office.

Alabama: Bldg. 600, Suite 341, 3322 Memorial Pkwy., Huntsville, AL 35801-5311, 205-544-5802.

Alaska: Federal Bldg., 701 C St., PO Box 22, Anchorage, AK 99513, 907-271-5821.

Arizona: U.S. Postal Service Bldg., 522 N. Central Ave., Rm. 120, Phoenix, AZ 85004, 602-261-4736.

Arkansas: (see Oklahoma listing).

California: Linder Bldg., Third Floor, 845 S. Figueroa, Los Angeles, CA 90017, 213-894-3360; 1029 J St., Second Floor, Sacramento, CA 95814, 916-551-1464; Federal Bldg., Rm. 4 S-9, 880 Front St., San Diego, CA 92188, 619-557-6165; PO Box 7405, San Francisco, CA 94120, 415-974-9725 (located at 211 Main St., Second Floor, Rm. 235).

Colorado: PO Box 25167, Denver, CO 80225, 303-236-4160 (located at 12345

W. Alameda Pkwy., Lakewood, CO). For job information in the following states, call: Montana, 303-236-4162; Utah, 303-236-4165; Wyoming, 303-236-4166.

Connecticut: Federal Bldg., Rm. 613, 450 Main St., Hartford, CT 06103, 203-240-3263.

Delaware: (see Philadelphia listing).

District Of Columbia: 1900 E St., N.W., Washington, DC 20415, 202-653-8468.

Florida: Commodore Bldg., Suite 150, 3444 McCrory Pl., Orlando, FL 32803-3701, 407-648-6148.

Georgia: Richard B. Russell Federal Bldg., Rm. 960, 75 Spring St., S.W., Atlanta, GA 30303, 404-331-4315.

Guam: Pacific Daily News Bldg., 238 O'Hara St., Rm. 902, Agana, GU 96910, 671-472-7451.

Hawaii: (all Hawaiian Islands and Overseas) Federal Bldg., Rm. 5216, 300 Ala Moana Blvd., Honolulu, HI 96850, 808-541-2791 and 808-541-2784 (overseas jobs).

Idaho: (see Washington listing).

Illinois: 175 W. Jackson Blvd., Rm. 530, Chicago, IL 60604, 312-353-6192.

Indiana: Minton-Capehart Federal Bldg., 575 N. Pennsylvania Ave., Indianapolis, IN 46204, 317-269-7161.

Iowa: (see Missouri listing — 816-426-7757).

Kansas: One-Twenty Bldg., Rm. 101, 120 S. Market St., Wichita, KS 67202, 316-269-6794. In Johnson, Leavenworth, and Wyandotte Counties call 816-426-5702.

Kentucky: (see Ohio listing).

Louisiana: 1515 Poydras St., Suite 608, New Orleans, LA 70112, 504-589-2764.

Maine: (see New Hampshire listing).

Maryland: Garmatz Federal Bldg., 101 W. Lombard St., Baltimore, MD 21202,

APPENDIX A   **215**

301-962-3833. If in the DC Metro area, contact the District of Columbia office.

Massachusetts: Thomas P. O'Neill Federal Bldg., 10 Causeway St., Boston, MA 02222-1031, 617-565-5900.

Michigan: 477 Michigan Ave., Rm. 565, Detroit, MI 48226, 313-226-6950.

Minnesota: Federal Bldg., Ft. Snelling, Twin Cities, MN 55111, 612-725-3430.

Mississippi: (see Alabama listing).

Missouri: Federal Bldg., Rm. 134, 601 E. 12th St., Kansas City, MO 64106, 816-426-5702; Old Post Office, Rm. 400, 815 Olive St., St. Louis, MO 63101, 314-539-2285.

Montana: (see Colorado listing).

Nebraska: (see Kansas listing).

Nevada: (see Sacramento, CA listing).

New Hampshire: Thomas J. McIntyre Federal Bldg., Rm. 104, 80 Daniel St., Portsmouth, NH 03801-3879, 603-431-7115.

New Jersey: Peter W. Rodino, Jr., Federal Bldg., 970 Broad St., Newark, NJ 07102, 201-645-3673. In Camden, call 215-597-7440.

New Mexico: Federal Bldg., 421 Gold Ave., S.W., Albuquerque, NM 87102, 505-766-5583. In Dona Ana, Otero and El Paso Counties, call 505-766-1893.

New York: Jacob K. Javits Federal Bldg., 26 Federal Plaza, New York City, NY 10278, 212-264-0422; James M. Hanley Federal Bldg., 100 S. Clinton St., Syracuse, NY 13260, 315-423-5660.

North Carolina: Federal Bldg., 4565 Fall Neuse Rd., PO Box 25069, Raleigh, NC 27609, 919-856-4361.

North Dakota: (see Minnesota listing).

Ohio: Federal Bldg., 200 W. Second St., Rm. 506, Dayton, OH 45402, 513-225-2720.

Oklahoma: 200 N.W. Fifth St., Second Floor, Oklahoma City, OK 73102, 405-

231-4948 (mail or phone only).

Oregon: Federal Bldg., Rm 376, 1220 S.W. Third St., Portland, OR 97204, 503-221-3141.

Pennsylvania: Federal Bldg., Rm. 168, PO Box 761, 228 Walnut St., Harrisburg, PA 17108, 717-782-4494; Wm. J. Green, Jr., Federal Bldg., 600 Arch St., Rm. 1416, Philadelphia, PA 19106, 215-597-7440; Federal Bldg., 1000 Liberty Ave., Rm. 119, Pittsburgh, PA 15222, 412-644-2755.

Puerto Rico: Frederico Degetau Federal Bldg., Carlos E. Chardon St., Hato Rey, PR 00918, 809-766-5242.

Rhode Island: John O. Pastori Federal Bldg., Rm. 310, Kennedy Plaza, Providence, RI 02903, 401-528-5251.

South Carolina: (see North Carolina listing).

South Dakota: (see Minnesota listing).

Tennessee: 200 Jefferson Ave., Suite 1312, Memphis TN 38103-2335, 901-521-3956.

Texas: Room 6B12, 1100 Commerce St., Dallas, TX 75242, 214-767-8035 (mail or phone only); Houston, 713-226-2375, (phone-recording only); 643 E. Durango Blvd., San Antonio, TX 78206, 512-229-6600 or 229-6611 (mail or phone only).

Utah: (see Colorado listing).

Vermont: (see New Hampshire listing).

Virginia: Federal Bldg., Rm. 220, 200 Granby St., Norfolk, VA 23510-1886, 804-441-3355. If in DC Metro Area, contact District of Columbia office.

Washington: Federal Bldg., 915 Second Ave., Seattle, WA 98174, 206-442-4365.

West Virginia: (see Ohio listing).

Wisconsin: Residents in counties of Gray, Iowa, Lafayette, Dane, Green, Rock, Jefferson, Walworth, Waukesha, Racine, Kenosha and Milwaukee should call 312-353-6189 for job information. Residents of other counties should refer to the Minnesota listing.

Wyoming: (see Colorado listing).

Appendix B
Networks and Other Groups

While the following groups serve a variety of purposes, most provide information about careers, including training requirements and job duties, salaries, and future opportunities. Many of these organizations provide memberships that offer the benefits described in Chapter 12.

The groups are listed alphabetically within 17 categories, the last one of which is reserved for general and miscellaneous organizations. Other helpful groups mentioned throughout this guide are not repeated in the listing that follows.

ADMINISTRATIVE AND MANAGERIAL OCCUPATIONS

American Bankers Association: Bank Personnel Division, 1120 Connecticut Ave., N.W., Washington, DC 20036, 202-663-5000.

American Management Association: 135 W. 50th St., New York, NY 10020, 212-586-8100.

American Society For Personnel Administration: 606 N. Washington St., Alexandria, VA 22314, 703-548-3440.

American Society Of Women Accountants: 35 E. Wacker Dr., Suite 2250, Chicago, IL 60601, 312-726-9030.

American Woman's Society Of Certified Public Accountants: 111 E. Wacker Dr., Chicago, IL 60601, 312-644-6610.

Association For Volunteer Administration: PO Box 4584, Boulder, CO 80306, 303-497-0238.

International Association For Financial Planning, Inc.: Two Concourse Pkwy., Suite 800, Atlanta, GA 30328, 404-395-1605.

National Association Of Bank Women, Inc.: 500 N. Michigan Ave., Suite 1400, Chicago, IL 60611, 312-661-1700.

National Association Of Credit Management: 520 Eighth Ave., New York, NY 10018-5070, 212-947-5070.

National Association For Female Executives: 1041 Third Ave., Second Floor, New York, NY 10021, 212-371-0740.

National Association Of Purchasing Management, Inc.: 2055 East Centennial Circle, PO Box 22160, Tempe, AZ 85282-0960, 602-752-0960.

National Mass Retailing Institute: 570 Seventh Ave., New York, NY 10018, 212-354-6600.

National Society Of Fund Raising Executives: 1101 King St., Suite 3000, Alexandria, VA 22314, 703-684-0410.

ADMINISTRATIVE SUPPORT OCCUPATIONS, INCLUDING CLERICAL

Air Line Employees Association, International: 5600 S. Central Ave., Chicago, IL 60638, 312-767-3333.

Meeting Planners International: Infomart Bldg., Suite 5018, 1950 Stemmons Fwy., Dallas, TX 75207, 214-746-5222.

National Association Of Executive Secretaries: 900 S. Washington St., Suite G13, Falls Church, VA 22046-4020, 703-237-8616.

Professional Secretaries International: 301 E. Armour Blvd., Kansas City, MO 64111-1299, 816-531-7010.

THE ARTS AND ENTERTAINMENT-RELATED OCCUPATIONS

American Art Therapy Association: 505 East Hawley St., Mundelein, IL 60060-2419, 312-949-6064.

American Association Of Museums: 1225 Eye St., N.W., Washington, DC 20005, 202-289-1818.

American Association For Music Therapy: PO Box 359, 66 Morris Ave., Springfield, NJ 07081, 201-379-1100.

American Society Of Interior Designers: 1430 Broadway, New York, NY 10018, 212-944-9220.

Graphic Artists Guild (National): 11 W. 20th St., 8th Flr., New York, NY 10011, 212-463-7730.

Institute Of Business Designers: 1155 W. Merchandise Mart, Chicago, IL 60654, 312-467-1950.

National Association Of Woman Artists, Inc.: 41 Union Square, Rm. 906, New York, NY 10003, 212-675-1616.

Professional Photographers Of America, Inc.: 1090 Executive Way, Des Plaines, IL 60018, 312-299-8161.

Women's Caucus For Art: Moore College of Art, 20th & the Parkway, Philadelphia, PA 19103, 215-854-0922

COMMUNICATIONS-RELATED OCCUPATIONS

American Society Of Journalists And Authors, Inc.: 1501 Broadway, Suite 1907, New York, NY 10036, 212-997-0947.

American Women In Radio And Television, Inc.: 1101 Connecticut Ave., N.W., Suite 700, Washington, DC 20036, 202-429-5102.

Business/Professional Advertising Association: 205 E. 42nd St., New York, NY 10017, 212-661-0222.

International Association Of Business Communicators: 870 Market St., Suite 940, San Francisco, CA 94102, 415-433-3400.

International Women's Writing Guild: Box 810, Gracie Station, New York, NY 10028, 212-737-7536.

National Federation Of Press Women, Inc.: Box 99, 1105 Main St., Blue Springs, MO 64015, 816-229-1666.

National League Of American Pen Women, Inc.: 1300 17th St., N.W., Washington, DC 20036, 202-785-1997.

Public Relations Society Of America, Inc.: 33 Irving Pl., Third Flr., New York, NY 10003, 212-995-2230.

PR Reporter: Dudley House, PO Box 600, Exeter, NY 03833 (PR information).

Society For Technical Communication: 815 15th St., N.W., Suite 400, Washington, DC 20005, 202-737-0035 (includes technical writing and illustrating).

Speech Communication Association: 5105 E. Backlick Rd., No. E, Annandale, VA 22003, 703-750-0533.

Women In Cable: 500 N. Michigan Ave., Suite 1400, Chicago, IL 60611, 312-661-1700.

Women In Communications, Inc.: PO Box 9561, Austin, TX 78766, 512-346-9875.

COMPUTER-RELATED OCCUPATIONS

American Federation Of Information Processing Societies, Inc.: 1899 Preston White Dr., Reston, VA 22091, 703-620-8900.

American Society For Information Science: 1424 16th St., N.W., Suite 404, Washington, DC 20036, 202-462-1000.

Associated Information Managers: 1776 E. Jefferson St., Suite 450, Rockville, MD 20852, 301-231-7447.

Data Processing Management Association: 505 Busse Hwy., Park Ridge, IL 60068, 312-693-5070.

Women In Information Processing: Lock Box 39173, Washington, DC 20016, 202-328-6161.

COUNSELING, TEACHING, AND TRAINING OCCUPATIONS

American Association Of Counseling And Development: 5999 Stevenson Ave., Alexandria, VA 22304, 703-823-9800.

American Federation Of Teachers: 555 New Jersey Ave., N.W., Washington, DC 20001, 202-879-4400.

American Society For Training And Development: 1630 Duke St., Box 1443, Alexandria, VA 22313, 703-683-8100.

Music Educators National Conference: 1902 Association Dr., Reston, VA 22091, 703-860-4000.

National Art Education Association: 1916 Association Dr., Reston, VA 22091, 703-860-8000.

National Association For The Education Of Young Children: 1834 Connecticut Ave., N.W., Washington, DC 20009, 800-424-2460.

National Education Association of the U.S.: 1201 16th St., N.W., Washington, DC 20036, 202-833-4000.

ENGINEERING, ARCHITECTURE AND CONSTRUCTION

American Institute Of Architects: 1735 New York Ave., N.W., Washington, DC 20006, 202-626-7300.

American Society Of Landscape Architects: 1733 Connecticut Ave., N.W., Washington, DC 20009, 202-466-7730.

Association Of Women In Architecture: 7440 University Dr., St. Louis, MO 63130, 314-621-3484.

National Association Of Women In Construction: 327 S. Adams St., Ft. Worth, TX 76104, 817-877-5551.

Society Of Women Engineers: 345 E. 47 St., Rm. 305, New York, NY 10017, 212-705-7855.

HEALTH-RELATED OCCUPATIONS

American Association Of Women Dentists: 211 E. Chicago Ave., Suite 948, Chicago, IL 60611, 312-337-1563.

American Dental Assistants Association: 666 N. Lake Shore Dr., Suite 1130, Chicago, IL 60611, 312-664-3327.

American Dental Hygienists Association: 444 N. Michigan Ave., Chicago, IL 60611, 312-440-8900.

American Dental Association, Council On Dental Education: 211 E. Chicago Ave., Chicago, IL 60611, 312-440-2500.

American Dietetic Association: 216 W. Jackson Blvd., Suite 800, Chicago, IL 60606, 312-899-0040.

American Medical Record Association: John Hancock Center, 875 N. Michigan Ave., Suite 1850, Chicago, IL 60611, 312-787-2672.

American Medical Technologists, Registered Medical Assistants: 710 Higgins Rd., Park Ridge, IL 60068, 312-823-5169.

American Medical Women's Association: 465 Grand St., New York, NY 10002, 212-533-5104.

American Nurses' Association: 2420 Pershing Rd., Kansas City, MO 64108, 816-474-5720.

American Occupational Therapy Association: 1383 Piccard Dr., Suite 300, Gaithersburg, MD 20850, 301-948-9626.

American Pharmaceutical Association: 2215 Constitution Ave., N.W., Washington, DC 20037, 202-628-4410.

American Physical Therapy Association: 1111 N. Fairfax St., Alexandria, VA 22314, 703-684-2782.

American Public Health Association: 1015 15th St., N.W., Washington, DC 20005, 202-789-5600.

American Society For Medical Technology: 3 Metro Center, Suite 750, Bethesda, MD 20814, 301-961-1931.

APPENDIX B

American Speech-Language Hearing Association: 10801 Rockville Pike, Rockville, MD 20852, 301-897-5700.

Association Of Physician Assistant Programs: 1117 North 19th St., Suite 300, Arlington, VA 22209, 703-525-4200.

Federation Of Nurses And Health Professionals: 555 New Jersey Ave., N.W., Washington, DC 20001, 202-879-4400.

National Council For International Health: 1701 K St., N.W., Suite 600, Washington, DC 20006, 202-833-5900.

National Health Council, Health Careers Program: 622- Third Ave., 34th Flr., New York, NY 10017-6765, 212-972-2700.

National League For Nursing, Career Information Services: 10 Columbus Circle, New York, NY 10019, 212-582-1022.

LAWYERS AND PARALEGALS

American Bar Association, Information Services: 750 N. Lake Shore Dr., Chicago, IL 60611, 312-988-5000.

National Association Of Women Lawyers: 750 N. Lake Shore Dr., Chicago, IL 60611, 312-988-6186.

LIBRARIANS

American Library Association: 50 E. Huron St., Chicago, IL 60611, 312-944-6780.

Special Libraries Association: 1700 18th St., N.W., Washington, DC 20009, 202-234-4700.

Women Library Workers: 2027 Parker, Berkeley, CA 94704, 415-540-6820.

MARKETING AND SALES OCCUPATIONS

American Marketing Association: 250 S. Wacker St., Suite 200, Chicago, IL 60606, 312-648-0536.

American Society of CLU and CHFC (Insurance): 270 Bryn Mawr Ave., Bryn Mawr, PA 19010, 215-526-2500.

American Society Of Travel Agents: 1101 King St., Alexandria, VA 22314, 703-739-2782.

National Association Of Insurance Women (International): 1847 E. 15 Street, PO Box 4410, Tulsa, OK 74159, 918-744-5195.

National Association For Professional Saleswomen: PO Box 255708, Sacramento, CA 95865, 916-484-1234.

National Association Of Realtors: 430 N. Michigan Ave., Chicago, IL 60611, 312-329-8200.

Women's Council Of Realtors: 430 N. Michigan Ave., Chicago, IL 60611, 312-329-8483.

RELIGIOUS WORKERS

National Assembly Of Religious Women: 1307 S. Wabash, Rm. 206, Chicago, IL 60605, 312-663-1980.

National Council Of Churches, Professional Church Leadership: 475 Riverside Dr., New York, NY 10115, 212-870-2511.

SCIENTISTS AND MATHEMATICIANS

American Chemical Society: 1155 16th St., N.W., Washington, DC, 20036, 202-872-4600.

American Meteorological Society: 45 Beacon St., Boston, MA 02108, 617-227-2425.

American Physical Society: 335 E. 45th St., New York, NY 10017, 212-682-7341.

American Physiological Society: 9650 Rockville Pike, Bethesda, MD 20814, 301-530-7164.

American Society For Microbiology: 1913 I Street, N.W., Washington, DC 20006, 202-833-9680.

APPENDIX B

American Statistical Association: 1429 Duke St., Alexandria, VA 22314, 703-684-1221.

Association For Women Geoscientists: c/o Resource Center for Associations, 10200 W. 44th Ave., Suite 300, Wheatridge, CO 80033.

Association For Women In Mathematics: PO Box 178, Wellesley College, Wellesley, MA 02181, 617-235-0320.

Association For Women In Science: 2401 Virginia Ave., N.W., Suite 303, Washington, DC 20037, 202-833-1998.

Geological Society Of America: PO Box 9140, 3300 Penrose Place, Boulder, CO 80301, 303-447-2020.

Society For Industrial And Applied Mathematics: 1400 Architects Bldg., 117 S. 17th St., Philadelphia, PA 19103, 215-564-2929.

SERVICE OCCUPATIONS

Associated Master Barbers And Beauticians Of America: 219 Greenwich Rd., Charlotte, NC 28211, 704-366-5177.

National Caterers Association: 942 N. Main St., Akron, OH 44310, 216-376-3900.

National Cosmetology Association: 3510 Olive St., St. Louis, MO 63103, 314-534-7980.

National Restaurant Association, The Educational Foundation: 250 S. Wacker Dr., Suite 1400, Chicago IL 60606, 312-782-1703.

SOCIAL SCIENTISTS AND SOCIAL WORKERS

American Anthropological Association: 1703 New Hampshire Ave., N.W., Washington, DC 20009, 202-232-8800.

American Economics Association: 1313 21st Ave., South, Nashville, TN 37212, 615-322-2595.

American Political Science Association: 1527 New Hampshire Ave., N.W., Washington, DC 20036, 202-483-2512.

American Psychological Association: 1200 17th St., N.W., Washington, DC 20036, 202-955-7600.

American Sociological Association: 1772 N St., N.W., Washington, DC 20036, 202-833-3410.

Association Of American Geographers: 1710 16th Street, N.W., Washington, DC 20009, 202-234-1450.

Linguistic Society Of America: 1325 18th St., N.W., Washington, DC 20036-6501, 202-835-1714.

Modern Language Association Of America: 10 Astor Pl., New York, NY 10003, 212-475-9500.

National Association Of Black Social Workers: 271 W. 125th St., New York, NY 10027, 212-749-0470.

National Association Of Business Economists: 28349 Chagrin Blvd., Suite 201, Cleveland, OH 44122, 216-464-7986.

National Association Of Social Workers: 7981 Eastern Ave., Silver Spring, MD 20910, 301-565-0333.

Organization Of American Historians: Indiana University, 112 N. Bryan St., Bloomington, IN 47401-3841, 812-335-7311.

Society For Historical Archaeology: PO Box 231033, Pleasant Hill, CA 94523, 415-686-4660.

SPORTS AND RECREATION WORKERS

National Association For Girls And Women In Sports: 1900 Association Dr., Reston, VA 22091, 703-476-3450.

National Recreation & Park Association: Division of Professional Services, 3101 Park Center Dr., Alexandria, VA 22302, 703-820-4940.

Women's Sports Foundation: 342 Madison Ave., Suite 728, New York, NY 10017, 212-972-9170.

APPENDIX B

GENERAL AND MISCELLANEOUS

American Association Of University Women: 2401 Virginia Ave., N.W., Washington, DC 20037, 202-785-7700.

American Business Women's Association: 9100 Ward Pkwy., Kansas City, MO 64114, 816-361-6621.

American Home Economics Association: 2010 Massachusetts Ave., N.W., Washington, DC 20036, 202-862-8300.

Association Of American Foreign Service Women: Box 8068, Washington, DC 20024, 202-223-5796.

Displaced Homemakers Network: 1411 K St., N.W., Suite 930, Washington, DC 20005; 202-628-6767.

Federally Employed Women: 1400 Eye St., N.W., Suite 425, Washington, DC 20005, 202-898-0994.

National Association Of Negro Business And Professional Women's Clubs: 1806 New Hampshire Ave., N.W., Washington, DC 20009, 202-483-4206.

National Association Of Women Business Owners: 600 S. Federal St., Suite 400, Chicago, IL 60605, 312-922-0465.

National Association Of Working Women 9 To 5: 614 Superior Ave., N.W., Cleveland, OH 44113, 216-566-9308.

National Federation Of Business And Professional Women's Clubs: 2012 Massachusetts Ave., N.W., Washington, DC 20036, 202-293-1100.

National Military Family Association: 2666 Military Rd., Arlington, VA 22207, 703-841-0462.

Society For International Development, Washington Chapter: 1401 New York Ave., N.W., Suite 1100, Washington, DC 20005, 202-347-1800.

Appendix C

Supplemental Reading Material & Publisher/Distributor Contact Information

To supplement the material in this book, use the resources listed here. The author has reviewed many, but not all, of the suggested resources. A listing, therefore, is not necessarily a recommendation.

The prices given are as of publication of this book and are subject to change. When you order a resource, send a check for the amount listed. However, you may be asked to remit a shipping fee because some of the prices do not include postage.

Before searching for these materials and other career development resources, you need to be aware of several things. Libraries and bookstores often do not have self-published, small-press books and books covering narrow topics. When you can't find a resource, either ask a bookstore to order it or place the order yourself using the publisher/distributor information at the end of this appendix. If you need more information, refer to the data on publishers in *Books in Print*, available in libraries.

For a free catalog of nearly 750 career-related books, including many of those listed here, contact Impact Publications, 10655 Big Oak Circle, Manassas, VA 22111, 703-361-7300.

The resources in this appendix are listed according to the following categories:

- Career Planning and Job Hunting
- Fields of Work and Jobs
- Organizations

- Alternative Patterns of Work
- Two-Career Family
- Business Start-Up and Operation
- Government Employment
- Job Market/Employment Trends
- Goal Setting and Time Management
- Skill Development
- Overseas Employment
- Resumes and Cover Letters
- Interviewing
- Dressing for Work
- Career Advancement

CAREER PLANNING AND JOB HUNTING

The books listed in this category also cover material relevant to many of the other categories, such as resume and cover letter writing, interviewing, and skill development. Rather than being listed in each category, most are listed only once.

Allen, Jeffrey, et al. *Finding the Right Job at Mid-Life.* New York, NY: Simon & Schuster. 1985. $12.95.

Bolles, Richard N. *The Three Boxes of Life and How To Get Out of Them.* Berkeley, CA: Ten Speed Press. 1981. $8.95. A comprehensive, 480-page introduction to life/work planning.

Bolles, Richard N. *What Color Is Your Parachute?* Berkeley, CA: Ten Speed Press. Revised annually; get most recent edition. $8.95. In addition to its other attributes, this resource has an excellent bibliography and an effective tool for skill assessment entitled "The Quick Job Hunting Map." If you only purchase one career resource, make it this one.

Catalyst. *What to Do With the Rest of Your Life: The Catalyst Career Guide for Women in the '80s.* New York, NY: Simon & Schuster. 1981. $12.95.

Cauley, Constance D. *Time for A Change: A Guide to Careers for Women in Non-Traditional Fields.* Garrett Park, MD: Garrett Park Press. 1981. $8.95.

Curtin, Bernadette M. and Hecklinger, Fred J. *Training for Life: A Practical Guide to Career and Life Planning.* Dubuque, IA: Kendall/Hunt Publishing Company. 1984. $16.95. An absolutely superb resource by two college career counselors.

Figler, Howard E. *The Complete Job Search Handbook: Presenting the Skills You Need to Get Any Job, and Have a Good Time Doing It.* New York, NY: Henry Holt & Company. 1988. $11.95. Deals with the skills actully used in the job search process.

Fox, Marcia R. *Put Your Degree to Work: Job-Hunting Success for the New Professional.* New York, NY: W.W. Norton Co. 1988. $8.95.

Holland, John. *Making Vocational Choices: A Theory of Vocational Personalities and Work Environments.* Palo Alto, CA: Counseling Psychologists Press. 1984. $20.

Irish, Richard. *Go Hire Yourself an Employer.* Garden City, NY: Anchor Press/Doubleday. 1987. $9.95. On how to propose the job you want to employers and get yourself hired.

Jackson, Tom. *The Hidden Job Market for the Eighties.* New York, NY: Times Books. 1981. $9.95. Among the best resources on career planning and job hunting.

Krannich, Ronald L. *Careering and Re-Careering: The Complete Guide to Planning Your Future.* Manassas, VA: Impact Publications. 1989. $11.95. With a down-to-earth approach, this book discusses the role of skills in the ongoing technological revolution.

Moore, Donna J. *Take Charge of Your Own Career.* Available from the author at Box 723, Bainbridge Island, WA 98110. 1981. $10.00. A career planning guide applicable to many, this resource has a special orientation toward federal or would-be federal employees.

Powell, C. Randall. *Career Planning Today.* Dubuque, IA: Kendall/Hunt Publishing Co. 1981. $14.50 postpaid. A comprehensive career planning resource directed at people pursuing managerial, technical, or professional positions.

Sher, Barbara and Gottlieb, Annie. *Wishcraft: How to Get What You Really Want.* New York, NY: Ballantine. 1987. $6.95. Refreshingly enthusiastic, this book offers a unique step-by-step plan to pinpoint your goals and make your dreams come true.

Viscott, David *Risking: How to Take Chances and Win.* New York, NY: Pocket Books, Inc. 1983. $3.95.

FIELDS OF WORK AND JOBS

The resources in this category cover qualifications required, job duties, salary ranges, outlook, etc.

American Guidance Service. *Guide for Occupational Exploration*, second edition. Circle Pines, MN: American Guidance Service. 1984. $27.50. Updates and expands the Department of Labor publication with the same name (see reference this section). Relates your interests, work values, leisure activities, school courses, and experience to job characteristics, which include work settings, physical demands, work activities, and preparation needed.

Appelbaum, Judith and Evans, Nancy. *How to Get Happily Published: A complete and Candid Guide.* New York, NY: New American Library. 1982. $7.95.

Bastress, Frances. *Teachers in New Careers: Stories of Successful Transitions.* Cranston, RI: Carroll Press Publishers. Available from Career Development Services, Box 30301, Bethesda, MD 20814. 1984. $11.95. First-person interviews with former teachers who share how and why they moved to a variety of new careers.

Berkner, Dimity S. and Sellen, Betty-Carol. *New Options for Librarians: Finding a Job in a Related Field.* New York, NY: Neal-Schuman Publishers, Inc. 1984. $27.95.

Bly, Robert W. and Blake, Gary. *Dream Jobs: A Selective Guide to Tomorrow's Top Careers.* New York, NY: John Wiley & Sons, Inc., 1983. $8.95. A career guide to nine fast-growing industries — training and development, advertising, biotechnology, cable TV, computers, public relations, telecommunications, travel, and consulting.

Career World Magazine. Northbrook, IL: General Learning Corporation. Monthly, September through May. $14.95 for nine issues. A guide to career and self-awareness for high school students but excellent job information for all ages.

Cavallaro, Ann. *Careers in Food Services.* New York, NY: Lodestar Books. 1981. $10.95.

Fins, Alice. *Opportunities in Paralegal Careers.* Skokie, IL: VGM Career Horizons (offers books on many fields of work). 1985. $9.95.

Green, Mary and Gillmar, Stanley. *How to be an Importer and Pay for Your World Travel.* Berkeley, CA: Ten Speed Press. 1986. $6.95. For the small do-it-yourself importer, this reference tells where to go to find products, how to pay for them and get them home and sell them for a profit.

Guiley, Rosemary. *Career Opportunities for Writers.* New York, NY: Facts On File, Inc. 1985. $12.95.

Half, Robert. *Making It Big in Data Processing.* New York, NY: Crown Publishers, Inc. Available from Impact Publications. 1987. $19.95.

Kendall, Bonnie. *Opportunities in Dental Care.* Skokie, IL: VGM Career Horizons. 1983. $9.95.

Lerner, Elaine with Abbot,, C. B. *The Way To Go: A Women's Guide to Careers in Travel.* New York, NY: Warner Books. 1982. $6.95.

Marrs, Texe W. *High Technology Careers.* Homewood, IL: Dow-Jones Irwin Co. 1985. $9.95.

McAdam, Terry W. *Careers in the Nonprofit Sector: Doing Well By Doing Good.* Washington, DC: The Taft Group. 1986. $19.95.

Munschauer, John L. *Jobs for English Majors and Other Smart People.* Published by Peterson's Guides. Available from Impact Publications, Manassas, VA. 1986. $8.95. Designed to help liberal arts and nontechnical job applicants cope with the realities of the job market.

U.S. Department of Labor.
- *Dictionary of Occupational Titles*, 1981, $11.50. Supplement 1986, $5.50.

- *Guide for Occupational Exploration*. 1979. $14. A more recent and comprehensive version is available from the American Guidance Service (see reference in this section).
- *Occupational Outlook Handbook*. Biennial. $20.
- *Occupational Outlook Quarterly*. Four issues per year. $5.

To order these, send check or money order payable to Superintendent of Documents, U.S. Government Printing Office, Washington, DC 20402.

Wright, John. *The American Almanac of Jobs and Salaries*. New York, NY: Avon Books. 1987. $12.95. An excellent 800-page resource about the going rates for jobs in a wide variety of fields and industries.

ORGANIZATIONS

Many of the following national, international, and local directories are available in public libraries.

American Export Reigster. Coral Springs, FL: B. Klein Publications. Lists manufacturers and export-import buying agencies by product class.

Current Technical Services Contracts and Grants Directory, October 1 (*year*) to September 30 (*year*). Agency of International Development (AID) annual publication. Identifies firms and individuals receiving AID contracts and grants. Available in the central library of the Agency for International Development, Rosslyn, VA, or at no charge from 703-875-1047. To order by mail, write M/SER/OP/PS/SUP, Rm. 1440, SA 14, AID, Washington, DC, 20523-1801.

Directory of AID Indefinite Quantity Contracts. Agency of International Development (AID). 1984, but periodically updated. Identifies firms that have short-term technical services contracts with AID. Available in AID library in Rosslyn, VA, or for purchase from User Services, as described on page 82 (PNAAR272-$22.62, hardcopy).

Directory of American Firms Operating in Foreign Countries. Three volumes, 11th edition. New York, NY: World Trade Academy Press. 1987.

Directory of Executive Recruiters. 16th Edition. Fitzwilliam, NH: Consultants News. 1986. $21. Information on 1,479 executive search firms in the United States, Canada, and Mexico. Offers tips on how to work with recruiters and what to look for in a search firm.

Directory of Executive Recruiters – International. Coral Springs, FL: B. Klein Publications. 1984. $32. Covers more than 1,400 recruiting firms handling executive openings; international coverage.

Dun & Bradstreet Million Dollar Directory. Dun & Bradstreet, 99 Church St., New York, NY 10007. Annual. A five-volume set containing the names and addresses of more than 50,000 businesses with over $1 million net worth.

APPENDIX C

The Europa Year Book: A World Survey. Two volumes. New York, NY: Taylor & Francis, Inc. Annual. A valuable source of political, economic, statistical, and commercial information on every nation of the world and principal international organizations.

Federation of Organizations for Professional Women (FOPW). *A Woman's Yellow Book.* 1989. $20. Available from FOPW, 2437 15th St., Ste. 309, N.W., Washington, DC 20009. A list of organizations concerned with women's issues.

U.S. Nonprofit Organizations in Development Assistance Abroad (known as the *TAICH Directory*). Eighth edition. New York, NY: Technical Assistance Information Clearing House. 1983. Available at large libraries, including the central library of the Agency for International Development, Rosslyn, VA. Available for purchase from User Services, as described on page 82 (PNAAN899 – $6.48 for microfiche or $76.04 for hard copy). A very comprehensive directory of 535 U.S. nonprofit organizations with overseas development programs.

Klein, Bernard, Editor. *Guide to American Directories.* 11th edition. Coral Springs, FL: B. Klein Publications. 1982. Lists directories published by business and reference book publishers; magazines; trade associations; chambers of commerce; and by city, state, and federal government agencies. Provides complete information on directories published in the United States including some major foreign directories that are categorized under 300 industrial, technical, mercantile, scientific, and professional headings.

Krannich, Ronald L. and Krannich, Caryl Rae. *The Complete Guide to Public Employment.* Manassas, VA: Impact Publications. 1986. $13.95. An excellent resource that details the whys, wheres, and hows of finding employment and advancing careers within federal, state, and local governments; international organizations; trade and professional associations; nonprofit organizations; contracting and consulting firms; foundations; research organizations; and political support groups.

Kruzas, Anthony T. and Thomas, Robert C., Editors. *Business Organizations and Agencies Directory.* Detroit, MI: Gale Research Company. First edition, 1980. A comprehensive and convenient guide to major sources of current information on American business and industry including trade, business, and commercial organizations; government agencies; stock exchanges; labor unions; chambers of commerce; diplomatic representation; trade and convention centers; trade fairs; publishers; data banks and computerized services; educational institutions; business libraries and information centers; and research centers.

Lesko, Matthew. *Information U.S.A.* New York, NY: Penguin Books. 1986. $22.95. A comprehensive inventory of sources of information.

Marlow, Cecilian and Thomas, Robert C., Editors. *The Directory of Directories.* Detroit, MI: Gale Research Company. Biennial; supplemented by *Directory*

Information Service.

Martin, Susan and Koek, Karin, Editors. *Encyclopedia of Associations.* Detroit, MI: Gale Research Company. Annual. A guide to national and international organizations, including: trade, business, and commercial; agricultural and commodity; legal, government, public administration, and military; scientific, engineering, and technical; educational; cultural; social welfare; health and medical; veteran, hereditary, and patriotic; hobby and avocational; athletic and sports; labor unions, associations, and federations; chambers of commerce; and Greek letter and related organizations. Volume IV, *International Organizations,* provides information on about 2,500 nonprofit organizations headquartered outside the United States.

McLean, Janice, Editor. *Consultants and Consulting Organizations Directory: A Reference Guide to Concerns and Individuals Engaged in Consultation for Business, Industry, and Government.* Detroit, MI: Gale Research Co. Triennial. Contact information for thousands of individuals and organizations in the United States and abroad.

The National Council for International Health (NCIH), *Directory of U.S. Based Agencies Involved in International Health Assistance.* Available from NCIH, 1701 K St., N.W., Suite 600, Washington, DC 20006, 202-833-5900. $35.00 for nonmembers. A geographic listing of more than 450 organizations with contract jobs in developing countries in the areas of health, nutrition, and population programs.

Renz, Loren, Editor. *The Foundation Directory.* 10th edition. New York, NY: The Foundation Center. 1985. The standard reference work for information about private grant-making foundations in the United States.

Russell, John J. and O'Shea, Argie, Editors. *National Trade and Professional Associations of the United States,* Washington, DC: Columbia Books. Annual. $60. Gives information on associations alphabetically, by area of specialty, and by geographic location.

Standard and Poor's Register of Corporations. Standard and Poor's Corporation, 25 Broadway, New York, NY 10004. Annual. A three-volume set with extensive information about corporations and their officers.

Thomas' Register of American Manufacturers and Thomas' Register Catalog File. Thomas Publishing Company, One Penn Plaza, New York, NY 10001. Lists more than 100,000 manufacturers, by product and location.

Voluntary Foreign Aid Programs: Report of American Voluntary Agencies Engaged in Overseas Relief and Development Registered with the Agency for International Development. Washington, DC: Agency for International Development (AID). Annual. Available on microfiche in AID library in Rosslyn, VA, or for purchase from User Services, as described on page 82 (1986 edition — PNAAW585 — $1.08 for microfiche or $3.12 for hard copy).

Watkins, Mary M., Editor. *Research Centers Directory.* Detroit, MI: Gale Research Company. A guide to thousands of university-related and other nonprofit research organizations based in the United States and Canada doing research in agriculture, business, conservation, education, engineering and technology, government, law, life sciences, math, area studies, physical and earth sciences, social sciences, and humanities.

Whiteside, R.M., Editor. *Major Companies of Europe,* Volumes 1, 2, and 3. Norwell, MA: Graham & Trotman, Inc. 1986.

Examples of other directories include the *Washington Information Directory, Directory of Business and Industry* (for Fairfax County, VA) and many others specific to geographic regions and subjects.

ALTERNATIVE PATTERNS OF WORK

Applegath, John. *Working Free: Practical Alternatives to the 9 to 5 Job.* New York, NY: AMACOM. 1982. $6.95.

Holtz, Herman. *How to Become a More Successful Consultant with Your Personal Computer.* Glenelg, MD: Bermont Books. 1985. $29.

Holtz, Herman. *How to Succeed as an Independent Consultant.* New York, NY: Wiley & Sons. 1983. $19.95.

Lee, Patricia. *The Complete Guide to Job Sharing.* New York, NY: Walker and Co. 1983. $6.95.

Olmsted, Barney and Smith, Suzanne. *The Job Sharing Handbook.* Berkeley, CA: Ten Speed Press. 1985. $7.95. How to share a full-time job with another person if you don't want to work full-time.

Schiffman, Stephen. *The Consultant's Handbook: How to Start and Develop Your Own Practice.* Boston, MA: Bob Adams, Inc. 1988. $12.95.

Simon, A.R. *How to Be a Successful Computer Consultant.* New York, NY: McGraw Hill Publishers. 1985. $16.95.

Waxman, Robert. *Moonlighting With Your Personal Computer.* New York, NY: Pharos Books. 1984. $7.95.

Work Times Newsletter. San Francisco, CA: New Ways to Work. Available, along with membership, for a donation, tax-free, of $25. An international information exchange on alternative work time.

TWO-CAREER FAMILY

Bird, Caroline. *The Two-Paycheck Marriage.* New York, NY: Pocket Books. 1982. $3.50.

Catalyst. *Human Factors in Relocation: Corporate and Employee Points of View.* New York, NY: Catalyst. 1983. $12. A 60-page report on a nationwide study of corporate relocation practices, including interviews with relocation professionals and transferred employees. Also includes recommendations for corporate policy on transferring employees.

Catalyst. *No False Moves: How to Make a Relocation Work for You.* New York, NY: Catalyst. 1985. $29.95. A self-guided audio cassette program and workbook designed to help make moving easier for relocating employees and their families. A section for two-earner couples is especially relevant for the accompanying spouse.

Catalyst. *Relocation: An Annotated Bibliography for Employers and Transferees.* New York, NY: Catalyst. 1985. $8. Contains brief descriptions of 34 articles and videotapes in four categories, including relocation and two-career couples.

Curley, Jayme, et al. *The Balancing Act II: A Career and a Family.* Chicago, IL: Chicago Review Press, Inc. 1981. $8.95.

Greiff, Barrie and Munter, Preston. *Tradeoffs: Executive, Family, and Organizational Life.* New York, NY: The New American Library. 1981. $3.50.

Kimball, Gayle. *The Fifty-Fifty Marriage.* Boston, MA: Beacon Press, Inc. 1983. $10.95.

Winfield, Fairlee E. *Commuter Marriage: Living Together, Apart.* New York, NY: Columbia University Press. 1985. $24.00. Deals with the dual-residence commuter lifestyle as an alternative to sacrificing one's career, and offers strategies for successful commuting.

BUSINESS START-UP AND OPERATION

Behr, Marion and Lazar, Wendy. *Women Working Home: The Homebased Business Guide and Directory.* Scarsdale, NY: WWH Press. 1983. $12.95. An excellent how-to book on getting a business started, plus names, addresses, and business experiences of home-based businesswomen.

Blake, Gary and Bly, Robert W. *How to Promote Your Own Business.* New York, NY: New American Library. 1983. $10.95. A practical primer to the ins and outs of advertising and publicity.

Connor, Richard A., and Davidson, Jeffrey P. *Marketing Your Consulting and Professional Services.* New York, NY: Wiley & Sons. 1985. $19.95.

Davidson, Jeffrey P. *Avoiding the Pitfalls of Starting Your Own Business.* New York, NY: Walker and Company. 1988. $21.95.

Davidson, Peter. *Earn Money at Home: Over 100 Ideas for Businesses Requiring Little or No Capital.* New York, NY: McGraw Hill Publishers. 1982. $6.95.

Hawken, Paul. *Growing a Business.* New York, NY: Simon & Schuster. Available from Impact Publications. 1988. $9.95. Reveals what it takes to be a successful entrepreneur.

Goodrich, Donna C. *How To Set Up and Run a Typing Service.* New York, NY: John Wiley & Sons. 1983. $8.95.

Homeworking Mothers, a quarterly newsletter for women who want to start their own businesses and work from their homes. $21 includes the newsletter, membership in Mother's Home Business Network and many other benefits. PO Box 423, East Meadow, NY 11554, 516-997-7394.

Kamoroff, Bernard. *Small-Time Operator: How to Start Your Own Small Business, Keep Your Books, Pay Your Taxes & Stay Out of Trouble.* Lytonsville, CA: Bell Springs Publishers. 1987. $10.95.

Maze, Rick. "Policy on Home Businesses Varies From Base to Base." *Army Times.* April 30, 1984.

Moran, Peg. *Running Your Business Successfully: A Woman's Guide to Surviving the First Two Years.* Garden City, NY: Doubleday. 1985. $10.95.

Mucciolo, Louis, Editor. *Small Business: Look Before You Leap.* New York, NY: Arco Publishing, Inc. 1981. $8.95. A catalog of sources of information to help you start and manage your own small business.

O'Beirne, Kathleen. "Portable Careers: You Can Take Them With You" (and other articles on home-based businesses by various authors). *Family Magazine.* New York, NY: Military Forces Features, Inc. December 1982.

Olsen, Nancy. *Starting a Mini-Business: A Guidebook for Seniors and Others Who Dream of Having Their Own Part-Time, Home-Based Business.* Sunnyvale, CA: Bear Flag Books. 1986. $8.95. Covers all aspects of beginning a part-time, home-based business, including financial record keeping, marketing, partnerships, legal issues, and price setting.

Small Business Reporter, Bank of America, Department 3631, PO Box 37000, San Francisco, CA 94137. Write to this address for free catalog on booklet series covering various businesses.

Shilling, Dana. *Be Your Own Boss: The Complete, Indispensable Hands-On Guide to Starting and Running Your Own Business.* New York, NY: Penguin Books. 1984. $8.95. Addresses most of the problems encountered by those now involved in setting up new businesses — from avoiding pitfalls to dealing with expansion.

Toffler, Alvin. *The Third Wave.* Des Plaines, IL: Bantam Books, Inc. 1981. $4.95. This well-known futurist includes, among other things, predictions about the future of work and the "electronic cottage."

Woy, Patricia A. *Small Businesses That Grow and Grow and Grow.* White Hall, VA: Better Way Publications. Available from Impact Publications. 1984. $9.95.

GOVERNMENT EMPLOYMENT

Cook, Betsy, Editor. *Federal Yellow Book.* Washington, DC: Monitor Publishing Company. Updated quarterly. $145. A directory with contact information for key agency personnel in Washington, DC.

Dumbaugh, Kerry and Serota, Gary. *Capitol Jobs: An Insider's Guide to Finding a Job in Congress.* Washington, DC: Tilden Press. 1986. $6.95. Two veteran Capitol Hill staffers outline the secrets of landing a job with Congress. Includes tips on where to meet "Hill types" and lists key telephone numbers.

Federal Career Opportunities. Vienna, VA: Federal Research Service, Inc. Biweekly 64-page magazine. $36 for six issues. Compilation, by a private firm, of current professional and semiprofessional vacancies within federal government agencies in the United States and abroad. Also includes articles on federal hiring trends and job-hunting tips.

"Federal Job Application Forms Kit." Vienna, VA: Federal Research Service, Inc. $3.50. Reproducible masters of the SF171, including expanded versions of pages 2, 3, and 4. In addition, the kit provides blank performance appraisal forms that will help you to fulfill the requirements of application to the Federal Government.

"Federal Jobs Overseas." A pamphlet available from federal job information/testing centers.

Federal Times. Springfield, VA: Times Journal Co. Weekly. $39 per year. Newspaper with articles and a listing of current domestic and overseas vacancies from the Department of Defense and some civilian agencies.

Handbook X-118 — Qualification Standards for White Collar Positions Under the General Schedule. Washington, DC: Government Printing Office. Available at federal job information/testing centers and personnel offices of many federal agencies. Reference book that describes the experience and education required for federal white collar jobs. Useful for its "buzz" words that you can adapt for your own descriptions.

Kocher, Eric. *International Jobs: Where They Are/How To Get Them.* Reading, MA: Addison-Wesley Publishing Co. 1983. $9.57. 40 pages on federal employment.

Krannich, Ronald L. and Krannich, Caryl Rae. *The Complete Guide to Public Employment.* Manassas, VA: Impact Publications. 1986. $15.95. An excellent resource that details the whys, wheres, and hows of finding employment and advancing careers within federal, state, and local governments; international organizations; trade and professional associations; nonprofit organizations; contracting and consulting firms; foundations; research organizations; and political support groups.

Mace, Don and Young, Joseph, Editors. *Federal Employees' Almanac, 1988.* Available from PO Box 7528, Falls Church, VA 22046-1428, 703-533-3031. Annual. $3.95. A reference on fringe benefits for federal government employees — retirement, life and health insurance, moving expenses, and more.

"The New Expanded SF171 Forms Kit." Washington, DC: Workbooks Inc. $5.95. 20 pages of attractively reconstructed experience blocks, plus instructions.

Position Classification Standards. Washington, DC: Government Printing Office. Available at federal job information/testing centers and personnel offices of many federal agencies. Civil Service reference books that describe the duties and responsibilities of each class of position at each grade level.

APPENDIX C

Shanahan, William F. *101 Challenging Government Jobs for College Graduates.* New York, NY: Arco Publishing, Inc. 1986. $8.95.

United States Government Manual. Washington, DC: Government Printing Office. Available at some public and government libraries and for sale by Superintendent of Documents. U.S. Government Printing Office, Washington, DC 20402-9325 (order number 069-000-000-15-1). Annual. $20. A directory of agencies and administrators in the executive branch of federal government with organizational charts and brief descriptions of each agency.

"U.S. Government Establishments With Positions Outside the Competitive Civil Service" (BRE-84). Pamphlet available from federal job information/testing centers.

Vogel, Stephen E. *Directory of Employment Opportunities in the Federal Government: What the Jobs Are and How to Get Them.* New York, NY: Arco Publishing Co. 1985. $24.95.

Waelde, David E. *How to Get a Federal Job.* Washington, DC: Fedhelp Publications. 1989. $15. A federal job hunter's guide to preparing a top-notch SF171, establishing civil service eligibility, and locating agency job openings.

Wood, Patricia B. *The 171 Reference Book.* Washington, DC: Workbooks Inc. 1987. $16.95 plus $1.50 postage. A step-by-step guide on how to write the application for federal employment.

Woodrum, Wil. *The Federal Executive Telephone Directory.* Washington, DC: Carroll Publishing Company. Bimonthly. $95 for single copy, $140 for a six-copy subscription.

Zehring, John W. *Careers in State and Local Government.* Garrett Park, MD: Garrett Park Press. 1980. $10.95.

JOB MARKET/EMPLOYMENT TRENDS

Krannich, Ronald L. *Careering and Re-Careering: The Complete Guide to Planning Your Future.* Manassas, VA: Impact Publications. 1989. $11.95.

Naisbitt, John. *Megatrends: Ten New Directions Transforming Our Lives.* New York, NY: Warner. 1983. $4.50.

Russell, John J. and O'Shea, Argie, Editors. *National Trade and Professional Associations of the United States.* Washington, DC: Columbia Books. Annual. $60. Associations can provide job market information.

Toffler, Alvin. *The Third Wave.* Des Plaines, IL: Bantam. 1981. $4.95. Information about the future.

U.S. Department of Labor. *Occupational Outlook Handbook*, biennial. $20. *Occupational Outlook Quarterly*, four issues per year. $9 per year. To order, send check or money order payable to: Superintendent of Documents, U.S. Government Printing Office, Washington, DC 20402.

World Future Society. *The Futurist.* Bimonthly magazine about the future. Available from 4916 St. Elmo Ave., Bethesda, MD 20814, 301-656-8274. $25 per year, single copies $3.50.

GOAL SETTING AND TIME MANAGEMENT

Lakein, Alan. *How to Get Control of Your Time and Your Life.* Bergenfield, NJ: The New American Library, Inc. (Signet). 1974. $3.95. Excellent; one of the classics.

Winston, Stephanie. *Getting Organized: The Easy Way to Put Your Life in Order.* New York, NY: Norton. $12.95. 1978. How to better organize your time, finances, paper, work space, closets, books, clothes, etc.

SKILL DEVELOPMENT

This section covers volunteering as well as traditional and nontraditional methods of education.

Audio Forum, a division of Jeffrey Norton Publishers, On the Green, 96 Broad St., Guilford, CT 06437, 203-453-9794. A large outlet for educational cassettes specializing in the Foreign Service Institute language courses. Also offers reasonably priced programs in 10 categories, such as history, psychology, and education. Free trial periods.

Bedrosian, Margaret M. *Speak Like a Pro: In Business and Public Speaking.* New York, NY: John Wiley & Sons, Inc., 1987. $12.95. A concise guide that demystifies the process of speech preparation and delivery.

Breger Video, 915 Broadway, New York, NY 10010, 212-254-3900. Videos about cooking available by mail or telephone orders. Free brochure.

Cohen, Marjorie. *Volunteer!: The Comprehensive Guide to Voluntary Service.* Yarmouth, ME: Intercultural Press, Inc. 1986. $6.50 Includes opportunities in the United States and abroad with more than 160 organizations, including major U.S. government and United Nations programs, the Peace Corps, and VISTA.

Dantes Independent Study Catalog and *Guide to External Degree Programs.* Pensacola, FL: Defense Activity for Nontraditional Educational Support. A catalog of high school and higher education courses. Available at military installations worldwide and several U.S. embassies, it is directed toward military personnel and dependents but probably could be used by foreign service spouses as well.

Directory of External Graduate Programs. Lists institutions, degrees offered, admissions criteria, availability of credit for prior learning, campus time required, learning formats, and costs. Available from Directory of External Graduate Programs, The Regents College, Cultural Education Center, Rm. 5D61, Albany, NY 12230. Make $5 checks payable to University of the State of New York.

Ekstrom, Ruth B. *Project HAVE Skills, Women's Workbook.* $7.95. (a *Counselor's Guide* is also available for $10). Princeton, NJ: Educational Testing

Service. 1981. An excellent resource for assessing skills picked up or sharpened as a volunteer or homemaker. See the *I CAN* listing that follows.

Family Liaison Office staff of Department of State. *Adult Educational Opportunities Abroad.* 1986. Available to foreign service spouses for no charge from Program Assistant, Family Liaison Office, State Department, 2201 C St., N.W., Washington, DC 20520.

Family Liaison Office staff of Department of State. *The External Degree Program.* 1982. Available to foreign service spouses at no charge from Program Assistant, Family Liaison Office, State Department, 2201 C St., N.W., Washington, DC 20520.

FlipTrack Learning Systems, Suite 200, 999 Main, Glen Ellyn, IL 60137, 800-222-FLIP. Offers audio instruction courses on using the Apple and IBM computers and their more complicated word processing and financial software packages. Free catalog.

Georgetown University Continuing Legal Education Center, 25 E St., N.W., Washington, DC 20001, 202-662-9510. Through audio tapes of their conferences, the center offers lawyers opportunities to keep abreast of new developments in their field.

Halterman, William J. *The Complete Guide To Nontraditional Education.* New York, NY: Facts On File, Inc. 1983. $7.95. Describes institutions, colleges, and government programs that allow people to receive degrees or continue their education off-campus, through correspondence programs, or outside the United States.

Haponski, William C. Haponski, Sandra G., Editors. *Directory of External Degrees from Accredited Colleges and Universities.* ETC Associates, 507 Rider Rd., Clayville, NY 13322. 1985. $12.95.

Haponski, William C. and McCabe, Charles E. *New Horizons: The Education and Career Guide for Adults.* Princeton, NJ: Peterson's Guides, Inc. 1985. $8.95. A comprehensive source of information to assist prospective adult students with methods of school and program selection, acquiring life and transfer credits, applying, getting accepted, financing, balancing family and study, and more.

Howard, Edrice, Editor. *Academic Year Abroad, 1988-89.* The Learning Traveler, New York, NY: Institute of International Education. 1988. $19.95. Describes more than 1,200 programs sponsored by accredited U.S. colleges and universities for study abroad.

Howard, Edrice, Editor. *Vacation Study Abroad, 1989,* The Learning Traveler, New York, NY: Institute of International Education. 1989. $22.95. Lists 1,000 short-term programs for people college age and above interested in broadening their educational experiences by attending a study program abroad sponsored by U.S. colleges and universities, foreign institutions, private and governmental organizations and agencies.

I CAN – Volunteer Development Workbook. Available through local Red

Cross chapters or General Supply Division, American Red Cross, 7401 Lockport Place, Lorton, VA 22079. 1981. ($6.50; Stock No. 320090). The excellent checklists of skills clustered by various roles help volunteers to identify the basic skills clustered by various roles help volunteers to identify the basic skills they have used in their volunteer work or as homemakers. Among the roles under which the skills are clustered are administrator/manager, financial manager, personnel manager, trainer, advocate/change agent, public relations/communicator, problem surveyor, researcher, fund raiser, and counselor. Two other resources for those who want to help recruit or train volunteers: *I CAN Advisor's Manual* ($2.85; Stock No. 320089) and *I CAN Administrative Guidelines* ($4.00; Stock No. 320088).

Mendelsohn, Pam. *Happier By Degrees: The Complete Guide for Women Returning to College or Just Starting Out.* Berkeley, CA: Ten Speed Press. 1986. $7.95.

National Home Study Council. *Directory of Accredited Home Study Schools* (free) and *We Succeeded Through Home Study* ($6). Both publications are available from NHSC, 1601 18th St., N.W., Washington, DC 20009, 202-234-5100. The second resource offers success stories from individuals who used home study to enter a variety of professions.

Nightingale-Conant Corporation, 7300 North Lehigh Ave., Chicago, IL 60648, 800-323-5552. This leader in the field of self-help and "inspirational" audio tapes offers a free catalog.

Ready, Barbara C. and Sacchetti, Raymond D., Editors. *The Independent Study Catalog, 1986-1988.* National University Continuing Education Association Guide to Independent Study Through Correspondence Instruction. Princeton, NJ: Peterson's Guides, Inc. Revised biennially. $8.95 plus $1.75 for shipping. A directory of more than 12,000 correspondence courses, elementary to graduate school, offered by 72 colleges nationwide.

Science Through Media Inc., Suite 803, 303 Fifth Ave., New York, NY 10016, 212-684-5366. Offers continuing education by audio tape for physicians, other health-care personnel, and engineers. Free brochure.

Simon & Schuster Communications, 108 Wilmot Road, Deerfield, IL 60015, 800-323-5343. Offers many video tapes for rental or purchase. Free catalog.

Stanton, Timothy and Ali, Kamil. *The Experienced Hand: A Student Manual for Making the Most of an Internship.* Cranston, RI: Carroll Press. 1982. $6.95. Sponsored by the National Society for Internships and Experiential Education, this resource offers advice, resources, instruction, contract samples, and case histories.

Sullivan, Eugene J., Editor. American Council on Education. *Guide to External Degree Programs in the United States.* New York, NY: Macmillan Publishing Co. 1983. $16.95 plus $1.50 postage. Outlines 100 colleges and universities offering external degree programs, with types of degrees and areas of study.

APPENDIX C 243

Tutor Tape, 107 Frace St., Toms River, NJ 08753, 201-270-4880. Offers a full line of courses for high school, college, and continuing-education students, some of which have study guides, tests, and workbooks. Free 15-day trial period for each course.

Videocraft Classics, 1790 Broadway, Ste. 701, New York, NY 10019, 212-246-9849. A video cassette leader in the cooking field, the firm sells the tapes directly or you can get them in some video stores.

OVERSEAS EMPLOYMENT

Directories covering overseas employment may be listed earlier in the section on Organizations.

Anthony, Rebecca, and Roe, Gerald. *Educator's Passport to International Jobs: How to Find and Enjoy Employment Abroad.* Princeton, NJ: Peterson's Guides, Inc. Available from Impact Publications. 1984. $11.95.

Bajkai, Louis A., Editor. *Teacher's Guide to Overseas Teaching.* San Diego, CA: Friends of World Teaching. 1983. $19.95.

Beckmann, David M., Mitchell, Timothy J., and Powers, Linda L. *The Overseas List: Opportunities for Living and Working in Developing Countries.* Minneapolis, MN: Augsburg Publishing House. Available from Impact Publications. 1985. $13.95. An excellent resource.

Cantrell, Will and Marshall, Terry. *101 Ways to Find an Overseas Job.* Published by Cantrell Corporations, PO Box 2018, Merrifield, VA 22116. 1987. $29.95.

Casewit, Curtis W. *Foreign Jobs: The Most Popular Countries.* New York, NY: Monarch Press/Simon & Schuster, Inc. Covers profiles of many countries, working for American corporations overseas, listing of job leads, and how to apply. 1984. $8.95.

Casewit, Curtis W. *How to Get a Job Overseas.* New York, NY: Arco. Available from Impact Publications. 1984. $8.95.

Cohen, Marjorie A. *Work, Study, Travel Abroad, 1986-1987.* New York, NY: St. Martin's Press. Available from Impact Publications. 1986. $8.95

Copeland, Lennie and Griggs, Lewis. *Going International: How to Make Friends and Deal Effectively in the Global Marketplace.* New York, NY: New American Library. 1986. $9.95. Among the topics covered are doing business in a foreign environment and women in international business.

Foreign Policy Association. *Guide to Careers in World Affairs.* New York, NY. Available from Impact Publications. 1987. $12.95.

Goodman, Ellen, Editor. *Teaching Abroad*, The Learning Traveler. New York, NY: Institute of International Education. 1988. $21.95. Provides basic information on available opportunities, including the scope of formal teacher exchange programs, faculty needs as reported by foreign governments, and the approximate number of faculty positions available annually with American and international schools abroad.

Kocher, Eric. *International Jobs: Where They Are/How To Get Them.* Reading, MA: Addison-Wesley Publishing Co. $9.57. 1983. The author, who was with the Foreign Service for 22 years, lists more than 500 job opportunities with government agencies, nonprofit organizations, businesses and banks, publishing companies, schools, and law firms. Discusses the preferred experience and education and how to apply.

Krannich, Ronald L. and Krannich, Caryl Rae. *The Complete Guide to Public Employment: Opportunities and Strategies for Federal, State, Local, and International Careers.* Manassas, VA: Impact Publications. 1986. $15.95.

Piet-Pelon, Nancy J. and Hornby, Barbara. *In Another Dimension: A Guide for Women Who Live Overseas.* Yarmouth, ME: Intercultural Press, Inc. 1985. $9.95. Illuminates the advantages of overseas living and offers practical suggestions to help women survive and enjoy participating in another culture.

Powers, Linda. *Careers in International Affairs.* Washington, DC: Georgetown University's School of Foreign Service. Available from Impact Publications. 1986. $12.95. Lists and describes international-related employment sources for professional positions in both the public and private sectors.

Schrank, Robert, Editor. *American Workers Abroad.* Cambridge, MA: The MIT Press. 1979. $8.95.

Ward, Ted. *Living Overseas: A Book of Preparations.* New York, NY: Free Press. 1984. $9.95. Gives useful advice for making a successful transition to overseas working and living.

RESUMES AND COVER LETTERS

Bolles, Richard N. *Tea Leaves: A New Look at Resumes.* Berkely, CA: Ten Speed Press. 1976. $.50. An excellent booklet describing the myths about and problems with resumes.

Jackson, Tom. *The Perfect Resume.* Garden City, NY: Anchor Press/Doubleday. 1981. $8.95.

Lathrop, Richard. *Who's Hiring Who.* Berkeley, CA: Ten Speed Press. 1980. $7.95. Job hunting strategies for the new job seeker.

Krannich, Ronald L. and Banis, William J. *High Impact Resumes and Letters.* Manassas, VA: Impact Publications, 1988. $12.95.

INTERVIEWING

Chapman, Jack. *How to Make $1000 a Minute: Negotiating Salaries and Raises.* Berkeley, CA: Ten Speed Press. Available from Impact Publications. 1987. $8.95.

Irish, Richard. *Go Hire Yourself An Employer.* Garden City, NY. Anchor Press/Doubleday. 1987. $9.95.

APPENDIX C   **245**

Jackson, Tom and Mayleas, Davidyne. *The Hidden Job Market for the Eighties.* New York, NY: Times Books. 1981. $9.95.

Krannich, Caryl Rae. *Interview for Success.* Manassas, VA: Impact Publications. 1988. $10.95.

Lathrop, Richard. *Who's Hiring Who.* Berkeley, CA: Ten Speed Press. 1980. $7.95.

Medley, Anthony H. *Sweaty Palms: The Neglected Art of Being Interviewed.* Belmont, CA: Lifetime Learning Publications. 1978. $7.95.

Wright, John. *The American Almanac of Jobs and Salaries.* New York, NY: Avon Books. 1987. $12.95. An excellent 800-page resource about the going rates for jobs in a wide variety of fields and industries.

Yate, Martin. *Knock 'em Dead. . . with Great Answers to Tough Interview Questions.* Boston, MA: Bob Adams, Inc. 1987. $6.95.

DRESSING FOR WORK

Jackson, Carole. *Color Me Beautiful.* New York, NY: Ballantine Books. 1987. $8.95.

Martin, Jean. *Fit to be Tied: Accessorizing with Scarves and Sashes.* A 52-page pictorial guide for scarf and sash tying. 1987. $7.50. Closet Assets, 1530 Vista del Monte, San Antonio, TX 78216, 512-492-5991.

Wallach, Janet. *Working Wardrobe: Affordable Clothes That Work for You.* New York, NY: Warner Books. 1982. $8.95.

CAREER ADVANCEMENT

Bardwick, Judith M. *The Plateauing Trap: How to Avoid It in Your Career. . . & Your Life.* New York, NY: Bantam. 1988. $9.95.

Block, Peter. *The Empowered Manager: Positive Political Skills at Work.* Jossey-Bass. 1987. $19.95.

Davidson, Jeffrey P. *Blow Your Own Horn: How to Market Yourself & Your Career.* New York, NY: AMACOM. 1987. $16.95.

Morrow, Jodie Berlin and Lebor, Myrna. *Not Just a Secretary: Using the Job to Get Ahead.* New York: Wiley & Sons. 1984. $8.95.

PUBLISHER/DISTRIBUTOR CONTACT INFORMATION

Bob Adams, Inc., 840 Summer St., Boston, MA 02127, 800-872-5627.

Addison-Wesley Publishing Co.: Jacob Way, Reading, MA 01867, 800-447-2226.

AMACOM Book Division, Division of American Management Association: Seranac Lake Distribution Center, Publication Services, PO Box 319, Seranac Lake, NY 12983, 518-891-1500.

APPENDIX C

American Guidance Service: Publishers' Building, Circle Pines, MN 55014-1796, 1-800-328-2560.

Anchor: (imprint of Doubleday).

Arco Publishing, Inc.: 200 Old Tappan Rd., Old Tappan, NJ 07675. 201-767-5937.

Augsburg Publishing House: 426 S. Fifth St., Box 1209, Minneapolis, MN 55440, 800-328-4648.

Avon Books: PO Box 767, Swanson Dr., Dresden, TN 38225, 800-238-0658.

Ballantine, Inc.: 400 Hahn Rd., Westminster, MD 21157, 800-638-6460 or 301-848-1900 (in MD).

Bantam Books: 414 E. Golf Rd., Des Plaines, IL 60016, 800-323-9872.

Beacon Press, Inc.: (order from Harper & Row Publishers, Inc.).

Bear Flag Books: 941 Populus Pl., Sunnyvale, CA 94086. 408-739-7508.

Bell Springs Publishers: PO Box 640, Laytonsville, CA 95454, 707-984-6746.

Bermont Books: PO Box 309, Glenelg, MD 21737, 301-531-3560.

Carroll Press Publishers: 43 Squantum St., Cranston, RI 02920, 401-942-1587.

Carroll Publishing Compnay: 1058 Thomas Jefferson St., N.W. Washington, DC 20007, 202-333-8620.

Catalyst: 250 Park Ave. South, New York, NY 10003, 212-777-8900.

Chicago Review Press, Inc.: 814 N. Franklin, Chicago, IL 60610, 312-337-0747.

Columbia Books: 1350 New York Ave., N.W., Suite 207, Washington, DC 20005, 202-737-3777.

Columbia University Press: 136 S. Broadway, Irvington-on-Hudson, NY 10533, 914-591-9111.

Consultants News: Templeton Rd., Fitzwilliam, NH 03447, 603-585-2200.

APPENDIX C

Counseling Psychologists Press: PO Box 60070, Palo Alto, CA 94306, 800-624-1765.

Crown Publishers, Inc.: 225 Park Avenue South, New York, NY 10003, 212-254-1600 or 800-526-4264.

Dell Publishing Company: 1 Dag Hammarskjold Plaza, 245 E. 47th St., New York, NY 10017, 212-605-3000 or 800-932-0070.

Dolphin: (imprint of Doubleday).

Doubleday and Co., Inc.: 501 Franklin Ave., Garden City, NY 11530, 516-294-4000.

Dow Jones-Irwin: 1818 Ridge Rd., Homewood, IL 60430, 800-323-4560.

Educational Testing Service: Rosedale Rd., Princeton, NJ 08541, 609-921-9000.

Facts On File, Inc.: 460 Park Ave. South, New York, NY 10016, 800-322-8755.

Federal Research Service, Inc.: PO Box 1059, Vienna, VA 22180-1059, 703-281-0200.

FedHelp Publications: PO Box 15204F, Washington, DC 20003.

Free Press: (distributed by Macmillan Publishing Company).

Friends of World Teaching: PO Box 1049, San Diego, CA 92112, 619-274-5282.

Gale Research Company: Book Tower, 645 Griswold, Detroit, MI 48226, 800-223-4253.

The Garrett Park Press: PO Box 190E, Garrett Park, MD 20896, 301-946-2553.

General Learning Corporation: PO Box 3060, Northbrook, IL 60065, 800-323-5471.

Harper & Row Publishers, Inc.: Keystone Industrial Park, Scranton, PA 18512, 800-242-7737.

Henry Holt & Company: PO Box 30135, Salt Lake City, UT 84130, 800-247-3912.

Impact Publications: 10655 Big Oak Circle, Manassas, VA 22111, 703-361-7300.

Impact Publishers: PO Box 1094, San Luis Obispo, CA 93406, 805-543-5911.

Institute of International Education: Publications Service, 809 United Nations Plaza, New York, NY 10017, 212-984-5412.

Intercultural Press Inc.: PO Box 768, Yarmouth, ME 04096, 207-846-5168.

Jossey-Bass Inc. Publishers: 433 California St., San Francisco, CA 94104, 415-433-1740.

Kendall/Hunt Publishing Company: 2460 Kerper Blvd., Dubuque, IA 52001, 319-589-2833.

B. Klein Publications: PO Box 8503, Coral Springs, FL 33065, 305-752-1708.

Lifetime Learning Publications: UNR Order Dept., 7625 Empire Dr., Florence, KY 41042. 606-525-6600.

Lodestar Books: (distributed by New American Library, Inc.).

Macmillan Publishing Company: Front and Brown Sts., Riverside, NJ 08370, 609-461-6500 or 800-257-5755.

McGraw Hill Publishers: 1221 Avenue of the Americas, New York, NY 10020, 212-512-2000.

Military Forces Features: 169 Lexington Ave., New York, NY 10157-0016, 212-532-0660.

MIT Press: 55 Haywood St., Cambridge, MA 02142, 617-253-2884.

Monarch Press: Gulf & Western Bldg., Gulf & Western Plaza, 16th Flr., New York, NY 10023, 212-373-8208.

Monitor Publishing Company: 1301 Pennsylvania Ave., N.W., Washington, DC 20004, 202-347-7757.

William Morrrow & Co., Inc.: Wilmor Warehouse, 39 Plymouth St., Fairfield, NJ 07006, 800-631-1199.

APPENDIX C   249

Neal-Schuman Publishers, Inc.: 23 Leonard St., New York, NY 10013, 212-925-8650.

New American Library, Inc.: 120 Woodbine St., Bergenfield, NJ 07621, 201-387-0600.

New Ways To Work: 149 Ninth St., San Francisco, CA 94103, 415-552-1000.

W.W. Norton & Co., Inc.: 500 Fifth Ave., New York, NY 10110, 800-233-4830.

Penguin Books, Viking Penguin Inc.: 40 W. 23rd St., New York, NY 10010, 800-631-3577.

Peterson's Guides, Inc.: Book Order Dept., Box 2123, Princeton, NJ 08543-2123, 800-225-0261.

Pharos Books: 200 Park Ave., New York, NY 10166, 212-692-3824.

Pocket Books, Inc.: 200 Old Tappan Rd., Old Tappan, NJ 07675, 201-767-5000 or 800-223-2336.

Prentice-Hall, Inc.: 200 Old Tappan Rd., Old Tappan, NJ 07675, 201-767-5054.

Putnam Publishing Group: 200 Madison Ave., New York, NY 10016, 800-631-8571.

Random House, Inc.: 400 Hahn Rd., Westminster, MD 21157, 301-848-1900 or 800-638-6460.

Signet: (imprint of New American Library, Inc.).

Simon & Schuster: 200 Old Tappan Rd., Old Tappan, NJ 07675, 800-223-2336.

The Taft Group: 5130 MacArthur Blvd., N.W., Washington, DC 20016, 202-966-7085 or 800-424-3761.

Ten Speed Press: Box 7123, Berkeley, CA 94707, 800-841-BOOK.

Tilden Press: 1001 Connecticut Ave., N.W., Suite 310, Washington, DC 20036, 202-659-5855.

Times Books: Imprint of Random House).

The Times Journal Company: 6883 Commercial Dr., Springfield, VA 22159, 703-750-2000.

VGM Career Horizons, Division of National Textbook Company: 4255 Touhy Ave., Lincolnwood, IL 60646, 312-679-5500.

WWH Press: 41 Hampton Rd., Scarsdale, NY 10583, 914-725-3632.

Walker and Company: 720 Fifth Ave., New York, NY 10019, 212-265-3632.

Warner Books: 666 Fifth Ave., New York, NY 10103, 212-484-2900.

John Wiley & Sons, Inc.: Eastern Distribution Ctr., 1 Wiley Dr., Somerset, NJ 08873, 201-469-4400; Western Distribution Ctr., 1530 S. Redwood Rd., Salt Lake City, UT 84101, 801-972-5828.

Workbooks Inc.: c/o The Resume Place, 1800 Eye St., N.W., Washington, DC 20006, 202-737-8637.

World Trade Academy Press: 50 E. 42nd St., New York, NY 10017, 212-697-4999.

Index

Aburdene, Patricia, 99
Academics, 135
Accountants, help from, 57-58
Accounting, employment in, 36, 37, 100, 106, 140
Action words, 12, 14, 156, 186
Administration, employment in, 36, 140
Advertising executive, employment as, 36
Aerobics, employment in, 31
Age Discrimination Employment Act, 196
Agriculture, employment in, 140
Air Force, 133
American Association of Counseling and Development, 32, 113, 120, 138
American Association of Zoological Parks and Aquariums, 81
American Family Member (AFM) appointment. *See under* U.S. Government (overseas)
American Friends Service Committee, 42, 139
American Library Association, 43
American Marketing Association, 56
American Psychological Association, 43
American Register of Exporters and Importers, 81
American Society of Association Executives, 83, 137
American Society for Training and Development, 43, 80-81, 120

American Woman's Economic Development Corporation, 59
AMIDEAST, 140
Anthropology, employment in, 36
Applications, employment, 12, 145, 178-191
  nongovernment, 178-180
  U.S. Government. *See* SF171 form
Apprenticeships, 10, 57, 129
Archives curator, employment as, 140
Army, 133
Art, employment in, 36, 37
Association of American Foreign Service Women, 135
Association of Part-Time Professionals, 142
Association Trends, 137
Aspen Institute, 43
Audio and video cassettes, 94, 115, 124-125
Bed and breakfast operation, ownership of, 30
Berlin Tariff Agreements. *See under* U.S. Government (overseas appointments)
Berlitz Language Center, 125
Bilateral work agreements, 135
Biotechnology, employment in, 100
Bolles, Richard, 151
Bookkeeping, employment in, 36
Books in Print, 228
Brookings Institute, 43

251

252　　INDEX

Bureau of Labor Statistics. *See* U.S. Department of Labor
Business Week, 39
CARE, 42
Career (defined), 1, 29
Career appointment (with U.S. Government), 69-71
Career centers, 83, 111-112
Career counselors, 111, 113, 127
Career information, 21. *See also under* Career planning assistance
Career planning assistance, 111-115. *See also* Employment assistance programs
　availability of, 11-112
　career resources, 115
　one-to-one counseling, 113-115
　workshops and courses, 112-113
Career-conditional appointment. *See under* U.S. Government employment
Careers compatible with children, 36
Careers in International Affairs, 73, 81
Careers in the Nonprofit Sector: Doing Well By Doing Good, 81
Career World, 32
Catalyst, 112, 130, 132
Catering, employment in, 37, 39, 58
Catholic Relief Services, 42
Census Bureau, 56
Central Intelligence Agency, 41, 67, 73
Chambers of commerce, 38, 83, 99, 111, 136, 210
Civic organizations, 10
Civil service status, 70
Clearinghouses, 143-144
Clergy, 135, 136
CODEL. *See under* Placement services
College Level Examination Program (CLEP), 122
College placement offices, 137, 144
Commerce Business Daily, 139, 142
Community development, employment in, 36
Commuter marriage, 25
Company publications, 83, 88, 137
Competitive civil service, 66, 67
Complementary careers, 31
Complete Guide to Public Employment: Opportunities and Strategies With Federal, State, Local, and International Careers, 39, 73, 82, 141
Compressed workweek, 46
Computerized guidance, 94
Computers
　employment using, 34, 39-40, 45, 52, 70, 100, 140
　skills with, 37, 119

Conference coordinator, employment as, 193
Construction, employment in, 140
Consultants and Consulting Organizations Directory, 81, 142
Consulting and contracting firms, 38-39, 44, 141
Consulting work and contract work, 38, 44, 70, 76, 139, 141, 142
Contacts, 66, 84-86, 92-93, 137, 146-148
Contract work. *See* Consulting work
Conventions, 138
Coopers and Lybrand, 38
Coordinator of cooperative education, employment as, 170
Corporations, 39
Corporations and Two-Career Families, 130
Counselor, employment as, 32, 100, 131
Course work, 10-11, 120-124. *See also under* Resumes; SF171
　correspondence courses, 121
　external degree programs, 121-122
　nontraditional, 122
　opportunities for military and foreign service spouses, 40, 122-123
　overseas, 47, 140
Cover letters, 151, 162, 163, 170-177
　appearance of, 171
　purpose of, 170
　samples, 175-179
Credentials, hidden, 14-15
Cultural affairs, employment in, 140
Current Federal Examination Announcements, 65
Current Local Announcements for Positions in the . . . Area, 65
Current Technical Services Contracts and Grants, 81
Dance, employment in, 31, 37
Decision making, 2, 3, 7, 79, 109
Department of Dependents School (DODDS) appointment. *See under* Military installations; U.S. Government (overseas)
Dependent hire appointment. *See under* U.S. Government employment (overseas)
Dictionary of Occupational Titles, 80
Dietitian, employment as, 37
Diplomatic community, 39-40
Diplomatic or official status, 39
Direct Marketing Association, 43
Directories, 137, 139, 147. *See also under* Reading to explore options.
Directory of AID Indefinite Quantity Contracts, 81

INDEX

Directory of American Firms Operating in Foreign Countries, 81, 139
Directory of Directories, 82
Directory of Executive Recruiters, 137
Directory of Executive Recruiters – International, 137
Directory of U.S. Based Agencies Involved in International Health Assistance, 81
DISCOVER for Adult Learners. *See* Computerized guidance
Documentation, 12-13
Dual-career couples, 2, 25
Dun and Bradstreet Million Dollar Directory, 147
Economic and social affairs, 139
Economic development commissions, 83, 99, 136, 210
Economics, employment in, 36, 140
Editing, employment in, 35, 129, 195
The Editor and Publisher Market Guide, 99
Education. *See* Course work
Education, employment in, 66, 103, 124. *See also* Teacher; Trainer
Educational Record, 10, 11, 17, 158, 188
Embassies and consulates, 41, 72, 139
Employee Relocation Council, 31
Employment (defined), 1
Employment Abroad. *See under* Placement services
Employment agencies, 132, 137, 139, 142, 144, 146
Employment assistance programs, 131-136
  corporations, 131-133
  Foreign Service, 134-135
  military, 133
  other, 135-136
Employment offices, state and local, 83
Employment trends, 97-101
Encyclopedia America, 99
Encyclopedia of American Cities, 99
Encyclopedia of Associations, 81, 86
Energy, employment in, 140
Engineers, 36, 37, 68, 140
Entertainment, employment in, 100
Entrepreneurial quiz, 50-51
  answers to, 61-62
Entry-level jobs, 29, 125-126
Equal Employment Opportunity Commission, 196, 197
Europa Year Book, 81
Excepted service (with the U.S. Government), 67
Executive Order 12585. *See under* U.S. Government employment
Executive search firms, 137

Exercise on Pros and Cons of Preferred Options, 105
Exercise To Narrow Your Options, 104
Exotic jobs of the future, 101
Export-Import Bank, 73
Family planning, employment in, 36
Federal Bureau of Investigation, 67
Federal Career Opportunities, 65
Federal civilian personnel offices, 66, 74, 83, 180
Federal Executive Telephone Directory, 66
Federal Highways Administration, 73
Federal job information centers, 65, 66, 83, 180, 213-216
Federal Register, 139
Federal Times, 65
Federal Yellow Book, 66
Fields of work, 30, 31
Finance, employment in, 39, 60, 140
Flexibility, 29, 36
Flextime, 46
Food for the Hungry, 42
Foreign and Domestic Teachers' Bureau. *See under* Placement Services
Foreign Service, 134-135
  exam, 40
  spouses, 37, 39-40, 72, 120, 122-123, 134-135, 139
Foreign Service Institute. *See under* U.S. Department of State
Fortune Magazine, 39
Foundation Directory, 81
Foundations, 40
The Futurist, 100
GS rating, 67
General Electric, 81
Goal setting, 102-110, 209
  achieving goal, 105-110
  defining goal, 103-105
  employment action plans, 106-108
Goodwill Industries International, 144
Government
  federal. *See* U.S. Government
  local, 41
  state, 40-41, 113, 131, 135
Graduate Record Exam, 124
Graphic design, employment in, 36
Guide for Occupational Exploration, 80
Guide to American Directories, 82
Guide to External Degree Programs in the United States, 124
Guide to the CLEP Examinations, 122
Gymnastics, employment in, 31
Handbook X-118 - Qualification Standards for White Collar Positions Under

Handbook X-118 (continued)
   the General Schedule, 183, 186
Harvard University's Fogg Art Museum, 43
Health care, employment in, 32-33, 36, 99
Heatlh-care facilities, 41
Hidden job market, 146
The Hidden Job Market, 22
High-tech jobs, 100-101
Hobbies, 10, 126. *See also under* Resumes
Holland, John, 20
Holt International Children's Services, 42
Home-based jobs, 36
Honors and awards. *See under* Resumes; SF171
Horticulture, employment in, 36
Host country firms, 141
How To Get A Federal Job, 69
How To Get Control of Your Time and Your Life, 108
Human resource development, 34-35, 80, 100
The Independent Study Catalog, 124
Institute for Cancer Research, 43
InterAction: American Council for Voluntary International Action, 139
Inter-American Development Bank, 140
Interest inventories, 21, 22
   Career Assessment Inventory, 22
   Self-Directed Search, 22
   Strong Campbell Interest Inventory, 22
Interests, 22-23. *See also under* Resumes
Internal Revenue Service, 58
International Association for Community Development, 44
International Association of Business Communicators, 147
International Employment Hotline, 141
International Employment Opportunity Digest. *See under* Placement services
International Federation of Health professionals, 44
International Health News, 143
International Jobs, 39
International Liaison, 144
International Monetary Fund, 140
International nonprofit organizations, 42, 44, 139
International Society for Human Rights, 44
International Trade Administration, 99
International trade jobs, 140
Internships, 10, 129, 158
Interviews, job, 7, 12, 131, 192-210
   dressing for, 199
   letters associated with, 203-207
      employment agreement, 203

Interviews, job *(continued)*
   panel, 194
   prior to relocating, 138
   questions for the interviewer, 66, 198
   questions from the interviewer, 195-197, 208-210
   that may discriminate, 196-197, 209
   salary negotiation, 193, 199, 202, 209-210
Jackson, Tom, 20
Job Description Records, 13, 15, 16, 17, 23, 152, 154, 179, 184
Job fairs, 83, 137
Job market, 29, 97-101, 136
Job objective. *See under* Resumes
Job Opportunities Bulletin, 141
Job search strategies, 136-148
   for alternative work arrangements, 142-144
   long-distance, 136-141
      overseas, 138-141
   self-directed, 146-148
   timing of, 3-4, 148
   traditional, 144-146
      disadvantages of, 145-146
Job search expenses, 144, 174
Job sharing, 46, 143
Journals, 66, 83, 86, 99, 129, 144
Kocher, Eric, 39
Krannich, Ronald and Caryl Rae, 39, 82, 141
Lakein, Alan, 108
Language skills, 37, 119, 125. *See also under* Resumes; SF171
Lawyers, 36, 58
Librarian, employment as, 37, 45, 100
Libraries, 66, 83, 137, 228
Library of Congress, 67
Licensing, 32, 33, 34, 56, 93
Life events, 9
Linguaphone, 125
Linguistics, employment in, 36, 103
Local hire, 74, 76
Lutheran World Ministries Volunteers, 144
Lutheran World Relief, 42
Major Companies of Europe, 81
Making Vocational Choices: A Theory of Careers, 20
Management, jobs in, 140, 153, 156, 190
Marine biology, employment in, 160
Marines, 133
Maryland (University), 34
Memberships, 86, 138. *See also under* Resumes; SF171
Military, 70
   installations, 41, 42, 120, 133

INDEX

Military - installations *(continued)*
   categories of employment on, 43, 75-76
   spouses, 42-43, 120, 122-123
Mobile career, 31
Mobile lifestyle, 32, 64-65, 129, 153
Model for documenting experience, 12-13, 184, 195-196
Moody's Principal International Businesses, 139
Moving To series, 99
Music, employment in, 31
Myers-Briggs Type Indicator, 22
Myers, Isabel Briggs, 22
Naisbitt, John, 99
National Association for the Cottage Industry, 59
National Association of Manufacturers, 43
National Association of Temporary Services, 143
National Board of Certified Counselors, 32, 113
National Council for International Health, 144
National Network of Career Resource Centers, 112
National Oceanic and Atmospheric Administration, 73
National trade and professional associations, 83, 138
National Trade and Professional Associations (directory), 43, 81, 86
Navy, 133
Networking, 86, 138-139, 146-147
Networks, 86
New Expanded 171 Forms Kit, 184
Newspapers, 83, 99, 137, 144, 145, 146, 147
New TransCentury Foundation, 141
New Ways to Work, 143
Nonappropriated Fund (NAF) Appointment. *See under* Military Installations; U.S. Government (overseas)
Noncompetitive eligibility, 182
Nongovernmental organizations. *See* International nonprofit organizations
Nursing, employment in, 23, 33, 45, 101, 120
Observation as a way to explore options, 79, 93
Occupational Outlook Handbook, 80
Occupational Outlook Quarterly, 37, 80

Office of Personnel Management (OPM), 66, 67, 68, 69, 70, 71, 73, 74, 77, 180, 182
Opportunities in Paralegal Careers, 80
Organization of American States, 139, 140
Overseas Development Network Opportunities Catalog, 81
Overseas Jobworld. *See under* Placement services
Overseas Limited Appointments. *See under* U.S. Government (overseas)
Overseas List: Opportunities for Living and Working in Developing Countries, 73, 81
Overseas Private Investment Corporation, 73
PACT. *See under* Placement services
Paralegal, employment as, 100-101
Part-time/Intermittent/Temporary (PIT) appointment. *See under* U.S. Government (overseas).
Part-time work, 10, 45, 56, 126, 142
Peace Corps, 73, 134, 144
Personality type, 20-21
Personal traits. *See under* skills
Personnel
   departments, 83, 144, 146, 147, 171, 199
   employment in, 40, 66, 78-79, 140, 201
Physical education, employment in, 31
Physical fitness instruction, employment in, 37
Placement services, 137
   and job listings for international nonprofits, 141
Political science, employment in, 36, 128
Portable careers, 31-36, 52
Portable skills, 37, 103, 129
Position Classification Standards, 186
Private voluntary organizations. *See* International nonprofit organizations
Professional organizations, 10, 137, 147
Program development, employment in, 36
Project HOPE, 144
Proposal for a job, 147
Psychology, employment in, 36
Public information specialist, employment as, 140
Quality ranking factors (with SF171 application), 186
Rand Corporation, 43

Reading to explore options, 79, 80-83
  books, 80
  Department of Labor Publications, 80
  directories, 81-82
  pamphlets and articles, 80-81
  sources of written information, 82-83
Real estate, employment in, 36, 93, 201
Reasons for leaving past employment, 179, 184
Recommendations. *See* References.
Recreation, employment in, 36
References, 17-18, 179, 199, 202. *See also* Applications; Resumes; SF171
Registers, civil service, 66, 68, 69
Reinstatement eligibility. *See under* U.S. Government employment
Reinventing the Corporation, 99
Relocation management firms, 132
Research Centers Directory, 81
Research, employment in, 37, 150
Research organizations, 43
Resumes, 7, 12, 48, 147, 149-169
  appearance of, 162-163
  contact information on, 151-152
  credentials, licenses, and special skills on, 158
  education, training, course work on, 157-158
  honors and awards on, 158
  how to critique, 163
  interests and hobbies on, 160-161
  job objective on, 161-162
  languages on, 160
  memberships on, 159-160
  personal data on, 161
  problems with, 145, 150-151
  publications on, 159
  purpose of, 149
  references on, 161
  samples, 164-169
  styles of, 152
    chronological, 152-153
    combination functional/chronological, 153-155
  work experience on, 152-156
    using the language of your future work, 155-156
Retailing, employment in, 36, 100
Risking, 26
Robotics, employment in, 100
Runzheimer and Co., 132
SF50 (Notification of Personnel Action), 73
SF171 (U.S. Government employment application), 66, 67, 68, 180-191
  attachments to, 181, 186
  education, training, coursework on, 188

SF171 *(continued)*
  expansion of, 184-5, 188, 190
  honors, awards, and fellowships on, 181, 189
  knowledge, skills, and abilities, 183
  languages on, 189
  length of, 184
  memberships on, 189, 190
  performance appraisal with, 191
  purpose of, 180
  references, 190
  special qualifications, skills, accomplishments on, 189
  supplementary statement to, 186, 187
  unemployment on, 188
  work experience on, 183-188
Salary negotiation. *See under* Interviews, job
Salary history, 179
Sales, employment in, 36, 37, 45, 194
Scientists, 140
Secretary, employment as, 30, 33, 37, 45, 68, 72, 101, 140
Security clearance, 71, 72
Selective placement factors (with SF171 application), 186
Self-development, 102, 129
Self-employment, 36, 41-42, 50-62, 129
  advantages and disadvantages, 51-54
  business failures, 52, 61
  business plan, 57
  entrepreneurial quiz, 50-51, 61
  groups to assist you, 59
  how to decide on a business, 54-57
  how to promote, 59
  legal and tax considerations, 5
  portable businesses, 55
Separate maintenance allowance, 25
Separate residences for marriage partners, 25
Service Corps of Retired Executives (SCORE), 59
Service jobs, 101
Skills, 8, 12, 20, 23. *See also* Portable skills
  personal traits (self-management skills), 23
  transferable or functional, 23
  ways to develop, 119-129
  work-content, 23
Small Business Administration, 57, 59, 129
Social work, employment in, 34, 150
Spouse, (defined), 1
SRI International, 43

INDEX

Standard and Poors Register of Corporations, 81, 137
System of Interactive Guidance and Information (SIGI). *See* Computerized Guidance.
TAICH Directory, 82
Talking with people to explore options, 66, 79, 83-93
   questions to ask, 88, 91
   ways to make contacts, 84-88, 89-90
Tandem couple arrangement (Foreign Service), 40
Teacher, employment as, 8, 34-35, 45, 98-99, 101, 136, 140, 155-156
Teachers in New Careers: Stories of Successful Transitions, 35, 80
Temporary appointment. *See under* U.S. Government employment
Temporary work, 10, 45-46, 66, 126, 147
   ways to locate, 142-143
Term appointment. *See under* U.S. Government employment
Thomas Register of American Manufacturers, 81
Time line, 9-10, 12, 15, 20, 23
Time management, 108-110, 129
   log, 110
Trade and professional associations, 38, 43-44, 56, 99, 144, 159
Trainer, employment as, 15, 35, 140
Training. *See* Course work
Transcripts, 10, 124
Transfers, 25, 30, 98, 130, 132
Transitional leave (from the U.S. Government), 71
Translating, employment in, 31, 37, 98
Travel, employment in, 36, 37, 99, 108
Unemployment, 98, 179. *See also* under SF171
U.S. Agency for International Development (AID), 39, 41, 73, 76, 82, 134, 141, 142
U.S. Chamber of Commerce, 43, 56, 139
U.S. Department of Agriculture, 41, 73
U.S. Department of Commerce, 32, 56, 66
U.S. Department of Defense, 41, 65, 73
U.S. Department of Labor, 66, 99, 100, 101
   publications, 80
U.S. Department of State, 41, 73, 132, 134-135. *See also* Foreign Service
   Family Liaison Office, 123, 134, 139
   Foreign Service Institute, 40
      career planning workshops, 135
      functional training, 40, 120, 123
      Overseas Briefing Center, 135

U.S. Government employment, 40-41, 65-77
   advantages of, 63-64
   disadvantages of, 64-65
   how to get, in the U.S., 66-73
      types of appointments, 69
   overseas, 73-77
      types of appointments, 75-76
   reinstatement eligibility, 69-71
   spouses of federal employees, 40-41, 64, 123
      direct appointment eligibility (Executive Order 12585), 71-73, 75, 76, 77, 182.
U.S. Government Establishments With Positions Outside the Competitive Service, 67
United States Government Manual, 81, 85
U.S. Information Agency, 73, 124, 134
U.S. Nonprofit Organizations in Development Assistance Abroad (TAICH Directory), 81-82
U.S. Postal Service, 67
U.S. Travel and Tourism Administration, 73
Urban Affairs Institute, 43
Urban planning, employment in, 157
Vacancy announcements, 65, 137, 18
Values, 10, 20,
   personal values, 20
   work values, 20
Veterans preference, 68
Voluntary Foreign Aid Programs, 82
Volunteer work, 10, 29, 47-48, 147
   for skill development, 15, 29, 127, 159, 200
   ways to locate, 143-144
Waelde, David, 69
Waitress, employment as, 197-198
Wall Street Journal, 39
Washington Information Directory, 81, 147
What Color Is Your Parachute?, 111
Women's centers, 111-112
A Women's Yellow Pages, 86
Work, (defined), 1
Work arrangements, alternative, 44-49
Work autobiography, 8
Work environment, 20
Work history, 12
Working on the local economy, 47
Work portfolio, 17-18, 179, 199
Work Research Information Sheet, 79
Work settings, 24, 37-44
World Bank, 140, 141

Writer, employment as, 29, 35-36, 45, 53, 159
YWCA, 111
Yearbook of International Organizations, 82

Notes

Notes

Notes

ORDER FORMS
(all prices include shipping and handling)

------------ Cut and Mail --------------

WOODLEY PUBLICATIONS
4620 DeRussey Parkway
Chevy Chase, MD 20815

Attention: Sales Department

Please send me a copy of *The Relocating Spouse's Guide To Employment*. I have enclosed my check or money order for $14.95 (tax deductible).

Please Print

Name _____
Street Address _____
City _____ State _____ Zip _____

------------ Cut and Mail --------------

WOODLEY PUBLICATIONS
4620 DeRussey Parkway
Chevy Chase, MD 20815

Attention: Sales Department

Please send me a copy of *Teachers in New Careers: Stories of Successful Transitions*. I have enclosed my check or money order for $12.95 (tax deductible).

Please Print

Name _____
Street Address _____
City _____ State _____ Zip _____

------------ Cut and Mail --------------

WOODLEY PUBLICATIONS
4620 DeRussey Parkway
Chevy Chase, MD 20815

Attention: Sales Department

Please send me a copy of *The Complete Guide to Public Employment*. I have enclosed my check or money order for $15.95 (tax deductible).

Please Print

Name _____
Street Address _____
City _____ State _____ Zip _____

ORDER FORMS
(all prices include shipping and handling)

------------- Cut and Mail ---------------

WOODLEY PUBLICATIONS
4620 DeRussey Parkway
Chevy Chase, MD 20815

Attention: Sales Department

Please send me a copy of *High Impact Resumes and Letters*. I have enclosed my check or money order for $13.95 (tax deductible).

Please Print

Name _____
Street Address _____
City _____ State _____ Zip _____

------------- Cut and Mail ---------------

WOODLEY PUBLICATIONS
4620 DeRussey Parkway
Chevy Chase, MD 20815

Attention: Sales Department

Please send me a copy of *Interview for Success*. I have enclosed my check or money order for $11.95 (tax deductible).

Please Print

Name _____
Street Address _____
City _____ State _____ Zip _____

------------- Cut and Mail ---------------

WOODLEY PUBLICATIONS
4620 DeRussey Parkway
Chevy Chase, MD 20815

Attention: Sales Department

Please send me a copy of *Careering and Re-careering for the 1990s*. I have enclosed my check or money order for $14.95 (tax deductible).

Please Print

Name _____
Street Address _____
City _____ State _____ Zip _____

Daphne B. Latimore